STRANGE NEIGHBORS

CITIZENSHIP AND MIGRATION IN THE AMERICAS
General Editor: Ediberto Román

Strange Neighbors

The Role of States in Immigration Policy

Edited by Carissa Byrne Hessick and Gabriel J. Chin

NEW YORK UNIVERSITY PRESS
New York and London

NEW YORK UNIVERSITY PRESS
New York and London
www.nyupress.org

References to Internet websites (URLs) were accurate at the time of writing.
Neither the author nor New York University Press is responsible for URLs that
may have expired or changed since the manuscript was prepared.

Library of Congress Cataloging-in-Publication Data

Strange neighbors : the role of states in immigration policy / edited by Carissa Byrne
Hessick and Gabriel J. Chin.
pages cm. — (Citizenship and migration in the Americas)
Includes bibliographical references and index.
ISBN 978-0-8147-3780-4 (hardback)
1. Emigration and immigration law—United States. 2. Emigration and immigration
law—United States—States. 3. Exclusive and concurrent legislative powers—United States.
4. States' rights (American politics) I. Hessick, Carissa Byrne, editor of compilation. II.
Chin, Gabriel J. (Gabriel Jackson), 1964- editor of compilation.
KF4819.S765 2014
325.73—dc23
                                    2013049128

New York University Press books are printed on acid-free paper, and their binding materials
are chosen for strength and durability. We strive to use environmentally responsible
suppliers and materials to the greatest extent possible in publishing our books.

Manufactured in the United States of America
10 9 8 7 6 5 4 3 2 1

Also available as an ebook

For Becca, Sarah, and Sue.
For John and Frances Qualteri, first-generation Americans who passed their love of this country on to their family.

Contents

Acknowledgments

This book would not have been possible without the hard work and support of many individuals. First and foremost, we would like to thank Marc Miller and Toni Massaro. Their collaboration on our early work about Arizona's S.B. 1070 laid the groundwork for many of the ideas we have included in this volume. We are also deeply indebted to Ediberto Román. His advice and encouragement as the editor of the Citizenship and Migration in the Americas series has been invaluable. Many thanks to Andy Hessick for reading drafts and providing very helpful suggestions. Jennifer Angeles, Nina-Marie Bell, Linda Cooper, Glenda McGlashan, Carol Ward, and Gina Wilson provided key administrative assistance.

Arizona State University's Sandra Day O'Connor College of Law was very supportive of this project. In addition to financial support, the school's willingness to sponsor a conference on the role of the states in immigration policy and enforcement in October of 2010 was invaluable. Several of the distinguished authors who contributed chapters to this volume spoke at that conference, and the interest and enthusiasm generated by the conference helped spark the idea of creating this volume. Many people at the law school helped tremendously in the organization and execution of that conference, including Janie Magruder, Amanda Breaux, Charles Calleros, Doug Sylvester, Chris Baier, and Shelli Soto. And Dean Paul Berman deserves special thanks for his enthusiastic support.

The University of Arizona James E. Rogers College of Law and the University of California, Davis School of Law are also gratefully acknowledged, in particular former dean Larry Ponoroff; dean emerita Toni Massaro, who supported this project as dean as well as a collaborator on related work; and UC Davis dean Kevin Johnson, who, in addition to supporting the project, authored immigration and constitutional law scholarship that has been immensely influential and helpful.

Introduction

GABRIEL J. CHIN AND CARISSA BYRNE HESSICK

In 2010, Arizona ignited a national controversy over state regulation of immigration. It did so by enacting S.B. 1070, a statute through which Arizona tried to encourage undocumented immigrants to "self-deport"—i.e., voluntarily leave the state—by creating an inhospitable environment.[1] While S.B. 1070 captured the nation's attention, it was not the first state effort, or indeed the first effort in Arizona, to influence immigration policy or enforcement. In the five years leading up to S.B. 1070, various state legislatures introduced thousands of immigration bills and enacted hundreds.[2] Arizona in particular had previously enacted several immigration-related measures, including an initiative requiring that undocumented noncitizens arrested for crimes be held without bail, a law denying them state benefits, and a law revoking the business licenses of Arizona employers who hired undocumented workers.[3]

In addition to drawing public attention to the increasingly active role of states in immigration, S.B. 1070 also spawned copycat legislation in a number of other states. Alabama, Georgia, Indiana, South Carolina, and Utah enacted similar laws in 2011. And a number of states introduced other omnibus immigration enforcement bills in 2012.[4] These state laws seek to restrict the number of undocumented immigrants in their states. Because direct efforts to regulate immigration have been deemed unconstitutional,[5] the states seek to accomplish this restriction indirectly, such as by making it more difficult to obtain employment or by creating state crimes for failure to comply with federal immigration requirements. Some state efforts also appear designed to place pressure on the federal government to increase immigration enforcement efforts by, for example, increasing the number of requests for immigration status verification through laws requiring law enforcement officers to verify status under various circumstances.

The increasingly active and visible role of states in the area of immigration has been framed as a response to a perceived inactivity on the part of the federal government. Congress has visibly failed to pass immigration reform, and the newly elected presidential administration was perceived as failing to rigorously enforce existing immigration laws.

The public debate over state involvement in immigration policy and enforcement was complicated by a lack of legal guidance from the courts. Although immigration is traditionally viewed as an area reserved for the federal government, the Supreme Court has said that the states have the power to take substantial action with respect to those individuals who are in the country illegally. But for years the Court failed to clarify the line between state and federal power. When Arizona passed S.B. 1070, the most recent guidance from the Supreme Court was decades old. State lawmakers and anti-immigration interest groups carefully crafted the Arizona legislation (as well as other omnibus state immigration legislation) to capitalize on the legal gaps left by the Court's inaction in this area.

Since the proliferation of omnibus state immigration legislation in 2010 and 2011, we have seen a sea change in the balance of power between the states and the federal government. The Supreme Court has decided two immigration cases, including the federal government's challenge to S.B. 1070. The Obama administration has used its executive power to diminish the states' roles in immigration. Not only did the administration file legal challenges to the omnibus state immigration legislation in Arizona, Alabama, South Carolina, and Utah,[6] but it also announced a partial termination of the 287(g) program in Arizona—the program that deputizes state and local police to function as federal immigration enforcement agents.[7] The administration also took steps toward federal immigration reform. In the face of congressional inaction on the DREAM Act[8]—legislation aimed at providing a path to legal residency for many undocumented immigrants who arrived in the country as minors[9]—the Department of Homeland Security adopted guidelines that mimicked some of the provisions in that legislation.[10]

Racial profiling has also been a visible issue in the recent battle over immigration policy between the states and the federal government.

The Department of Justice took the unusual step of filing a lawsuit alleging civil rights violations against Arizona sheriff Joe Arpaio after negotiations between the DOJ and the Sheriff's Office broke down. And the ACLU prevailed in a similar federal lawsuit in the spring of 2013; a federal judge concluded that the Sheriff's Office had engaged in racial profiling, a finding that will undoubtedly be revisited on appeal. Interestingly, although fears of racial profiling prompted significant public concern in the debate over Arizona's S.B. 1070, that issue was not raised by the federal government in the litigation that made it to the Supreme Court. Presumably, the administration did not want to raise the issue, given that it has actively defended its own practice of using race as a factor in immigration enforcement.[11]

In addition to these legal and political changes, U.S. immigration has also undergone dramatic demographic changes. Recent demographic studies show that migration from Mexico to the United States has essentially ceased.[12]

This book traces the significant and visible role that states have assumed in immigration policy and enforcement. It also presents a first look at the way the Supreme Court responded to that state involvement in its 2012 decision in *Arizona v. United States*. While it is always difficult to predict what the Supreme Court will do, it is possible that this case may represent only the beginning of the Court's involvement in the complicated and complicating role the states now play in immigration policy and enforcement. Before previewing the contents of the book, we first provide a brief summary of the Supreme Court's recent opinion.

* * *

Arizona v. United States,[13] which tested the constitutionality of Arizona's S.B.1070, is unquestionably the most important immigration decision in decades.[14] The Supreme Court had upheld a different Arizona law, the Legal Arizona Workers Act, which punished Arizona employers for hiring undocumented workers, in 2011, but that case was less significant because federal law explicitly authorized state regulation, and the only question was whether Arizona's law went too far.[15] These laws were part of an explicit policy to make Arizona less hospitable to undocumented workers so they would self-deport. As stated in Section 1 of S.B.1070,

"The legislature declares that the intent of this act is to make attrition through enforcement the public policy of all state and local government agencies in Arizona. The provisions of this act are intended to work together to discourage and deter the unlawful entry and presence of aliens and economic activity by persons unlawfully present in the United States."

S.B. 1070 is a long and complex statute, attempting to achieve its goals through a variety of new provisions and amendments to existing Arizona law dealing with immigration. But by the time the case reached the Supreme Court, four parts of the law were at issue:

Section 2 applies whenever state or local police lawfully stopped or detained a person and there was "reasonable suspicion" that that person was undocumented. In such cases, police are required to make "a reasonable attempt . . . when practicable, to determine the immigration status of the person, except if the determination may hinder or obstruct an investigation." Also, the law provides that "[a]ny person who is arrested shall have the person's immigration status determined before the person is released." An Arizona driver's license and certain other forms of identification are presumptive evidence of legal status.[16]

Section 3 makes it an Arizona crime for an undocumented non-citizen to fail to register with the federal government or, having registered, to fail to carry the documents provided by the federal government.[17] Failure to register and failure to carry immigration documents that have been issued to a non-citizen are federal crimes, albeit ones rarely prosecuted.

Section 5(C) makes it an Arizona crime to work in the state if not authorized by federal law.[18] In contrast to Section 3, this section did not mirror a federal crime.

Section 6 authorizes Arizona police to arrest people who had committed crimes making them civilly deportable.[19] Federal cases dating back to Prohibition recognized the power of local police to arrest for federal crimes, including immigration crimes. Section 6 broke new ground by allowing arrests for civil immigration violations, with neither supervision by, nor the request of, federal authorities.

The case started when the U.S. Department of Justice sued, arguing that many of the provisions were preempted by federal law. U.S. District Judge Susan Bolton struck down the four sections described above, although she allowed others to stand, and the United States did not appeal. The U.S. Court of Appeals for the Ninth Circuit affirmed. All three judges on the panel agreed that Sections 3 and 5(C) were void, but one judge, Carlos Bea, contended that Sections 2 and 6 were valid.

One measure of the significance of the case is the amicus curiae briefs it attracted: some states, members of Congress and state legislatures, current and former law enforcement officials, and advocacy and policy groups filed briefs supporting the United States; a different set of the same entities filed briefs supporting Arizona. Mexico and a number of other Central and South American states also filed briefs, supporting the United States.

In the U.S. Supreme Court, Justice Kagan, who had been involved in the case as Solicitor General before being appointed to the Court, recused herself and did not participate. Accordingly, of the eight justices participating, five were generally regarded as conservative and only three as part of the liberal wing of the Court. Nevertheless, by a comfortable margin, the Court struck down Sections 3, 5(C), and 6 in an opinion written by Justice Kennedy and joined by Chief Justice Roberts, and Justices Breyer, Ginsburg, and Sotomayor. One suspects that Justice Kagan would have agreed with the majority, so it is likely that six of the current justices support the outcome.[20]

The Court struck down Sections 3, 5(C), and 6 "on their face," that is, without waiting to see how they were actually applied. All eight justices declined to strike down Section 2 on its face, concluding that it could constitutionally be applied. But they recognized that additional challenges could be raised later depending on the way the law was actually implemented.

Justice Kennedy's opinion for the Court began with a discussion of the reasons for federal authority over immigration, which traditionally has been exclusive. The Court noted, "Immigration policy can affect trade, investment, tourism, and diplomatic relations for the entire Nation, as well as the perceptions and expectations of aliens in this country who seek the full protection of its laws." At the same time, "Perceived mistreatment of aliens in the United States may lead to harmful reciprocal treatment of American citizens abroad." Because of the relationship between immigration and foreign policy, "It is fundamental that foreign countries concerned about the status, safety, and security of their nationals in the United States must be able to confer and communicate on this subject with one national sovereign, not the 50 separate States."[21] These concerns suggest that states have only a limited scope for enacting their own immigration-related laws.

The Court also noted that immigration enforcement was discretionary; it did not involve automatic prosecution of everyone who committed an immigration crime, or even automatic removal of every noncitizen who was not entitled to be in the United States. A person might not be charged because of "immediate human concerns. Unauthorized workers trying to support their families, for example, likely pose less danger than alien smugglers or aliens who commit a serious crime. The equities of an individual case may turn on many factors, including whether the alien has children born in the United States, long ties to the community, or a record of distinguished military service." The Court also noted that a noncitizen might avoid charges on the basis of national security or foreign policy grounds: "Some discretionary decisions involve policy choices that bear on this Nation's international relations."[22]

On the basis of these general principles, the Court invalidated Section 3, requiring registration and carrying of documents. The core difficulty for the validity of this section was that in 1941, in *Hines v. Davidowitz*,[23] the Supreme Court struck down a Pennsylvania law attempting to impose criminal sanctions for failure to register, because federal law was exclusive. "The framework enacted by Congress leads to the conclusion here, as it did in *Hines*, that the Federal Government has occupied the field of alien registration."[24]

Section 5(C) (penalizing noncitizens for working without federal authorization) was invalidated because it was contrary to a congressional choice. The Court determined, as had the courts below, that Congress specifically decided not to criminally punish individual unauthorized workers when, in the Immigration Reform and Control Act of 1986, it set up the basic system of employer sanctions and eligibility verification. "This comprehensive framework does not impose federal criminal sanctions on the employee side (i.e., penalties on aliens who seek or engage in unauthorized work). Under federal law some civil penalties are imposed instead. . . . Congress made a deliberate choice not to impose criminal penalties on aliens who seek, or engage in, unauthorized employment."[25]

The Court also invalidated Section 6, allowing Arizona police to arrest without a warrant for any public offense that made an individual removable from the United States, even a past offense for which a person had already been convicted and sentenced. The Court first noted that "[a]s a general rule, it is not a crime for a removable alien to remain present in the United States."[26] Accordingly, being an unauthorized migrant, in and of itself, is not evidence of a criminal offense, and would not justify an arrest under this section.

The problem with the section, according to the Court, was that it gave the state discretion to override federal choices and policies about who should be deported.

> This state authority could be exercised without any input from the Federal Government about whether an arrest is warranted in a particular case. This would allow the State to achieve its own immigration policy. The result could be unnecessary harassment of some aliens (for instance, a veteran, college student, or someone assisting with a criminal investigation) whom federal officials determine should not be removed. This is not the system Congress created.[27]

The Court also addressed an important statute authorizing state law enforcement officers to "cooperate with the Attorney General in the identification, apprehension, detention, or removal of aliens not lawfully present in the United States."[28] This, the Court said, did not authorize independent police action. "There may be some ambiguity as to what constitutes cooperation under the federal law; but no coherent understanding of the term would incorporate the unilateral decision of state officers to arrest an alien for being removable absent any request, approval, or other instruction from the Federal Government."[29]

The Court, however, rejected the claim that Section 2—the controversial section that media reports often referred to as the "show me your papers" provision—was invalid on its face. The Court concluded that Congress had authorized the states to gather and report information about the immigration status of noncitizens. Accordingly, they rejected the idea that investigating the status of arrestees and reporting it to federal immigration authorities, in and of itself, was inconsistent with federal law.

The Court did recognize a potential problem with the statute, which seemed to authorize or require delaying "the release of some detainees for no reason other than to verify their immigration status."[30] That is, if a person were stopped for a traffic offense and issued a ticket, but the investigation of his or her immigration status was not complete, then perhaps Section 2 required the detention of that person solely to investigate his or her citizenship and circumstances of entry into this country. Such a scenario, the Court said, would be problematic: "Detaining individuals solely to verify their immigration status would raise constitutional concerns. And it would disrupt the federal framework to put state officers in the position of holding aliens in custody for possible unlawful presence without federal direction and supervision. The program put in place by Congress does not allow state or local officers to adopt this enforcement mechanism."[31]

However, in language that bears all of the hallmarks of a pointed suggestion, the Court explained how Section 2 could be interpreted in such a way as to avoid constitutional difficulty. As to the requirement of checking status during a stop, "The state courts may conclude that, unless the person continues to be suspected of some crime for which he may be detained by state officers, it would not be reasonable to prolong the stop for the immigration inquiry."[32]

S.B. 1070's requirement of verifying status before releasing an arrested person was less qualified and more explicit than the duty applicable after a mere stop. Nevertheless,

> State courts may read this as an instruction to initiate a status check every time someone is arrested, or in some subset of those cases, rather than as a command to hold the person until the check is complete no matter the circumstances. Even if the law is read as an instruction to complete a check while the person is in custody, moreover, it is not clear at this stage and on this record that the verification process would result in prolonged detention.[33]

Having given Arizona a way out, the Court noted, "This opinion does not foreclose other preemption and constitutional challenges to the law as interpreted and applied after it goes into effect."[34]

At bottom, then, the Court approved seeking information and reporting to the federal government, but not necessarily any other actions, such as detention. Justice Alito's concurrence on this point may have been correct. He noted that this section "adds nothing to the authority that Arizona law enforcement officers, like officers in all other States, already possess under federal law,"[35] the right to ask questions (but not necessarily the right to compel answers) and to communicate information (but not necessarily the right to demand action).

The Court concluded with a tribute to immigration and a reaffirmation of federal power:

> The history of the United States is in part made of the stories, talents, and lasting contributions of those who crossed oceans and deserts to come here. The National Government has significant power to regulate immigration. With power comes responsibility, and the sound exercise of national power over immigration depends on the Nation's meeting its responsibility to base its laws on a political will informed by searching, thoughtful, rational civic discourse. Arizona may have understandable frustrations with the problems caused by illegal immigration while that process continues, but the State may not pursue policies that undermine federal law.[36]

As this introduction is being written, the full impact of the Supreme Court's opinion in *United States v. Arizona* is still unknown. Lower courts will interpret the opinion and decide whether it requires that the copycat legislation in Alabama, Georgia, South Carolina, Utah, and elsewhere be struck down. Lower courts will also have to decide whether the Court's language about the need for uniform immigration policy should be interpreted to forbid other recent state forays into immigration law and policy. It is also possible that the U.S. Supreme Court will hear additional state immigration cases, such as challenges to the state proposals to deny birthright citizenship to those children born in the United States to noncitizen and undocumented parents.

* * *

Whatever the immediate and distant future hold for state immigration involvement, the flurry of state omnibus immigration legislation in the past few years and the Supreme Court's recent immigration decisions indicate that we may be at a turning point in the relationship between the states and the federal government with respect to immigration.

This book provides legal, empirical, and historical analysis of state and local immigration regulation. It also provides both a defense and a critical evaluation of such regulation, with particular emphasis on the state actions taken over the past decade. While the chapters address a number of different topics and include a number of different methodological approaches, each chapter demonstrates that the role of the states in immigration policy and enforcement has historically been and continues to be pluralistic. The chapters also demonstrate that a number of empirical assertions in the immigration debate are inaccurate.

The book begins with an empirical examination of the recent spate of state and local immigration regulation. In the most comprehensive study of subfederal immigration regulation to date, "Measuring the Climate for Immigrants: A State-by-State Analysis," Professors Huyen Pham and Pham Hoang Van construct an index of state and local laws enacted from 2005 to 2009. The index notes whether each law is detrimental or beneficial to immigrants, and it weights each law according to the scope of the regulation's content and its geographic reach. For example, a local ordinance is weighted less than a statewide law; and a law that affects only one aspect of an immigrant's life (such as a requirement that all commercial transactions be conducted in English) is weighted less than a law that affects multiple aspects or more important aspects of immigrants' lives.

Some results of the Pham and Van study are surprising. While it is perhaps expected that Arizona tops their list as the most restrictive state for immigrants, California's score as among the least restrictive is unexpected. And while those states with relatively large immigrant populations tend to be more active in enacting immigration laws, there is no discernible relationship between the amount of regulation and whether those regulations are detrimental to or beneficial for immigrants.

Chapter 2 provides an empirical and historical overview of immigration from Mexico to the United States. In "How Arizona Became Ground Zero in the War on Immigrants," Professor Douglas Massey presents data on the migration patterns between the United States and Mexico, as well as the immigration enforcement efforts of the United States. He uses this data to demonstrate how the controversial state efforts to regulate immigration in Arizona can be traced to federal immigration legislation and enforcement policies over the past fifty years.

Professor Massey explains that, although Mexico-U.S. migration stabilized in the 1970s, the increasing politicization of immigration has generated a self-perpetuating cycle of immigration legislation and enforcement. Each new restrictive piece of legislation or policy has led to more immigration apprehensions, and the higher number of apprehensions has led to political pressure for more restrictive legislation and policies, and so on. What is more, while most migration between the United States and Mexico previously consisted of a circular flow of male Mexican workers, these restrictive policies have encouraged undocumented migrants to remain in the United States with their families because the policies have increased the costs and risks of border crossing.

Professor Massey's migration data demonstrates not only that the policies of the United States have helped create the immigration crisis but also why Arizona is a focal point. As he explains, the large number of undocumented migrants entering Arizona was an unintended consequence of the federal government's decision to concentrate enforcement resources at the two historically popular border crossings in San Diego and El Paso.

Chapter 3 places the current state and local efforts in historical context. Tom Romero's chapter, "'A War to Keep Alien Labor out of Colorado': The 'Mexican Menace' and the Historical Origins of Local and State Anti-Immigration Initiatives," provides a detailed account of Colorado's efforts to deter immigrant labor from Mexico during the 1930s. Professor Romero describes the American Southwest's dependency on Mexican and Mexican American agricultural labor, as well as the way the exploitative practices of the agricultural industry resulted in bleak financial prospects for Latino families. Those families were often forced to rely on private charity and public relief. When the Great Depression hit, Latinos found themselves in direct competition with Whites for scarce employment opportunities and public relief funds. The question of Latino labor in the fields became entangled with a national discourse of nativism and immigration restriction in the early decades of the twentieth century. Contemporary commentators criticized the federal government for failing to patrol the border and enforce the newly enacted immigration laws. And beginning in 1931, the Hoover administration enlisted state and local governments to deport and "repatriate" "Mexicans" (including Mexican American citizens born in the United States) back to Mexico.

The historical backdrop that Professor Romero paints seems eerily similar to the current situation—an economic crisis precipitating an immigration crisis, a federal government criticized for lack of action, and some cooperative actions between federal and state governments. It was against this backdrop, in 1935, that Governor Ed Johnson directed a local sheriff to detain "Alien Mexicans" who were en route to Colorado's sugar beet fields. Johnson had proposed establishing a "concentration camp" for all "aliens" on public relief so that the state could institute deportation proceedings. The sheriff ultimately detained thirty-two Latinos, whom he escorted to the New Mexico border and expelled, even though the federal government had taken no action. At the beginning of the sugar beet season in 1936, Governor Johnson deployed the National Guard to Colorado's southern border. He declared martial law and required that all travelers seeking to enter Colorado through its southern border demonstrate citizenship and financial security.

As Romero explains in detail, Governor Johnson's war on "the Mexican menace" was ultimately unsuccessful. The federal government did not permit Johnson to act completely unchecked, and public opinion eventually turned against him, especially as his policies were shown to affect not only Latinos. Johnson failed, Professor Romero concludes, because the attempt to carve out a new role for state involvement in immigration was too radical given the legal and political standards of the time. Although the Colorado efforts to restrict Mexican migration during the Great Depression were ultimately unsuccessful, there are striking similarities between the events that precipitated Governor Johnson's dramatic steps to restrict Mexican migration and those that have precipitated current state governments in Arizona, Alabama, and elsewhere to enforce their own regulations against immigrants.

A defense of state and local efforts to regulate immigration is presented in chapters 4 and 5. Chapter 4 is an updated version of Kris Kobach's highly influential article "Reinforcing the Rule of Law: What

States Can and Should Do to Reduce Illegal Immigration." First published in 2008, the article presents a blueprint for active state involvement in immigration that has obviously shaped the recent spate of state and local immigration regulation. Indeed, Kobach was one of the principal drafters of Arizona's S.B. 1070. Kobach has updated the text of the article to account for additional legislative and judicial developments since 2008.

Kobach explains that illegal immigration imposes a significant fiscal burden on states, and he identifies several areas in which states or local governments can constitutionally act in the field of immigration reform. In particular, Kobach advocates prohibitions on the employment of undocumented aliens through licensing sanctions and mandatory usage of the E-Verify system; the creation of state-level crimes that mirror federal crimes, such as alien smuggling and alien harboring; the cooperation of state and local law enforcement with federal immigration officials by the use of "inherent arrest authority," entrance into Section 287(g) agreements, and prohibition of sanctuary cities, as well as other state efforts. Recent years have seen challenges to such state actions. Some of Kobach's recommendations have been vindicated, such as the employment prohibitions, which were upheld by the Supreme Court in 2011. Others have not fared as well, such as the Supreme Court's analysis of state officers' authority to arrest on the basis of removability in *United States v. Arizona*. But many of Kobach's proposals have not yet been tested in the Supreme Court, and their constitutionality and appropriateness continue to spark much public and legal debate.

In chapter 5, "The States Enter the Illegal Immigration Fray," Professor John Eastman defends a number of state efforts to regulate immigration: Arizona's S.B. 1070, Alabama's new law requiring public schools to determine the immigration status of enrolling students, and recent state efforts to revoke birthright citizenship for the children of undocumented immigrants. In his analysis of S.B. 1070 and the court opinions surrounding the federal government's preemption challenge, Professor Eastman notes his disagreement with the statutory construction from both the district court and the Supreme Court, as well as the Court's focus on executive decision making in its preemption analysis. Eastman notes that this shift in focus from what Congress intended to what enforcement policies federal executive officials adopt represents a break from previous preemption doctrine.

In his defense of the new Alabama law, Professor Eastman argues not only that the law is consistent with the Supreme Court's 1982 opinion in *Plyler v. Doe* but also that it is designed to provide the very information that the *Plyler* justices said was missing in that case—namely, information about how the education of undocumented children affects the quality and cost of education for other students.

Professor Eastman's analysis of birthright citizenship—that is, the conventional interpretation of the Fourteenth Amendment as conferring citizenship on those individuals born on U.S. soil—describes and endorses the recent legislative initiative undertaken by a number of states to limit the grant of automatic citizenship. He points to legislative history and early Supreme Court cases to support a narrower view of the Fourteenth Amendment. As with his defense of the Arizona and Alabama laws, Professor Eastman states that the Supreme Court's decisions in this area leave much more room for state action than is commonly believed, and that these state actions represent the states functioning as "laboratories" in our federal system. Such state-level experimentation is desirable, Eastman argues, because it will allow us to assess, on the basis of actual experience in the different states, some of the difficult policy concerns that are implicated by illegal immigration.

The final three chapters of the book provide a critical evaluation of the new state and local regulations. Professors Gabriel Chin and Marc Miller critique the "mirror image" theory of immigration regulation championed by Kris Kobach in chapter 6, "Broken Mirror: The Unconstitutional Foundations of New State Immigration Enforcement." Although the Supreme Court held that those portions of Arizona's S.B. 1070 that mirrored federal law were preempted, Chin and Miller note that the Court did not specifically address the mirror-image theory and a narrow reading of the opinion would permit state efforts that mirror federal law in other discrete immigration areas.

The mirror-image theory is, however, according to Chin and Miller, an insufficient basis for states to create their own immigration crimes. They distinguish the power to arrest—a power that state officers often possess in immigration matters—from the power to prosecute and legislate, arguing that the executive power to choose whether to charge and what charges to bring is as much a part of the law as the statutory texts. They base this conclusion on the federal power to regulate immigration, federal statutes, and a historical presumption that federal courts have the exclusive authority to prosecute federal crimes. Chin and Miller conclude not only that states currently do not possess the power to enact criminal immigration laws that mirror federal policies but also that Congress does not have the authority to confer such a power on the states.

In chapter 7, "The Role of States in the National Conversation," Professor Rick Su argues that the role of states in immigration policy has been oversimplified as a binary relationship with the federal government. Su argues that the states' role is better understood as that of an intermediary between the national government and the intrastate governments of counties, cities, and municipalities. Using Arizona as an example, Su notes that the conventional account of S.B. 1070 framed the controversy as a dispute between the federal and state government, a classic struggle between federal power and states' rights. Overlooked in this account, according to Su, is the fact that much of the legislation was directed downward at local governments within the state. The law forbade sanctuary cities and forced all communities within the state to prioritize immigration enforcement. The state legislature's decision to conscript local resources to enforce immigration-related goals led to significant intrastate conflict, including complaints about the law's unfunded mandate, and it resulted in police chiefs and cities within Arizona supporting the federal government in its lawsuit against the state.

Professor Su's nuanced account of the state's role in the immigration debate also recognizes that state responses to immigration often reflect the beginning of a national conversation, not the end. State efforts to regulate immigration often result in a discussion of the wisdom of federal policy that is said to preempt the state law in question. And those discussions have repeatedly resulted in changes to federal laws and policies, even when the state efforts have been successfully challenged and rejected. In light of this, Professor Su advocates taking affirmative steps to include the states in the discourse on immigration, rather than continuing to attempt to exclude states from the conversation in the name of federal exclusivity.

In her chapter, "Post-Racial Proxy Battles over Immigration," Professor Mary Fan also highlights the importance of the way the immigration debate is framed. She states that the recent spate of state immigration legislation is a proxy for racialized anxiety about a foreign "other" during times of economic turmoil. She bases that conclusion on current statements and policies, as well as the parallels between the present climate and the hostility faced by Chinese immigrants in the late nineteenth century. Fan draws parallels between the politics and policies in California during the recession of the 1870s and the current attrition-by-enforcement legislation (such as S.B. 1070) and birthright citizen efforts.

Although Fan's critique of these two forms of state immigration efforts is based on the racialized perception and stereotypes of undocumented immigrants, she does not turn to antidiscrimination law as a solution. Because equal protection challenges present legal difficulties, Fan advocates using alternative frames, such as preemption analysis, to challenge these immigration efforts. She argues that this reframing will highlight shared national interests rather than racial differences, and the appeal of national interest will be greater, especially during times of economic and political turmoil.

* * *

State involvement in immigration policy has generated significant debate in the past several years, and we anticipate that the debate is likely to continue for the foreseeable future. Those opposed to immigration have formed a number of advocacy groups that support state and local legislation aimed at the undocumented, and it is clear that those advocacy groups have found a willing audience in many state legislatures. And while the Supreme Court is typically the final arbiter of questions regarding the balance of state and federal power, the Justices seem content to address these issues in the immigration context piecemeal, if at all.

Recent and ongoing events highlight the uncertain and unstable role of the states in immigration policy and enforcement. The existing law, the relevant history, and the empirical evidence surrounding immigration and the states are both murky and unsettled. It is our hope that readers of this volume will appreciate that the simplistic views of immigration policy and enforcement advanced by each side of the immigration debate fail to appreciate a number of complicating facts and factors. As these chapters demonstrate, there are few easy answers regarding the appropriate role of the states in immigration policy.

NOTES

1. For a detailed description and analysis of the law, see Gabriel J. Chin, Carissa Byrne Hessick, Toni Massaro, and Marc L. Miller, *A Legal Labyrinth: Issues Raised by Arizona Senate Bill 1070*, 25 Georgetown Immigration Law Journal 47 (2010), http://papers.ssrn.com/sol3/papers.cfm?abstract_id=1617440.

2. 2009 State Laws Related to Immigrants and Immigration, Nat'l Conference of State Legislatures, http://www.ncsl.org/default.aspx?tabid=19232.

3. *See* Gabriel J. Chin, Carissa Byrne Hessick, and Marc L. Miller, *Arizona Senate Bill 1070: Politics through Immigration Law*, in Arizona Firestorm: Global Immigration Realities, National Media, and Provincial Politics 74–76 (Otto Santa Ana and Celeste González de Bustamante eds., 2012).

4. State Omnibus Immigration Legislation and Legal Challenges, Nat'l Conference of State Legislatures, http://www.ncsl.org/issues-research/immig/omnibus-immigration-legislation.aspx (identifying Kansas (H2576), Mississippi (H488 and S2090), Missouri (S590), Rhode Island (H7313), and West Virginia (S64)).

5. *See* Hines v. Davidowitz, 312 U.S. 52 (1941); Chy Lung v. Freeman, 92 U.S. 274 (1876).

6. State Omnibus Immigration Legislation and Legal Challenges, Nat'l Conference of State Legislatures, http://www.ncsl.org/issues-research/immig/omnibus-immigration-legislation.aspx.

7. Jeremy Duda, *Homeland Security revokes 287(g) agreements in Arizona*, AZ Capitol Times (June 25, 2012).

8. Elisha Barron, *The Development, Relief, and Education for Alien Minors (DREAM) Act*, 48 Harv. J. on Legis. 623, 636 (2011).

9. S. 3992, 111th Cong. (2010).

10. Memorandum from Janet Napolitano, Secretary of Homeland Security, to David V. Aguilar, Acting Commissioner, U.S. Customs and Border Protection, et al. (June 15, 2012), *available at* http://i2.cdn.turner.com/cnn/2012/images/06/15/s1-exercising-prosecutorial-discretion-individuals-who-came-to-us-as-children.pdf.

11. *See* Gabriel J. Chin and Kevin R. Johnson, *Profiling's enabler: High court ruling underpins Arizona immigration law*, Wash. Post, July 13, 2010, at A15.

12. Jeffrey Passel, D'Vera Cohn, and Ana Gonzalez-Barrera, *Net Migration from Mexico Falls to Zero—and Perhaps Less*, Pew Hispanic Center (May 3, 2012), *available at* http://www.pewhispanic.org/2012/04/23/net-migration-from-mexico-falls-to-zero-and-perhaps-less.

13. 132 S. Ct. 2492 (2012).

14. Modern important decisions include *Plyler v. Doe*, 457 U.S. 202 (1982), holding, 5-4, that states violated equal protection when they excluded undocumented children from free K-12 education, and *De Canas v. Bica*, 424 U.S. 351 (1976), holding, 9-0, that states could prohibit employers from hiring those not authorized to work under federal law. The Immigration Reform and Control Act of 1986 occupied the field of employer sanctions, with an exception that was addressed in *Chamber of Commerce v. Whiting*, 131 S. Ct. 1968 (2011).

15. Chamber of Commerce v. Whiting, 131 S. Ct. 1968 (2011).

16. Ariz. Rev. Stat. § 11-1051(B).

17. Ariz. Rev. Stat. § 13-1509.

18. Ariz. Rev. Stat. § 13-2928(C).

19. Ariz. Rev. Stat. § 13-3883(A)(5).

20. Justice Alito agreed that Section 3 was unconstitutional, but concluded that Sections 5(C) and 6 were valid. By contrast, Justices Scalia and Thomas believed that all four sections were valid.

21. 132 S. Ct. at 2498 (citations omitted).

22. *Id.* at 2499.

23. 312 U.S. 52 (1941).

24. 132 S. Ct. at 2502.

25. *Id.* at 2504

26. *Id.* at 2505.

27. *Id.* at 2506.

28. 8 U.S.C. §1357(g)(10)(B).

29. 132 S. Ct. at 2507.

30. *Id.* at 2509.

31. *Id.* (citations omitted).

32. *Id.*

33. *Id.*

34. *Id.* at 2510.

35. *Id.* at 2525 (Alito, J., concurring in part and dissenting in part).

36. *Id.* at 2510.

PART I

The Recent Spate of State and Local Immigration Regulation

1

Measuring the Climate for Immigrants

A State-by-State Analysis

HUYEN PHAM AND PHAM HOANG VAN

Introduction

In the fierce debate about subfederal immigration regulation, Arizona has become the focus of national attention. Its Senate Bill 1070, which gives police broad authority to detain people for immigration violations, has been described as "the nation's toughest bill on illegal immigration."[1] And Arizona itself has been characterized as "the state most aggressively using its own laws to fight illegal immigration."[2] Are these descriptions accurate? Is Arizona the most restrictive state in the realm of immigration regulation? How would such a measurement be made? And how do other states and local jurisdictions that have also enacted subfederal immigration regulation compare?

That state and local governments have become actively involved in immigration regulation is well known. There are almost daily media reports about immigration laws enacted by subfederal governments and about the legal and policy debates that these laws have created.[3] What is not known, however, is the precise extent of this subfederal involvement. Having a complete picture of subfederal immigration regulation is crucial to understanding our nation's treatment of immigrants; though we ostensibly have a unitary national immigration policy, these subfederal immigration laws create very different climates for immigrants, depending on their geographical location.

In the most comprehensive study of this issue, we construct a state-by-state index to measure the climates created by subfederal immigration regulation. This Immigrants' Climate Index (ICI) analyzes laws enacted from 2005 to 2009, including laws enacted at both the state and local government levels. The ICI then assigns a score to each law, negative if the law is restrictive and positive if the law benefits immigrants. A state's climate score is based on the sum of its scores for individual laws.

The ICI is designed to provide a comprehensive and accurate picture of subfederal immigration regulation. In collecting data, we used a broad definition of subfederal regulation, including laws that are often ignored in the policy debates. Specifically, we include immigration regulations enacted by cities and counties ("local" laws), as well as by states, and immigration regulations that benefit immigrants, as well as those that are restrictive. All of these laws are essential to calculating accurate climate scores but are rarely considered together in analyses of subfederal immigration regulation.[4]

In constructing the ICI, we recognize that different types of laws can have significantly different effects. For example, a law requiring that all government transactions be conducted in English only is not as significant as a law authorizing local police to enforce federal immigration laws. Similarly, a statewide law will affect more people than a law enacted in a single city or county. Thus, we used a system that weights laws on the basis of their scope (with laws affecting multiple aspects of immigrants' lives weighted more heavily than laws affecting single or less important aspects) and their geographic reach (weighting statewide laws more heavily than local laws). Weighting laws, rather than merely counting them, yields more accurate climate scores.

We found some interesting results: While Arizona's ICI score as the most restrictive state may be expected, California's ICI score as among the least restrictive states (second only to Illinois) may surprise some. Our other results are presented herein.

I. The Phenomenon of Subfederal Immigration Regulation

Subfederal immigration regulation has generated much debate and analysis.[5] In the midst of this controversy, it is crucial to understand what it is that we are debating. Guided by our purpose of measuring the climate created by these laws, we define subfederal immigration regulation as simply the laws enacted by cities, counties, and states to regulate immigrants within their jurisdictions.[6]

Using this definition has several benefits. First, it puts the focus squarely on immigration regulation, on laws that have a special link to immigrants, as compared with other populations in the jurisdiction. Usually, the immigration link is explicit, as when a law authorizes housing for migrant farm workers.[7] Sometimes, however, a law does not mention immigrants or immigration in its text, but we include it in our analysis because the law has a special impact on immigrants. For example, the typical English-only law does not reference immigrants,[8] but its impact will be felt most strongly among immigrants, who are less likely than the native born to be fluent in English.

This definition also has the benefit of clarity. Though a law's enactment does not guarantee its enforcement, our definition provides a bright-line rule for analysis. Tracking enforcement of these laws is not workable as different political subdivisions have different ways of allocating resources and recording government activity. Even if it is not rigorously enforced, the mere enactment of a law can contribute to the jurisdiction's climate for immigrants. Finally, as mentioned earlier, our definition includes immigration regulation enacted at the city and county levels, as well as at the state level. This broader approach has the benefit of providing a more complete picture of subfederal regulation.

Using our definition, we see that there has been a very clear increase in subfederal immigration regulation in recent years. The National Conference of State Legislatures, a bipartisan organization that provides research and other assistance to state legislatures, has tracked a substantial increase in immigration-related legislation during the period 2005–2009.[9] Our own tracking of local immigration laws—enacted at the city and county levels—shows a similar surge during this time period.[10]

Many of these laws have been challenged in court. Most of the lawsuits have contested the legality of restrictive immigration laws, but there have also been a handful of lawsuits challenging positive immigration laws.[11] The plaintiffs are varied, including immigrants, landlords, employers, business associations, and advocacy groups, both conservative and liberal. The legal arguments that have been raised echo many of the policy debates about these laws. The most common objection invokes federal preemption, claiming that a particular subfederal immigration regulation is invalid because it conflicts with existing federal law.[12] Plaintiffs have also raised conflict with existing state law as grounds for invalidating subfederal regulations.[13] Another objection from plaintiffs is that enforcement of the regulations, either generally or in particular cases, violates the plaintiffs' constitutional rights (e.g., through racial or ethnic profiling).[14]

These lawsuits have had mixed results. For example, in 2010, the Tenth Circuit struck down employer sanction provisions in the Oklahoma Taxpayer and Citizen Protection Act on preemption grounds.[15] But in 2009, the Ninth Circuit upheld similar provisions in the Legal Arizona Workers Act, ruling that its employer-sanction provisions were not preempted by federal law,[16] a decision that the Supreme Court recently affirmed.[17]

This flurry of activity—in legislatures and courts—shows that there is a growing phenomenon of subfederal immigration regulation. Our purpose here is to sketch out the quantitative dimensions of the phenomenon in a way that is both informative and useful.

II. Constructing the ICI

The Immigrants' Climate Index sums up each state's scores, positive and negative, on immigration regulations. ICI scores are important for several reasons. First, they organize lots of data (the many subfederal laws enacted by various political entities) into useful pieces of information. Essentially, a state's ICI score quantifies the environment for immigrants that a state and its cities and counties have created with their immigration regulations. Moreover, because subfederal regulation affects so many different aspects of immigrants' lives, the ICI scores help us to understand more accurately the environment that immigrants in the United States face.

The ICI is the first study to quantify subfederal regulation, to include laws enacted at both the state and local levels, and to conduct these evaluations over a multiple-year timeline.[18]

A. Data Collection

As an introduction, we provide some general parameters about our data collection. First, we considered laws that were enacted over a five-year period, from 2005 to 2009. Certainly there was some subfederal activity before 2005,[19] but not in the numbers that we saw in 2005 and subsequent years. The data collection efforts by the National Conference of State Legislators (NCSL), our source for state regulations, support our timeline. The NCSL did not compile immigration-related laws until 2005 and estimates that from 1999 to 2004, only 50–100 such laws were introduced by state legislatures.[20] Our tracking of local regulations shows a similar pattern.[21]

Because our purpose is to measure the climate for immigrants, we excluded certain categories of laws from our analysis that do not have a practical effect on immigrants' lives or that have only a tangential relationship to immigrants.[22] Using these criteria, we excluded *de minimis* laws like Wyoming's HB 144, enacted in 2006, that allows a foreign passport or green card to be used as identification to rent a keg of beer.[23] Another *de minimis* example is Indiana's HB 1182, a 2009 bill that details health care reimbursement rates for prisoners without private health care coverage, a group that also includes unauthorized prisoners.[24]

For these reasons, we also excluded immigration-related resolutions. A resolution can certainly express a collective opinion on immigrants, either positive or negative, but unless the enacting political entity actually has authority to implement the act that is being endorsed by the resolution, the resolution is merely symbolic. As such, it does not have a practical effect on immigrants' lives and therefore is excluded from our climate study. Examples of excluded resolutions include Illinois' HR 913, adopted in 2006, urging Congress to enact the DREAM Act,[25] and Richmond, California's 2006 resolution asking Congress to adopt comprehensive immigration reform.[26]

1. STATE LAWS

Our source for state laws is the National Conference of State Legislatures, which, since 2005, has collected and categorized immigration-related state legislation. As noted earlier, we use a more specific definition of immigration regulation than that used by NCSL.[27] We also use some different categorizations. The benefits category is broadly defined to include access, based on immigration status, to welfare programs, workers' compensation, health care, public housing, naturalization and refugee assistance, and education. By regulation, the state can choose to limit that access (for example, by limiting the benefit to U.S. citizens or those who can prove legal presence) or to enhance that access (for example, by funding medical clinics for migrant workers or granting in-state tuition rates to undocumented college students).

The employment category consists of laws controlling access to employment or employment benefits on the basis of immigration status. Sample laws range from requirements that employers must verify the lawful immigration status of their employees generally to requirements that an applicant for a specific professional license (like a certified public accountant license) prove legal immigration status. The law enforcement category includes laws that enhance or restrict a police department's authority to enforce immigration laws or laws that change a defendant's treatment in the criminal justice system on the basis of immigration status. There are also categories for housing (affecting the ability of immigrants to obtain private housing), voting (making it easier or more difficult for immigrants to vote), and legal services (typically, laws that regulate the legal market to prevent immigrants from being defrauded).

One category of state regulation that we did not include in our analysis is the human trafficking law.[28] Though trafficking laws would definitely affect the climate for immigrants, the net effect would probably be neutral. At first glance, human trafficking laws would seem to benefit immigrants because the laws offer protection from the abuses of trafficking. But by clamping down on trafficking, the laws also limit a channel that immigrants use to reach the United States. Others who have studied subfederal regulation have taken opposite views about the effects of trafficking laws on immigrants,[29] reinforcing our decision to exclude them from our analysis.

2. LOCAL LAWS

The compilation of local laws was more complicated, because there is no centralized source like the NCSL that collects and analyzes laws enacted by cities and counties. We started our data collection with lists of local laws compiled by advocacy organizations that track these laws.[30] We then combined these with DOJ information about subfederal governments that have agreed to allow their police to enforce various aspects of federal immigration laws (known as 287(g) agreements).[31] We also did our own searches, using electronic news databases, to find other immigration laws enacted during the period 2005–2009. From these sources, we created a master list and then contacted each subfederal governmental entity to confirm that it had enacted the law(s); wherever possible, we obtained a written copy of the law(s). Once enactment was confirmed, the local governments were entered into our legal database for analysis.

We used the same categories for local laws as we did for state laws. As described in section 3, the frequency of certain types of laws changes, as we shift from state to local levels of analysis.

B. Scoring Laws

In calculating ICI scores, we recognize that different types of immigration regulations will have different effects on immigrants' lives. For example, Utah's 287(g) agreement[32] will have much more impact on immigrants in that state than Texas's law requiring mortgage broker applicants to show proof of U.S. citizenship or legal permanent resident status will have on immigrants in Texas.[33] To obtain a more nuanced picture of the environment that immigrants face in different states, we assigned points to the subfederal laws on the basis of the impact that the laws could be expected to have on immigrants' lives.

We divided the laws, state and local, into the following four tiers:

Tier 4:
> *Definition:* laws that affect many aspects of life for immigrants, laws that will have the motierst impact on climate.
> *Examples:* laws related to law enforcement, including laws that authorize or prohibit subfederal police from enforcing federal immigration laws.
> *Score:* ± 4 points.

Tier 3:
> *Definition:* laws that affect a crucial aspect of life for immigrants, an aspect that is difficult to avoid or replace.
> *Examples:* laws that make it harder or easier for immigrants to obtain private housing (as contrasted with government-provided housing), identification (like driver's licenses), or any kind of employment.

Score: ± 3 points.

Tier 2:

> *Definition:* laws that affect an important but not crucial aspect of life for immigrants, an aspect that can be replaced with alternatives (albeit, not easily).
>
> *Examples:* laws that make it harder or easier for immigrants to obtain specific jobs (including work as day laborers), specific work licenses, or access to social welfare benefits like education and health care.
>
> *Score:* ± 2 points.

Tier 1:

> *Definition:* laws that affect a practical aspect of immigrants' lives but in a less important or less significant way.
>
> *Examples:* English-only laws, laws that make it harder or easier for immigrants to vote, or legal services laws.
>
> *Score:* ± 1 point.

Besides assigning points based on type of law, we also assigned different weights to the scores of local laws, to reflect their more limited jurisdiction, as compared with state laws. A local law may be in the same tier as a statewide law (e.g., Tier 3), but its impact on the environment of immigrants within that state will be limited to immigrants who live in that particular local jurisdiction. Accordingly, its score is adjusted to reflect that more limited impact.

As a more concrete example, Barnstable County, Massachusetts, has signed a 287(g) with the Department of Justice. The negative four points that the law receives under the tier system described above is weighted to reflect the county's smaller population, as compared with the larger population of the state.

221,151 (population of Barnstable County)

  ÷ 6,593,587 (population of Massachusetts)

  × -4 tier points

    = -0.13 points

In calculating Massachusetts' ICI, this 287(g) agreement will contribute -0.13 points to the state's total score. A corollary of this weighting system is that the laws of larger local governments (like Los Angeles County) will have a more significant effect on their states' ICI scores than will the laws of smaller local governments.

III. Immigrant Climate Results

The purpose in undertaking this analysis was to flesh out the quantitative dimensions of subfederal immigration regulation so that we could understand the contours of this phenomenon and its variations across the United States. Our results, both in the data patterns and the ICI scores themselves, support some of the conventional wisdom about this topic but also have some unexpected implications.

A. Patterns in Subfederal Immigration Regulation

The focus of our analysis is on the ICI scores, but the legal data that was collected to tabulate those scores is also interesting. Table 1.1 below summarizes key information about subfederal immigration regulation.

Some general patterns are worth noting. First, states were more active in this realm, enacting over two-thirds of the immigration laws. Moreover, approximately two-thirds of the laws enacted at both the state and local levels were restrictive in nature. But the flip side of these statistics is also significant: A third of the immigration laws are enacted by cities and counties and a third of the laws benefit immigrants. Readers who read or listen to media coverage of this topic might be surprised by the relatively high incidence of local laws and positive laws.

There are several interesting differences between immigration regulation at the state level and immigration regulation at the local level. As a percentage of the total laws enacted, state governments enacted more positive laws than local governments (39% versus 18%). Many of the state benefits, however, are limited to legal permanent residents and others who can demonstrate legal immigration status. Another interesting difference is that while benefit laws made up a whopping 52% of state-level laws, they only accounted for 6% of local regulation.[34] And though employment laws are popular with both state and local governments, the content of the laws is different. At the local level, 72%

Table 1.1. State and Local Immigration Laws Enacted 2005–2009

	Negative Laws	Positive Laws
Total Number of State Laws	296	187
By Type:		
Law Enforcement	60	3
Employment	110	30
Language	1	-
Housing	-	2
Benefits	114	137
Voting	9	1
Legal Services	2	14
Total Number of Local Laws	183	39
By Type:		
Law Enforcement	58	27
Employment	78	4
Language	26	-
Housing	15	-
Benefits	6	8

Source: Authors' compilation.

of the employment provisions regulate day laborers, mostly by restricting their ability to solicit work. State employment laws, by contrast, focus on employers (e.g., rescinding business licenses or government contracts for employers who hire unauthorized workers) or on specific groups of workers (e.g., requiring proof of legal immigration status for certain professional licenses).

B. ICI Scores

As noted earlier, a state's ICI score is calculated by adding up the individual scores, positive and negative, of immigration regulations enacted by the state and its cities and counties. Table 1.2 shows the ICI scores by state, and figure 1.1 shows the geographical distribution of scores.

Overall, two-thirds of the states received negative ICI scores. Arizona clearly has the most negative climate for immigrants, with a score of -60, which is almost twenty points lower than the next most negative state, Missouri.[35] After Arizona, the next six states have closely clustered negative scores (Missouri, Virginia, South Carolina, Utah, Oklahoma, and Georgia), the result of highly restrictive state laws, with very few, if any, positive laws at the state or local level.

At the opposite end of the index are Illinois and California, whose positive scores (+38 and +33, respectively) are more than twenty points higher than the next most positive state, Connecticut (+10). Illinois' score is largely the result of positive state-level laws,[36] while California's score is bolstered by a combination of positive laws at both the state and local level.[37] After California and Illinois, the next seven states with the highest positive scores are Connecticut, Minnesota, Washington, New Mexico, Maryland, Pennsylvania, and Iowa, which are scattered throughout the United States.

Significantly, there is a 98–point difference between Arizona and Illinois, representing the gulf between the extreme positions on subfederal immigration regulation. To give context to these numbers, ninety-eight points is equivalent to twenty-four statewide law enforcement provisions, plus one statewide benefit law. Thus, an immigrant in Arizona faces a drastically more negative climate than an immigrant in Illinois. In Arizona, an immigrant would be subject to, among other things, local and state enforcement of federal immigration laws, increased punishment for immigration offenses, and the requirement to prove legal status to get a business license, a liquor license, or any public benefits. In Illinois, by contrast, an immigrant can use a consular identification card as proof of identity, has access to a variety of state-funded services for immigrants, and, perhaps most significantly, is not subject to state or local enforcement of immigration laws.

What kinds of patterns exist in these ICI scores? Arizona's position on the U.S.-Mexico border and its large unauthorized population[38] might suggest a link to its high negative score. But our analysis found no statistically significant correlation between a state's ICI score and the size of its unauthorized population. Figure 1.2 shows that states with large unauthorized populations do not necessarily have negative ICI

Table 1.2. Immigrant Climate Index (ICI) Scores Based on State and Local Legislation Enacted 2005–2009

	State	ICI Score		State	ICI Score
1	Arizona	-60	26	New Hampshire	-4
2	Missouri	-43	27	North Carolina	-4
3	Virginia	-40	28	New Jersey	-3
4	South Carolina	-39	29	North Dakota	-3
5	Utah	-37	30	Delaware	-2
6	Oklahoma	-35	31	South Dakota	-2
7	Georgia	-30	32	West Virginia	-2
8	Colorado	-25	33	Wyoming	-2
9	Arkansas	-22	34	Alaska	0
10	Tennessee	-21	35	Rhode Island	0
11	Texas	-19	36	Vermont	0
12	Alabama	-16	37	Indiana	1
13	Florida	-15	38	Ohio	1
14	Nebraska	-14	39	Massachusetts	2
15	Michigan	-13	40	New York	2
16	Hawaii	-11	41	Wisconsin	3
17	Mississippi	-11	42	Iowa	4
18	Louisiana	-10	43	Pennsylvania	4
19	Montana	-10	44	Maryland	5
20	Idaho	-9	45	New Mexico	5
21	Kansas	-9	46	Washington	7
22	Oregon	-9	47	Minnesota	8
23	Maine	-7	48	Connecticut	10
24	Kentucky	-6	49	California	33
25	Nevada	-4	50	Illinois	38

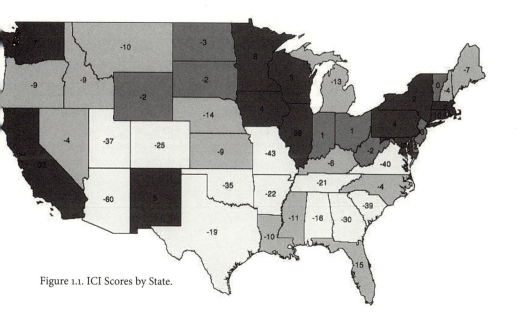

Figure 1.1. ICI Scores by State.

scores. For example, Nevada, California, and New Jersey, states with three of the largest unauthorized populations, have positive ICI scores.

However, there is a statistically significant correlation between the *magnitude* of a state's ICI score and the size of its unauthorized population. Figure 1.3 (correlation coefficient = 0.34, p-value = 0.016) shows that the intensity of the climate, either positive or negative, increases as the size of the unauthorized population increases.

Figures 1.2 and 1.3, taken together, suggest that states with higher numbers of unauthorized immigrants (relative to state population) tend to be more active in enacting immigration laws. However, there is no discernible pattern in the direction of those laws, whether the laws will be restrictive or integrative in tenor.

While the size of a state's unauthorized population does not portend a negative ICI score, we did find a statistically significant negative correlation between ICI score and the *growth* of a state's unauthorized population. Figure 1.4 shows a negative relationship (correlation coefficient = -0.25, p-value = 0.08) between growth in undocumented population as tracked from 2005 to 2009 and ICI score. That is, states that experienced higher growth in their unauthorized populations tended to have more negative ICI scores.

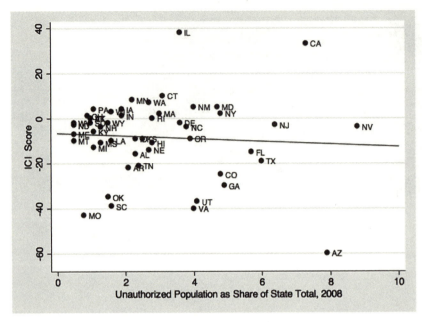

Figure 1.2. ICI Score and Unauthorized Immigrant Population.

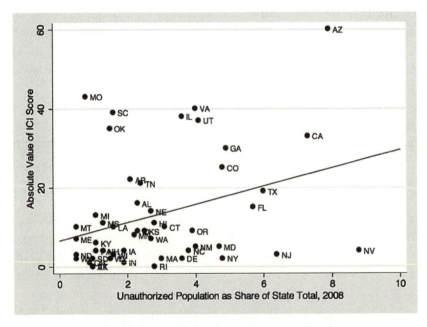

Figure 1.3. Magnitude of ICI Score and Unauthorized Immigrant Population.

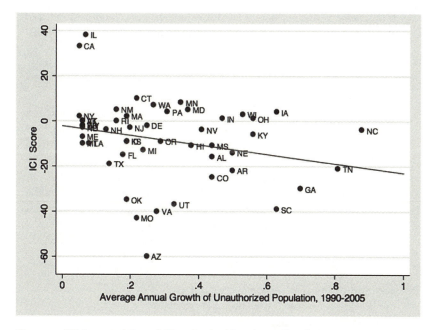

Figure 1.4. ICI Score and Growth Unauthorized Immigrant Population.

These are some initial exercises. With ICI scores that track legislation over time, we can see the evolution of states on immigration issues. We hope to use this information to study the interaction between these laws and economic growth, demographic movement, and other outcomes.

NOTES

1. Randal C. Archibold et al., *Arizona Enacts Stringent Law on Immigration*, N.Y. Times, Apr. 24, 2010, at A1, *available at* 2010 WL 8495626.

2. *Ariz. Immigration Law Would Be among Strictest*, Seattle Times, Apr. 15, 2010, *available at* http://seattletimes.nwsource.com/html/nationworld/2011609060_immigration15.html.

3. *See, e.g.,* Julia Preston, *Political Battle on Illegal Immigration Shifts to States*, N.Y. Times, Jan. 1, 2011, at A1, *available at* http://www.nytimes.com/2011/01/01/us/01immig.html.

4. *See, e.g.,* Jorge M. Chavez & Doris Marie Provine, *Race and the Response of State Legislatures to Unauthorized Immigrants*, 623 annals am. acad. pol. & soc. Sci. 78 (2009) (looking exclusively at state laws, positive and negative); S. Karthick Ramakrishnan & Tom Wong, *Partisanship, Not Spanish: Explaining Municipal Ordinances Affecting Undocumented Immigrants*, *in* Taking Local Control:

Immigration Policy Activism in U.S. Cities and States, 73 (Monica Varsanyi ed., 2010) (looking exclusively at local laws, positive and negative); Huyen Pham & Pham Hoang Van, *The Economic Impact of Local Immigration Regulation: An Empirical Analysis*, 32 Cardozo L. Rev. 485 (2010) (looking exclusively at negative local laws).

5. *See, e.g.*, Michael A. Olivas, *Immigration-Related State and Local Ordinances: Preemption, Prejudice, and the Proper Role for Enforcement*, 2007 U. Chi. Legal F. 27 (opining that though subfederal laws aimed at regulating general immigration functions are constitutionally preempted, there should be an exception carved out for subfederal laws that govern only subfederal interests and do not trigger federal preemption powers); Cristina M. Rodríguez, *The Significance of the Local in Immigration Regulation*, 106 Mich. L. Rev. 567 (2008) (arguing that because state and local governments are responsible for the integration of immigrants, they should have a significant role in immigration regulation); Michael J. Wishnie, *State and Local Police Enforcement of Immigration Laws*, 6 U. Pa. J. Const. L. 1084, 1091–95 (2004) (contesting the proposition that state and local police have inherent authority to enforce civil immigration laws, beyond the authority specifically granted by Congress).

6. We use the terms "law," "ordinance," and "regulation" interchangeably.

7. 2009 Mich. Pub. Acts 119.

8. *See, e.g.*, Dare County, N.C., Resolution 08-04-6 (Apr. 7, 2008) (establishing English as the official language) and Carpentersville Village, Ill., Resolution R07-84 (June 19, 2007) (requiring that all written government transactions be conducted in English).

9. In 2005, state legislatures introduced three hundred immigration bills and enacted thirty-eight, with six bills vetoed. The numbers for subsequent years show a sharp increase: 2006 (570 bills introduced, 84 enacted, 6 vetoed), 2007 (1,562 bills introduced, 240 enacted, 12 vetoed), 2008 (1,305 bills introduced, 206 enacted, 3 vetoed), and 2009 (1,500 bills introduced, 222 enacted, 20 vetoed). 2009 State Laws Related to Immigrants and Immigration, Nat'l Conference of State Legislatures, *available at* http://www.ncsl.org/default.aspx?tabid=19232 (last visited Oct. 28, 2010). Because we use a different definition of immigration regulation, we do not consider all of these enacted laws in our analysis. *See* notes 13–17 and accompanying text.

10. The pattern for local laws is very similar: 2005 (twenty enacted), 2006 (sixty-five enacted), 2007 (eighty-five enacted), 2008 (forty-nine enacted), and 2009 (nineteen enacted).

11. Legal challenges to positive immigration laws have targeted state laws granting in-state tuition rates to unauthorized college students. *See, e.g.,* Martinez v. Regents of the Univ. of Cal., 83 Cal. Rptr.3d 518 (Cal. Ct. App. 2008), *rev'd*, 241 P.3d 855 (Cal. 2010) (holding that state statute granting in-state tuition to unauthorized college students did not violate federal law); Day v. Sebelius, 376 F. Supp. 2d 1022 (D. Kan. 2005), *aff'd sub nom.* Day v. Bond, 500 F.3d 1127 (10th

Cir. 2007) (dismissing a challenge to Kansas's in-state tuition law because the plaintiffs lacked standing); Timberly Ross, *Nebraska Judge Tosses Kobach Suit over Illegal-Immigrant Tuition,* Wichita Eagle, Dec. 18, 2010, *available at* http://www.kansas.com/2010/12/18/1638667/neb-judge-tosses-kobach-suit-over.html.

12. Subfederal restrictions on employment have been challenged on the grounds that the laws are preempted by 8 U.S.C. § 1324a(h)(2), which expressly preempts all state laws "imposing civil or criminal sanctions (other than through licensing and similar laws)" for the hiring of undocumented workers. *See* notes 3–4 *infra.*

13. Reynolds v. City of Valley Park, No. 06-CC-3802, 2007 WL 857320 (Mo. Cir. Ct. Mar. 12, 2007) (holding that the city's law requiring landlords to check immigration status of tenants violated state housing laws).

14. *See, e.g.,* Rene Romo, *Otero Sheriff Settles Immigration Suit over Rights,* Albuquerque Journal, April 10, 2008, at C1, *available at* 2008 WL 6705713 (discussing settlement of a lawsuit in which Hispanic plaintiffs alleged that local law enforcement violated their civil rights in carrying out immigration raids).

15. Chamber of Commerce of U.S. v. Edmondson, 594 F.3d 742, 747 (10th Cir. 2010).

16. Ariz. Contractors Ass'n v. Candelaria, 534 F. Supp. 2d 1036, 1048–49 (D. Ariz. 2008) (rejecting a preemption challenge to the state's employer sanctions law), *aff'd sub nom.* Chicanos Por La Causa, Inc. v. Napolitano, 558 F.3d 856, 866 (9th Cir. 2009).

17. Chamber of Commerce v. Whiting, 131 S. Ct. 1968 (2011).

18. In 2008, the Progressive States Network issued a report that divided states into six categories, ranging from "inactive" to "punitive," depending on whether the state enacted punitive or integrative policies toward immigrants. This report, which did not assign numerical scores, was based on state-level legislation enacted in 2008 only. Progressive States Network, The Anti-Immigrant Movement that Failed: Positive Integration Policies by State Governments Still Far Outweigh Punitive Policies Aimed at New Immigrants (2008), *available at* http://www.progressivestates.org/files/reports/immigrationSept08.pdf.

19. A prominent example would be California's Proposition 187, a political initiative adopted in 1994 that denied a wide variety of benefits to unauthorized immigrants living in the state. The initiative was challenged in court, and the case was settled in mediation. Bob Egelko, *Prop. 187 May Show Arizona Law's Fate,* S.F. Chron., April 26, 2010, at A1, *available at* 2010 WL 8586836.

20. E-mail from Ann Morse, Program Dir., Immigrant Policy Project, Nat'l Conference of State Legislature, to Huyen Pham, Professor of Law, Texas A&M Univ. Sch. of Law (Aug. 12, 2009, 11:47 EST) (on file with author).

21. *See* note 10 *supra.*

22. Thus, the number of state laws in our analysis is smaller than the numbers cited by NCSL as being enacted during these years. *See* note 9 *supra.*

23. Wyo. Stat. Ann. § 144 (2006).

24. Ind. Code § 1182 (2009).

25. H.R. 913, 94th Gen. Assem., Reg. Sess. (Il. 2006). The DREAM Act would offer a pathway to citizenship for undocumented young people who attend college or serve in the military. Teresa Watanabe, *House of Representatives Narrowly Approves DREAM Act: Senate Must Now Vote on Immigration Bill*, L.A. Times, Dec. 8, 2010, *available at* http:// latimesblogs.latimes.com/lanow/2010/12/dream-act.html.

26. Richmond, Cal., Resolution 11-07 (Feb. 6, 2007).

27. *See* notes 22–26 *supra.*

28. Colorado's human trafficking law, enacted in 2009, is typical of the trafficking laws enacted by states: it revises the criminal offense of involuntary servitude to include the act of withholding or threatening to destroy a person's immigration documents and the act of threatening to notify federal immigration authorities of a person's illegal immigration status. Colo. Rev. Stat § 18-13-129 (2009).

29. *See* Progressive States Network, *supra* note 18 (concluding that human trafficking laws benefit immigrants and thus were evidence of a state's integrative policies toward immigrants); Jorge M. Chavez & Doris Marie Provine, *Race and the Response of State Legislatures to Unauthorized Immigrants*, 623 Annals Am. Acad. Pol. & Soc. Sci. 78, 84 (2009) (characterizing human trafficking laws as restrictionist legislation because they increase penalties for those who assist unauthorized immigrants).

30. These organizations include the American Civil Liberties Union, the Mexican American Legal Defense and Education Fund, Latino Justice, the Puerto Rican Legal Defense and Education Fund, the National Day Laborer Organizing Network, and the Ohio Jobs and Justice PAC.

31. The term "287(g)" is taken from the numbered provision in the Immigration and Nationality Act that authorizes the federal-subfederal agreements. 8 U.S.C. § 1357(g) (2006). Under these agreements, DOJ provides training to local and state police officers; it is, however, the responsibility of the subfederal police departments to pay these officers, during both training and actual enforcement duties.

32. Utah Code Ann. § 17-22-9.5 (2008).

33. Tex. Fin. Code Ann. § 156.204 (Vernon 2009).

34. This difference may reflect the limited control that local governments have over social benefit programs, many of which are administered at the state or federal level.

35. Because our data collection ends in 2009, Arizona's score does not include the controversial SB 1070, which was enacted in 2010 and has been described as "the nation's toughest bill on illegal immigration." *See* note 1.

36. One example is Senate Bill 133, which encourages employers to consider the accuracy of E-Verify (a federal system for verifying the work eligibility of potential employees) before using it and prohibiting localities from requiring employers to use the system. 820 Ill. Comp. Stat. Ann. 55/12 (2010).

37. *See, e.g.,* San Jose, Cal., Resolution 73677 (Mar. 6, 2007) (city council resolution prohibiting police from making arrests solely for illegal immigration presence and inquiring about the immigration status of crime victims or witnesses).

38. In 2005, approximately 7.9% of Arizona's population was unauthorized, second only to California's population. Jeffrey S. Passel & D'Vera Cohn, A Portrait of Unauthorized Immigrants in the United States i-ii (2009), Pew Hispanic Ctr., *available at* http://pewhispanic.org/files/reports/107.pdf (listing unauthorized population by state).

2

How Arizona Became Ground Zero in the War on Immigrants

DOUGLAS S. MASSEY

The nation's current immigration crisis and Arizona's controversial role in it didn't just happen. Both outcomes are a direct result of poorly conceived immigration and border policies implemented by the United States over the past fifty years, which have created today's large undocumented population. More than 60% of all unauthorized migrants in the United States today come from Mexico. The next closest country is El Salvador at 5%, followed by Guatemala at 4% and Honduras at 3% (Hoefer, Rytina, and Baker 2010). No other country accounts for more than 2%, which is the rough share comprised by Ecuador, the Philippines, Korea, and India. Brazil comes in at 1%, as does China. The overwhelming majority of undocumented migrants thus come from Latin America, and Mexico dwarfs all other source countries, with more than twelve times the number of undocumented migrants as the next largest contributor.

Mexican immigration to the United States is nothing new, of course. Large-scale flows date to the early twentieth century, and except for a brief hiatus during the Great Depression, Mexicans have been migrating to the United States continuously from 1907 to the present (Massey, Durand, and Malone 2002). The modern era of immigration begins in 1942, when the United States started recruiting temporary workers from Mexico under the auspices of the Bracero Accord, a binational program that sought to revive immigration flows that had died in the deportation campaigns of the 1930s (Calavita 1992). The program grew slowly at first, but expanded dramatically in the 1950s after employers complained about labor shortages and citizens reacted against undocumented migration.

At that time, there were no numerical limits on the number of resident visas available to Latin Americans, and by the late 1950s around a half-million Mexicans were legally entering the United States each year, 90% temporarily as guest workers and 10% as permanent residents. Bracero migration was overwhelmingly male and focused heavily on growers in California, and to a lesser extent on agricultural employers in Texas. Braceros and legal immigrants also went to work sites in Illinois, particularly Chicago, where Mexican migrants had established a foothold in the 1920s (Arrendondo 2008). As temporary and permanent migration from Mexico grew during the 1950s, social networks evolved and ramified to connect workers in Mexico with employers in the United States, and by 1960 the movement of male workers back and forth was fully institutionalized and well integrated into social structures on both sides of the border. This mass movement was entirely legal, and unauthorized migration was close to nonexistent. For most Americans, Mexican migration, despite its volume, was invisible, and the presence of Mexicans in the country was uncontroversial.

The Rise of Undocumented Migration

This picture of tranquility along the border came to an end in 1965, when the U.S. Congress undertook two actions that greatly reduced the legal possibilities for entry into the Untied States from Latin America, especially from Mexico. Politically, these actions were not framed as anti-immigrant measures so much as civil rights reforms. As the civil rights movement gained momentum during the 1960s, pressure grew to eliminate racism from the U.S. immigration system, and in 1965 Congress responded, first by passing landmark amendments to the Immigration and Nationality Act and second by terminating the Bracero Program, despite strenuous objections from Mexico.

The 1965 amendments eliminated long-standing prohibitions on immigration from Asia and Africa and discarded the discriminatory national-origins quotas that had been levied against southern and eastern Europeans in the early 1920s. In their place, a new nondiscriminatory quota system was substituted. Each country in Europe, Africa, Asia, and the Pacific would be given an annual quota of no more than twenty thousand resident visas to be allocated on the basis of U.S. labor needs and family reunification criteria. The Bracero Program was shut down entirely because, in the context of an expanding civil rights movement, it came to be seen as an exploitive labor system on a par with sharecropping in the South.

Although both actions were undertaken for understandable, even laudable reasons, legislators at the time gave little thought to the potential effects of their actions on the large and by then well-established North American immigration system. Under the new legislation, numerical limits were placed on immigration from the western hemisphere for the first time in history, and by 1976 nations in the Americas were also subject to the individual country quota limitation of twenty thousand visas per year. Whereas in the late 1950s, some 450,000 Mexicans had entered the United States each year as Braceros and 50,000 as permanent residents, by the late 1970s the Bracero Program was gone and legal visas were capped at 20,000.

After decades of mass movement back and forth across the border, the North American migration system by the 1960s had acquired a strong momentum rooted in well-developed migrant networks that operated to connect specific employers in the United States with specific sending communities in Mexico. Under the auspices of the Bracero Program, millions of Mexicans had established strong connections to the United States and accumulated significant amounts of time north of the border. As a result, when the avenues for legal entry suddenly disappeared in 1965, the migratory flows did not cease, but simply continued under other auspices. In the absence of legal channels of entry, migrants entered the country without authorization, often going to the same employers for whom they had worked as Braceros.

Thus, the inevitable result of U.S. immigration reforms launched during the civil rights era was a sustained increase in the volume of undocumented migration between Mexico and the United States. The shift in the legal composition of Mexican migration is documented in figure 2.1, which uses official statistics from the U.S. Department of

Homeland Security (2011) to assess Mexican migration to the United States in three categories: legal permanent residents, legal temporary workers, and illegal border crossers. Legal immigration is indicated by the number of Mexicans admitted to permanent residence, guest worker migration by the number of entries made by temporary workers, and undocumented migration by the annual number of apprehensions divided by the number of Border Patrol officers (expressed per thousand). The latter indicator—apprehensions per thousand officers— is a proxy for the volume of undocumented migration in any given year, one that standardizes for the intensity of the enforcement effort, which as we shall see has varied greatly over time.

As can be seen, in 1959 guest worker migration was just under 450,000 per year, and during the early 1960s legal immigration fluctuated around 50,000 per year. Apprehensions, meanwhile, were occurring at around 10,000 per officer per year. With the elimination of the Bracero program in 1965, however, and the progressive imposition of more restrictive limits on legal immigration from the Americas, undocumented migration rose dramatically, with the number of apprehensions per officer increasing from around 30,000 in 1965 to 464,000 in 1977. Legal immigration increased more slowly, rising from around 40,000 in 1965 to reach 135,000 in 1978.

Although the 20,000-visa cap took full effect in 1977, immigrants increasingly were able to overcome this limitation by acquiring U.S. citizenship. Whereas legal residents have the right to sponsor the entry of spouses and minor children subject to quota limitations, once they become U.S. citizens they obtain the right to sponsor the entry of these relatives outside of the quotas. Newly naturalized citizens also acquire the right to sponsor the entry of parents without restriction, as well as the right to sponsor the entry of brothers and sisters subject to numerical limitations. In other words, each new U.S. citizen tends to create additional legal immigrants in years to come, and as more Mexicans have attained U.S. citizenship, the volume of legal immigration has continued to grow and has remained well above the annual cap of twenty thousand visa entries for decades.

As suggested by figure 2.1, the migratory system stabilized during the late 1970s, and the volume of both documented and undocumented immigrants stopped rising. From 1976 to 1986, apprehensions fluctuated

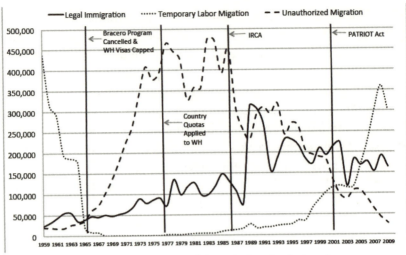

Figure 2.1. Mexican migration to the United States in three legal categories.

between 330,000 and 470,000 per officer, dropping during Mexico's oil boom of 1978–1982 and rising with the onset of the peso crisis in 1982, but with no consistent trend over time. Over the same period, legal immigration fluctuated between 73,000 and 150,000 entries per year and followed much the same temporal pattern, but again with no secular trend. In practical terms, the North American migratory system had reestablished itself by the late 1970s, but with the crucial difference that most of the movement was unauthorized.

In essence, the United States after 1965 shifted from a *de jure* labor system based on the annual circulation of legal temporary workers and a small number of legal permanent residents to a *de facto* system based on the circulation of undocumented workers and a somewhat larger number of permanent residents. According to estimates by Massey and Singer (1995), 85% of all undocumented entries between 1965 and 1985 were offset by departures, and among legal immigrants more than one-third of arrivals were offset by departures (Jasso and Rosenzweig 1982). The system was thus largely circular, and once the status quo ante of seasonal migration had been reestablished in the late 1970s, there was no real change in the volume of either documented or undocumented migration up to the passage of the Immigration Reform and Control Act (IRCA) in 1986.

As shown in figure 2.1, after the passage of IRCA, undocumented migration dropped while legal immigration rose. Legal immigration from Mexico increased because of IRCA's amnesty and farm worker legalization programs, which ultimately admitted 2.3 million former undocumented migrants to legal permanent residence. IRCA also required legalizing immigrants to take English and civics courses and pushed them toward citizenship, which as we have seen simply produced more legal immigration in years to come. In the aftermath of the legalization, the volume of undocumented migration dropped dramatically as migrants stopped circulating and remained in the United States to file applications for legalization. Thus, from 1988 through 1996, annual apprehensions fluctuated between 250,000 and 300,000 per officer, and legal immigration fluctuated between 150,000 and 200,000 per year.

In 1976, Congress had quietly reinstated temporary worker migration under the H-visa program, but the number of such visas issued to Mexicans remained small until 1996. The number of temporary admissions from Mexico rose from just 2,000 in 1977 to 26,000 in 1995. As shown in figure 2.1, however, temporary worker migration surged in the late 1990s to reach 120,000 in the first years of the new century, and then surged again after 2005 to peak at 361,000 in 2008, the largest number of temporary entries from Mexico since the Bracero Program. In that year entries by legal permanent residents totaled 192,000, bringing the total number of Mexican entries to 553,000. As opportunities for legal entry rose, the number of apprehensions steadily fell, decreasing from 319,000 per officer in 1993 to just 28,000 in 2009. By the time of the great recession of 2008, undocumented migration had all but stopped.

Rise of the Latino Threat Narrative

Although Mexico-U.S. migration may have stabilized in the late 1970s and the growth in undocumented migration had essentially ceased, the annual circulation of hundreds of thousands of undocumented migrants and the large number of annual border apprehensions offered a tempting opportunity for political entrepreneurs to mobilize around the issue of illegal migration. In 1976, annual apprehensions along the Mexico-U.S. border totaled some 780,000, and in October of that year the head of the U.S. Border Patrol published an article in *Reader's Digest* entitled "Illegal Aliens: Time to Call a Halt!"(Gutierrez 1995). In it he alleged that for every migrant apprehended, two successfully evaded apprehension, and that the undocumented population had reached twelve million and was rapidly rising. To stop illegal immigration, he unsurprisingly called for a massive increase in funding for his agency.

Because so many migrants were now "illegal," they were easily framed as "criminals" and portrayed as "threatening" to American society. Politicians looking for an issue to mobilize voters seized on the rise in apprehensions as evidence of an unprecedented "alien invasion" in which "outgunned" Border Patrol officers "fought" to "hold the line" against "banzai charges" of "alien hordes" (Dunn 1996; Rotella 1998). Likewise, journalists looking for a sensational story to grab headlines warned of a "rising tide" of "illegals" that would "flood" the United States to "inundate" American society and "swamp" its culture (Andreas 2000; Chavez 2001).

After 1965 the description of Latino immigration was increasingly framed in such threatening martial and maritime metaphors (Massey and Sanchez 2010). Politicians and journalists were provided with a steady stream of sensational stories, images, and statistics by Border Patrol officials eager to increase their budgets and expand their bureaucratic influence (Rotella 1998; Massey, Durand, and Malone 2002). To measure the rise of what Chavez (2008) calls "the Latino threat narrative," I used the Proquest database to search articles published in the *New York Times, Wall Street Journal, Washington Post*, and *Los Angeles Times* from January 1965 through December 2009 and counted the number of times "undocumented," "illegal," or "unauthorized" "migrants" or "aliens" were paired with "Mexico" or "Mexicans" and with the words "crisis," "flood," or "invasion." The resulting data were smoothed using three-year moving averages to yield the plots shown in figure 2.2.

As revealed by the figure, the use of threatening marine and martial metaphors in connection with Mexican immigration was close to zero in 1965. As the number of apprehensions steadily rose in the ensuing years to render Mexican migrants more visible and seemingly more threatening, the use of these metaphors rose exponentially, from an average of just 0.5 in 1965 to a peak of 36 in 1979. After this date, the frequency of threatening metaphors, like the trend in apprehensions itself, stopped rising and began to fluctuate, falling during periods of economic expansion in the United States and rising during periods of economic decline.

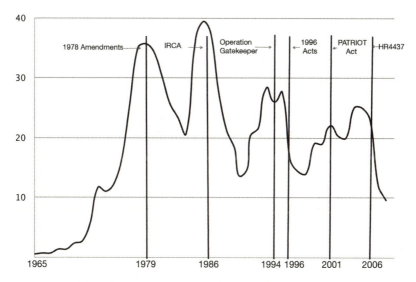

Figure 2.2. Mentions of Mexican immigration as a crisis, flood, or invasion in leading U.S. newspaper.

Each peak, however, coincided with the passage of a new piece of anti-immigrant legislation or the implementation of a new restrictive border policy. In 1978, for example, amendments to the Immigration and Nationality Act were passed to eliminate the separate quota for the western hemisphere, essentially forcing Mexicans to compete for visas with immigrants worldwide. Likewise, at the peak in 1986, the Immigration Reform and Control Act (IRCA) was passed to criminalize undocumented hiring and expand the Border Patrol. Then, in 1994, Operation Gatekeeper undertook a full-scale militarization of the busiest border sector in San Diego; in 2001 the PATRIOT Act further augmented enforcement resources and streamlined removal proceedings; and finally, in 2006, the Sensenbrenner Bill (HR 4437) sought to make undocumented status a felony and dramatically ramp up enforcement efforts not only at the border but throughout the United States. (Although this legislation passed the House, however, it failed in the Senate and was never enacted.)

Thus, rising undocumented migration from 1965 to 1975 and its perpetuation thereafter set off a self-feeding cycle of ever greater border enforcement and more restrictive immigration legislation (Andreas

2000; Massey, Durand, and Malone 2002). Increased restrictions and greater enforcement generated more apprehensions, which generated more political pressure for more restrictive measures, which produced still more apprehensions, which justified more enforcement, and so on—all this despite the fact that the volume of undocumented entries had, in fact, peaked by the late 1970s. During the 1980s and 1990s, immigration enforcement increasingly fed off itself.

The War on Immigrants

This powerful feedback cycle could only yield one result—an exponential increase in border enforcement—and this is precisely what we observe in figure 2.3, which shows trends in three indicators of the intensity of enforcement along the Mexico-U.S. border: the number of Border Patrol officers, the number of linewatch hours officers spend patrolling the border, and the size of the Border Patrol budget. In order to standardize the curves and put them on the same scale, each series was divided by the value in 1986, when the militarization of the border began in earnest. The numbers plotted after that date thus indicate the number of times an enforcement indicator has increased since 1986.

In each series, we observe little upward movement before 1986; but after the passage of IRCA we witness an acceleration in the enforcement effort, which quickens again after the 1994 launching of Operation Gatekeeper in San Diego. Enforcement accelerates once more after 1996 with the passage of the Illegal Immigrant Reform and Immigrant Responsibility Act and other pieces of anti-immigrant legislation, and then rises dramatically after the passage of the PATRIOT Act in 2001. By 2009 the number of Border Patrol officers was 5.5 times the number in 1986, the number of linewatch hours had increased 8.6 times since that date, and the Border Patrol budget had risen twenty-three times.

As dramatic as the rise in border enforcement was, the increase in internal enforcement was even steeper, as indicated in figure 2.4, which shows the trend in the annual number of Mexicans deported from within the United States. From 1965 to 1985, the annual number of deportations fluctuated in the tens of thousands, with no clear trend. After the passage of IRCA, deportations begin to rise slowly; but with the passage of the Antiterrorism and Effective Death Penalty Act in

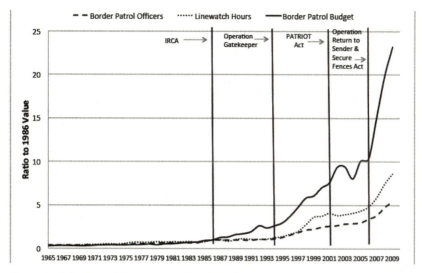

Figure 2.3. Indicators of the intensity of border enforcement.

1996, they abruptly increased and plateaued at 150,000 in 1999–2001. They increased exponentially thereafter to reach 283,000 in 2009. From 1986 to 2009, the annual number of Mexicans deported from the United States rose by a factor of twenty-six, even though over the same period the estimated size of the undocumented Mexican population increased by a factor of just three.

Consequences of the War on Immigrants

The tripling of the number of undocumented Mexicans between 1986 and 2009 is nothing to scoff at, of course, and the presence of 6.5 million undocumented Mexicans (plus 4.7 million non-Mexicans) carries serious implications for U.S. society. It would also seem to contradict my earlier assertion that the Mexican migration system had stabilized by the middle 1970s and that the volume of undocumented migration experienced no sustained increase thereafter. This seeming contradiction is resolved by an understanding of the effect that border enforcement had on the behavior of undocumented migrants. To put it bluntly, restrictive U.S. immigration and border policies paradoxically acted to transform what had been a circular flow of male Mexican workers going to three states into a settled population of Mexican families living in fifty states. What changed was not so much the number of

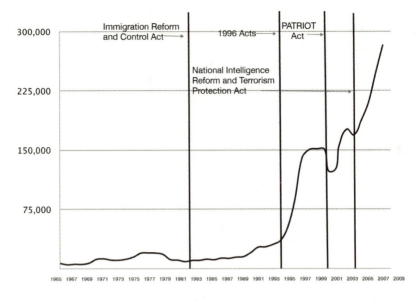

Figure 2.4. Number of Mexicans deported from the United States.

undocumented migrants arriving and crossing the border each year, but where they crossed, where they went after getting in, and how long they stayed at their new places of destination. All of these behaviors changed dramatically as a result of the War on Immigrants.

Likelihood of Leaving for the United States

Unauthorized migration from Mexico naturally begins with a decision to set out for the border and attempt to cross it without proper documentation. Because such migration is clandestine, official statistics offer little information about the migration decision itself. Undocumented migrants are included in the U.S. Census and Current Population Survey, and given data on the number of legal entries, mortality trends, emigration patterns, and undercount rates, one can derive an indirect estimate of the size of the undocumented population (see Warren and Passel 1987). Indeed, using such an approach, the Department of Homeland Security (Hoefer, Rytina, and Baker 2010) and the Pew Hispanic Center (Passel and Cohn 2011) now regularly produce estimates of the stock of undocumented migrants living in the United States.

Useful as they are, aggregated estimates of the number of undocumented migrants reveal little about changes in migratory behavior over time. For that information, we turn to the Mexican Migration Project (MMP), a binational study that each year surveys Mexicans on both sides of the border and adds the information they provide to a cumulative database on patterns and processes of documented and undocumented migration (http://mmp.opr.princeton.edu). The database currently contains life histories of 21,475 household heads, and each history includes a complete history of migration and border crossing, which can be used to compute annual probabilities of undocumented migration to and from the United States (Massey, Durand, and Pren 2009).

Prior work indicates that the likelihood that someone who has never migrated before will take a first undocumented trip to the United States is much lower than the likelihood that an experienced migrant will take an additional trip (Massey et al. 1987). Figure 2.5 thus displays two trends: the probability that a Mexican household head took a first trip to the United States and the probability that a household head took an additional trip after at least one trip had already occurred. As expected, the likelihood of initiating undocumented migration is much lower than the likelihood of migrating again without documents. On average, the probability of taking a first undocumented trip is just 0.008, whereas the probability of taking another trip is 0.039.

In terms of trends, the probability of taking a first undocumented trip begins at just 0.003 in 1965, but consistent with the trend in apprehensions observed earlier in figure 2.1, it rises steadily to peak at .012 in 1979. This is a fourfold increase in a little over a decade. After this date, the probability of initiating undocumented migration stabilizes and fluctuates around .010 through the year 2001. It then drifts downward to reach zero by 2009. In contrast, the probability of taking an additional undocumented trip fluctuates around 0.040 from 1965 through 1992, but once Operation Blockade and Operation Gatekeeper are launched in 1993 and 1994, the probability rises abruptly to peak at around .055 in 2000. The militarization of the two busiest border crossings thus seems actually to have *encouraged* rather than discouraged experienced migrants to undertake an additional U.S. trip. Knowing that border crossing was becoming more difficult, migrants in the know sought to get in while the getting was good. The probability of

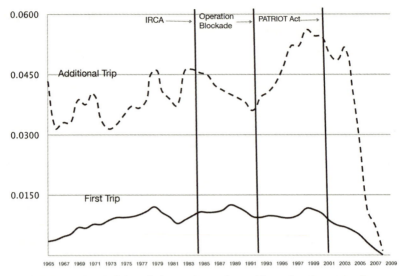

Figure 2.5. Annual probability of taking a first and an additional undocumented trip to the United States.

migration remained high until 2004, and then plummeted to zero between then and 2009.

According to these data, therefore, the massive increase in border enforcement during the late twentieth century had little effect on the likelihood of initiating undocumented migration, at least through 2000, and may even have increased the likelihood of continuing undocumented migration among experienced migrants between 1993 and 2005. Consistent with the apprehension statistics analyzed in figure 2.1, however, both likelihoods drop to zero by 2009. As already noted, in the context of a severe recession and given the greatest access to legal visas since the 1950s, undocumented migration from Mexico has effectively ceased.

Likelihood of Returning to Mexico

The growth of the undocumented population depends not only on the number of unauthorized entries, of course, but also on the number of undocumented departures. In addition to computing the likelihood of leaving for the United States, MMP data can be used to compute the probability of going back to Mexico. Figure 2.6 shows trends in the probability that an undocumented migrant returned to the United States within twelve months of entering on first and later trips. As one might expect, migrants are more likely to return from later trips than first trips. Those migrants with prior trips are likely already to have settled into a strategic pattern of recurrent migration (Massey et al. 1987). From 1965 to 1986, the likelihood of returning from an additional trip fluctuated around 0.80, whereas the likelihood of returning from a first trip varied between 0.55 and 0.60.

In neither case, however, do we see any evidence of a trend before the passage of IRCA in 1986. After that date, both return probabilities undergo a rapid decline that pauses briefly during the period 1995–1999 but accelerates thereafter. By 2009 the probability of returning from a first trip had dropped to zero, while the probability of returning from a later trip had fallen to 0.30. Return migration fell because the militarization of the border dramatically increased the costs and risks of undocumented border crossing. According to Massey, Durand, and Malone (2002), IRCA tripled the death rate among border crossers, and estimates computed by Massey, Durand, and Pren (2009) suggest that smuggling fees increased by a factor of six, rising from an average of around $500 before IRCA to around $3,000 in 2008 (in constant 2008 dollars). In order to minimize the costs and risks of border crossing, undocumented migrants quite rationally stopped crossing the border, not by deciding to remain in Mexico in the first place but by hunkering down and staying longer in the United States once they had managed to get in.

To this point, the data clearly indicate that the probability of undocumented entry remained stable or increased slightly from the late 1970s through the year 2000, despite the massive increase in border enforcement, but that the likelihood of out-migration fell markedly after 1986. The coincidence of these two trends necessarily implies an increase in *net* undocumented migration. Arithmetically, net migration equals in-migration minus out-migration, so that if undocumented in-migration persists while undocumented out-migration falls, net undocumented migration must rise. If we apply the probabilities shown in figures 2.5 and 2.6 to annual counts of Mexico's population, we can derive an

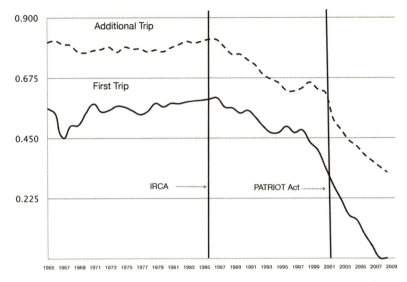

Figure 2.6. Probability of returning within 12 months of entry on first and additional undocumented trips.

estimate of total net annual migration. Figure 2.7 shows the results of this exercise.

As shown in the figure, net undocumented migration rose sharply after 1965, but by 1979 had stabilized and fluctuated around 380,000 net entries per year. Net migration fell during Mexico's oil boom to reach 270,000 in 1982, but with the onset of economic crisis in that year it rose back up to 380,000, where it persisted from1985 through 1987. With the implementation of IRCA, however, the net rate of undocumented migration began to rise, not because more people were coming to the United States without authorization but because fewer undocumented migrants were going home, a trend that accelerated after the implementation of the border blockades in 1993 and 1994, ultimately reaching a net of 922,000 entries in 2004. The area between the dashed horizontal line and the curve of net entries represents the number of additional entries caused by the militarization of the border. If enforcement efforts had remained at pre-1986 levels, there would have been around 5.3 million fewer net undocumented entries thereafter. To a large and very significant extent, the growth of the undocumented population was an artifact of U.S. policies.

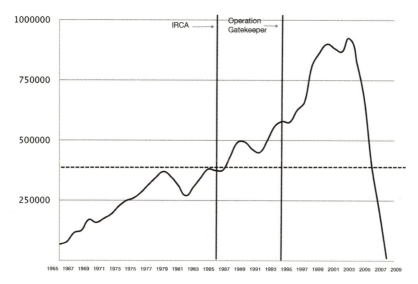

Figure 2.7. Estimated net undocumented migration on first and later trips.

Changing Geography of Migration

Not only did American policies backfire by discouraging return migration; they also radically transformed the geography of undocumented migration. Historically, the vast majority of Mexican migrants crossed into the United States along the border between San Diego and Tijuana, and to a lesser extent between El Paso and Juarez. When IRCA began the expansion of border enforcement after 1986, enforcement resources were naturally concentrated in these two sectors; and when these measures failed to stop the inflow, U.S. authorities implemented a full-scale militarization in El Paso in 1993 and in San Diego in 1994, complete with steel walls, watch towers, motion detectors, air surveillance, and additional Border Patrol officers. As the costs and risks of crossing in these sectors rose, migrants quite rationally began crossing elsewhere, mostly through the Sonoran desert into Arizona.

The changing geography of undocumented border crossing is depicted in figure 2.8, which draws on MMP data to show trends in the state of crossing from 1965 to 2009. Up until the border militarization began, undocumented migration had been focused increasingly on

California. The percentage of crossings into California rose from 57% in 1965 to peak at 71% in 1988. After this date, the share of border crossings into California underwent a sustained decline that only accelerated after the launching of Operation Gatekeeper in 1994, ultimately reaching a nadir of 20% in 2003 before experiencing a brief revival to 30% in 2006 and then falling back down to 14% in 2008

As entries into California steadily fell, crossings into Arizona correspondingly rose. Prior to 1988 the Arizona-Sonora border had been a quiet backwater, accounting for just 5–8% of all border crossings. After this date, crossings into Arizona rose quite rapidly to peak at 47% in 2003. From a quiet backwater Arizona had become the busiest sector along the entire border. With the launching of the Arizona border initiative in 2004, however, crossing there became more costly, risky, and difficult. Thus, migrants once again shifted their attention to other sectors along the border, and crossings into Arizona decreased to around 20% by 2009. Despite the rapid decline, however, crossings into Arizona still remained well above the historical level of 6% to 8%.

The deflection of undocumented migrants away from California left them far from traditional destinations at a time when employment opportunities elsewhere were surging, and undocumented migrants responded by proceeding in growing numbers to new destination areas throughout the country rather than heading back to California. Figure 2.9 uses MMP data to show trends in the state of destination for undocumented migrants from 1965 to 2009. Prior to IRCA, the vast majority of undocumented Mexicans went to just three states: California, Illinois, and Texas. As shown in the figure, the percentage going to these states fluctuated between 85% and 90% from 1965 through 1988, with no particular trend.

Afterward, however, migration to traditional destinations underwent a sustained decline, and by 2009 only 54% of all undocumented migrants went to one of the three principal states. Almost all of the shift came at the expense of California. Whereas two-thirds of all Mexicans who arrived in the United States between 1985 and 1990 went to California, ten years later only one-third who arrived between 1995 and 2000 went to that state, a fraction that persisted for Mexicans who arrived between 2000 and 2005 (Massey and Capoferro 2008). The hardening of the border in San Diego may have reduced the flow of undocumented

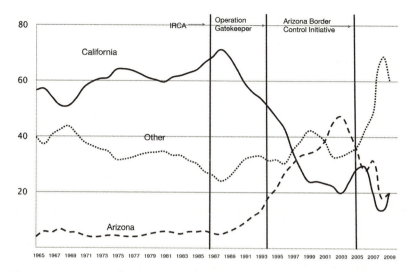

Figure 2.8. Percentage of undocumented border crossings by state.

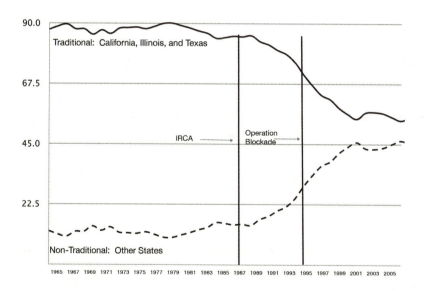

Figure 2.9. Percentage of undocumented migrants going to traditional and non-traditional destinations.

migrants into California, but it did not reduce the flow into the United States, and by 2009 nearly half of all undocumented migrants were going to nontraditional destinations. As a result, the most rapidly growing Mexican communities in the United States are no longer in California, Texas, or Illinois, but in North Carolina, South Carolina, Georgia, Iowa, Nebraska, and Minnesota. In other words, U.S. border policies transformed Mexican immigration from a regional to a national issue.

Arizona as Ground Zero

Arizona's recent emergence as a center of anti-immigrant protest, xenophobia, and nativism is thus part of a much larger transformation of the American immigration system. It is also a direct result of U.S. policy actions and initiatives. The launching of the War on Immigrants and the consequent militarization of the border transformed what had been a stable circular flow of Mexican male workers going to three states into a much larger population of Mexican families living in fifty states. Arizona emerged as a border hotspot and new destination area because U.S. policies blocked pathways to California. In 1992, on the eve of the American border blockades, Arizona accounted for under 100,000 apprehensions, and its undocumented population was just 50,000. Eight years after Operations Blockade and Gatekeeper had deflected the flows away from El Paso and San Diego, the number of apprehensions exceeded 700,000 and Arizona's undocumented population had risen to 330,000. Eight years after that the undocumented population peaked at 560,000 in 2008, with 320,000 apprehensions along Arizona's southern border.

Arizona continues to mirror national trends in the present day. As already noted, undocumented migration to the United States has effectively ceased. According to estimates by Hoefer, Rytina, and Baker (2009, 2010), the undocumented population of the United States fell from 11.6 million to 10.8 million between January 1, 2008, and January 1, 2009, and Arizona's undocumented population alone dropped from 560,000 to 460,000. According to more recent estimates published by Passel and Cohn (2011), Arizona's population dropped by another 60,000 persons between 2009 and 2010, reaching just 400,000 in the latter year. Clearly, undocumented populations in Arizona and elsewhere in the United States have stopped growing, and flows have dropped to zero or below. In other words, after twenty-five years of steadily rising border enforcement, the border by any measure is now "under control." At the same time, as we have seen, legal immigration and guest worker immigration from Mexico have both risen to record levels, with temporary legal entries from Mexico averaging 331,000 per year and entries of legal permanent residents, around 178,000 per year.

As in the late 1950s, therefore, the United States is taking in roughly 500,000 Mexican migrants per year in legal status, and undocumented migration has virtually disappeared. The proponents of immigration reform have long articulated four basic goals: gaining control of the border, creating a large guest worker program, expanding quotas for legal immigration from Mexico, and legalizing undocumented residents already present in the United States. In a very real way, three of the four goals have already been achieved. Undocumented migration has ended, legal immigration has expanded to nearly 180,000 per year, and guest worker entries are at levels not seen since the height of the Bracero Program.

The only piece of unfinished business at this point is the legalization of the estimated 11.2 million undocumented residents now living in the United States, 6.5 million of whom are Mexican. During a time when undocumented migration has ceased, legalizing these people and integrating them into American society should be the focus of future policy efforts at both the state and national levels. The undocumented population of the United States was created by U.S. policies, and U.S. policy actions are required to solve the problem. The longer we put off this day of political reckoning, the worse the situation will get for all concerned. Undocumented migrants currently comprise 4% of the population, 8% of the labor force, a third of the foreign born, and 60% of Mexican immigrants. The United States cannot continue to function well as a democratic republic with such large shares of people lacking social, economic, and civic rights.

BIBLIOGRAPHY

Andreas, Peter. 2000. *Border Games: Policing the US-Mexico Divide*. Ithaca, NY: Cornell University Press.

Arrendondo, Gabriela F. 2008. *Mexican Chicago: Race, Identity, and Nation, 1916–39.* Urbana: University of Illinois Press.

Calavita, Kitty. 1992. *Inside the State: The Bracero Program, Immigration, and the I.N.S.* New York: Routledge.

Chavez, Leo R. 2001. *Covering Immigration: Population Images and the Politics of the Nation.* Berkeley: University of California Press.

———. 2008. *The Latino Threat: Constructing Immigrants, Citizens, and the Nation.* Stanford, CA: Stanford University Press.

Dunn, Timothy J. 1996. *The Militarization of the U.S.-Mexico Border, 1978–1992: Low-Intensity Conflict Doctrine Comes Home.* Austin: Center for Mexican American Studies, University of Texas at Austin.

Gutiérez, David G. 1995. *Walls and Mirrors: Mexican Americans, Mexican Immigrants, and the Politics of Ethnicity.* Berkeley: University of California Press.

Hoefer, Michael, Nancy Rytina, and Bryan C. Baker. 2009. *Estimates of the Unauthorized Immigrant Population Residing in the United States: January 2008.* Washington, DC: Office of Immigration Statistics, U.S. Department of Homeland Security.

———. 2010. *Estimates of the Unauthorized Immigrant Population Residing in the United States: January 2009.* Washington, DC: Office of Immigration Statistics, U.S. Department of Homeland Security.

Jasso, Guillermina, and Mark R. Rosenzweig. 1982. "Estimating the Emigration Rates of Legal Immigrants Using Administrative and Survey Data: The 1971 Cohort of Immigrants to the United States." *Demography* 19:279–90.

Massey, Douglas S., Rafael Alarcón, Jorge Durand, and Humberto González. 1987. *Return to Aztlan: The Social Process of International Migration from Western Mexico.* Berkeley: University of California Press.

Massey, Douglas S., and Chiara Capoferro. 2008. "The Geographic Diversification of U.S. Immigration." Pp. 25–50 in Douglas S. Massey, ed., *New Faces in New Places: The Changing Geography of American Immigration.* New York: Russell Sage Foundation.

Massey, Douglas S., Jorge Durand, and Nolan J. Malone. 2002. *Beyond Smoke and Mirrors: Mexican Immigration in an Age of Economic Integration.* New York: Russell Sage Foundation.

Massey, Douglas S., Jorge Durand, and Karen Pren. 2009. "Nuevos Escenarios de la Migración México-Estados Unidos: Las Consecuencias de la Guerra Antiinmigrante." *Papeles de Población* 61:101–28.

Massey, Douglas S., and Magaly Sánchez R. 2010. *Brokered Boundaries: Creating Immigrant Identity in Anti-Immigrant Times.* New York: Russell Sage Foundation.

Massey, Douglas S., and Audrey Singer. 1995. "New Estimates of Undocumented Mexican Migration and the Probability of Apprehension." *Demography* 32:203–13.

Passel, Jeffrey S., and D'Vera Cohn. 2011. "Unauthorized Immigrant Population: National and State Trends, 2010." Washington, DC: Pew Hispanic Center

Rotella, Sebastian. 1998. *Twilight on the Line: Underworlds and Politics at the U.S.-Mexico Border.* New York: Norton.

U.S. Department of Homeland Security. 2011. Website of the Office of Immigration Statistics. http://www.dhs.gov/files/statistics/immigration.shtm. Accessed February 14, 2011.

Warren, Robert, and Jeffrey Passel. 1987. "A Count of the Uncountable: Estimates of Undocumented Aliens Counted in the 1980 US Census." *Demography* 24:375–96.

PART II

Historical Antecedents to the Modern State and Local Efforts to Regulate Immigration

3

"A War to Keep Alien Labor out of Colorado"

The "Mexican Menace" and the Historical Origins of
Local and State Anti-Immigration Initiatives

TOM I. ROMERO II

Introduction

In the early months of 1935, the governor of Colorado, "Big" Ed Johnson, initiated the first of several measures intended to deter undocumented immigrant labor from Mexico from entering the state. Animated by speculation that an "alien menace" from Mexico not only exacerbated the economic crisis gripping the nation but also directly contributed to the financial meltdown several years earlier, Governor Johnson, himself the son of immigrants, felt the need to act in the face of what he perceived as a federal inability to control the nation's borders.[1] First, Governor Johnson sent letters to the federal government demanding the deportation of "alien labor." The governor then declared that if the federal authorities refused to enforce its immigration laws, he would deploy the Colorado National Guard to do the job.[2] In anticipation of such a call, Governor Johnson approved a plan to establish a "concentration camp" for the Mexican "aliens" at the National Guard's training facility on the western outskirts of the Denver metropolitan area.[3] Under the plan approved by Governor Johnson and opposed only by "a group of local communists," all aliens on relief were to be placed in the camp in preparation for their eventual deportation.[4]

As the opening shot in a war to keep alien labor out of Colorado, Governor Johnson encouraged both local and statewide efforts to enforce the nation's immigration laws. From the deputization of local sheriffs to round up and summarily deport "aliens" to the deployment of the National Guard to police Colorado's border with New Mexico to the tacit endorsement of vigilantes to keep "Mexicans" out of the state, the state of Colorado during the Great Depression became one of the earliest flashpoints in the debate over the precise authority and jurisdiction of a state to enforce federal immigration law independent of federal cooperation. Although the United States Supreme Court would remain conspicuously silent on such issues until its 2012 decision in *Arizona v. United States*, the actions taken by Colorado in the mid-1930s were extraordinary and unprecedented in their scope and orientation. Of questionable legality from its inception, Colorado's decision to chart its own course of immigration enforcement provides important lessons about the challenges of state-level immigration enforcement.

This chapter details Colorado's experiment in the local enforcement of immigration law and policy. Starting with the state's as well as the entire American Southwest's dependency on Mexican American and Mexican agricultural labor, the chapter examines the relationship of labor markets, labor conditions, law, and policy to the creation of a "Mexican problem" in the American Southwest. It also explores how and in what ways state and local government authorities sought to define and respond to the "Mexican menace" as the failed enforcement of federal immigration law. Though there had long been a history of local and state cooperation with federal authorities concerning the migration of foreign nationals into the United States, Colorado's efforts raised critically important questions about the scope and authority of state governments to enforce federal immigration law without the consent of federal authorities. Much like local and state-level attempts to enforce federal immigration law today, Colorado's Depression-era immigration "law and policy" not only challenged Congress's seemingly settled absolute power to determine who had license and permission to be in the United States but it also questioned who had the authority to define and extend the benefits of citizenship.

The chapter then examines how the question of citizenship embedded in Colorado's ultimately futile efforts at immigration control contributed to the production of a color line in a United States where categories of Whiteness and Blackness were becoming increasingly insufficient.[5] Though Governor Johnson's policies were contested by federal officials (who had their own shifting immigration agenda), the Mexican consulate, other state governments, Mexican Americans, segments of organized labor, and agricultural business, Colorado's attempt to stop the "Mexican menace" highlighted the way the question of immigration was intricately connected to deep-rooted and changing patterns of racial bias and inequity. Like similar local and state enforcement against "illegal immigration" both then and now, the state's policies set into motion a series of events that gave legal cover to the social and economic harassment of Latinos—regardless of their status as American citizens. The legal construction of "illegal" Mexicans in Colorado and other states—whether they were American citizens or legally admitted under federal law—under the guise of a failure of federal authorities to enforce immigration law cast Latinos as permanently foreign, unassimilable, and directly threatening to the racial homogeneity of the state and the nation. Then, as now, a local or state government's attempt to police and deport the "illegal alien" with the use of its county sheriffs, the state patrol, or its National Guard highlighted the problematic extent to which local and state governments exercised their most disciplinary powers of sovereignty (policing) against Latinos, subject to the most minimal standards of judicial review (immigration law).

Because the vast majority of those "Mexicans" rounded up were American citizens as well as because of the unquestioned illegality (at the time) of the state's policy, Governor Johnson was quietly forced to stop the militarization of immigration enforcement altogether. Nevertheless, Colorado's Depression-era experiment with immigration control exposed inherent cracks in the edifice of immigration law as it came to be reconstructed in the early decades of the twentieth century. As the federal government instituted rigid control of borders, passports, and restrictions on entry and exit during this time, and as the Supreme Court declared immigration law to be an expression of the sovereign's right to determine its own membership and right of self-preservation, it should be no surprise that individual state governments would fixate on immigration. Indeed, Colorado's belligerent and over-the-top response to perceived failures of the federal government to police and control its borders would become a common trope in the emerging struggle between states and federal authorities over immigration issues. By the start of 1937, the "Mexican Menace" in Colorado had abated, though its consequences would linger for years to come.

I. "The Problem of the Mexican Wage Earner"

In the spring of 1930, Thomas Mahony, chairman of the Mexican Welfare Committee for the Colorado State Council of the Knights of Columbus, addressed a large audience at the Catholic Conference on Industrial Problems. The subject of his address was the "problem of the Mexican wage earner" in Colorado's sugar industry. Mahony described in great detail the inner workings of the sugar industry. At the top were the sugar companies that purchased and refined the sugar beets, which were grown by local growers throughout the state. The grower, "to make a profit at the price he gets, must have low wage labor or else he won't grow beets; and without beets the sugar companies could not operate their factories and make a profit."[6] The harvesting of the sugar beets, however, was not easy. It required intensive cultivation during most of the seven-month growing season.[7]

What made this particular form of labor unique, according to Mahony, was the fact that "it is dependent upon the labor of the family: the father, the mother, and little children."[8] As one sugar company circular noted, "an inexperienced man can work 9 acres, a woman 7 acres, and children in proportion to age."[9] Mahony stressed that this was not work that "native Americans," either as individuals or as families, were likely to seek or want. Due to pervasive discrimination in manufacturing and service work, the beginnings of restrictions on immigration from Southern and Eastern Europe in 1917, and sugar company–sponsored propaganda that said the Mexicans were especially well suited for sugar beet cultivation and harvest,[10] Mexican American and Mexican families were pushed into this narrow segment of the labor market—providing over two-thirds of the sugar beet laborers in Colorado.[11] Every winter and early spring, representatives of the sugar companies would travel throughout the American Southwest and northern Mexico to recruit Latino families for the sugar beet harvest. Contrary to the sugar companies' propagation of the notion that sugar beet laborers were docile and foreign "Mexicans," a vast majority of the families were in fact American citizens, born and reared largely in Colorado, New Mexico, and Texas.[12]

With few economic opportunities, these Latino families had little choice but to sign the standard beet labor contract.[13] The father would sign the contract on behalf of the family; and the size of the acreage assigned to the family in the contract would be based upon the proportional share to which every member of the family could be expected to work. The company unilaterally established the conditions under which the contract was to be performed. It left all disputes between grower and laborer to the company's final judgment; it provided no guarantee that the laborer would receive pay when work was completed; nor did it stipulate when the work season ended. In regard to this final point, Mahony noted that in the fall of 1929, Latino workers were "compelled to work in the field until late in the winter, under terrible weather conditions, without extra pay, and under penalty of losing the money they have already earned, if they stop work before 'all the crop is harvested.'"[14]

Though beet labor contracts typically included clauses providing that "children under 11 years of age" shall not be allowed to work in the fields, Mahony cited a long list of "open" and "flagrant" violations of these provisions.[15] It was common for children as young as six years old to be working in the fields, not only preventing them from attending school but also posing a direct threat to their lives. According to one study of the Arkansas Valley cited by Mahony, nearly 30% of the children died among a group of 140 beet labor families working in the sugar beet fields.[16]

Further exacerbating the tenuous existence of Latino families, sugar companies secured the next season's labor supply by giving credit for food and supplies to these same families during the winter. The problem, as Mahony noted, was that the credit was to be paid out of the next season's work. In this "system of Peonage" reminiscent of sharecropping in the American South, the Latino family would "start work in the spring handicapped by a debt to the sugar company which will reduce the amount coming to [them] in the fall."[17] Other families, recognizing the endless cycle of debt, "flocked to Denver, Pueblo, and to some of the smaller Colorado towns" seeking support from private charities and public agencies.

The question of Latino labor in the beet fields and beyond became wrapped up in the national discourse of nativism, racism, and immigration restriction in the early decades of the twentieth century. Though this period saw a general rising of nativism, fears about the "alienizing of America" fell unevenly on the Latino labor force.[18] Mexicans and other Latin Americans were exempt from the wholesale exclusion imposed on the Chinese and other Asians, and ultimately large-scale restrictions on southern and eastern Europeans, and thus Mexican immigrants as well as Mexican Americans filled the "vacuum" left by the embargo on cheap European and Asian labor. Latinos, according to one contemporary critic, were called upon to do the "work no white man will do."[19] Proponents of Mexican immigration in the first decade of the twentieth century, particularly those in the agribusiness and railroad industries, "insisted that Mexicans were an inferior race . . . well suited for hard labor . . . [who would] return to Mexico when their labor was no longer needed."[20]

Though there were no maximum quotas on immigration from Mexico, Mexican immigrants were subject to federal immigration laws and jurisprudence that applied to all immigrants, regardless of their country of origin. The Naturalization Acts of 1790 and 1870, for example, required that one be either White or Black in order to become a citizen.[21] In 1924, as part of its sweeping restrictions on immigration, Congress restricted immigration to only those persons "eligible for citizenship,"[22] and it formed the Border Patrol, which policed almost exclusively the United States' border with Mexico.[23] Aliens found to be anarchists, public charges, prostitutes, or guilty of a crime of "moral turpitude" were subject to deportation at any time after their entry into the United States. Federal law provided that immigrants who entered the country illegally were subject to deportation for up to three years after their entry. In 1929, the law was amended so as to make reentry after a previous deportation a felony. Anyone guilty of the felony of reentry was subject to deportation at any time.[24]

United States employers recruited Mexican families precisely because they did not have many of the legal "conditions" that prevented entry into the United States. Nevertheless, anti-Mexican restrictionists railed against the "illegality" of the Mexican. One critic, for example, argued that in the decade after World War I, "the number of Mexicans entering this country illegally . . . far exceeded the number who came legally."[25] This critic echoed contemporary commentators on all sides of the immigration debate who loudly criticized the failure of federal authorities to patrol the border, physically prevent undocumented entry, or enforce a burgeoning body of existing immigration law.[26] Collectively, the dramatically new edifice of immigration law and enforcement enacted by the federal government during the 1910s and 1920s, as well as public sentiment against immigration, created the conditions for Mexican immigrants and Mexican Americans to move from state to state "not as laborers with a set of enforceable protections but as fugitives targeted and chased" first by the U.S. Border Patrol[27] and soon thereafter by other agents of local, state, and federal government.

II. "Mexicans in Our Midst"

The suddenly intense focus on the "problem" of Mexican labor was a direct result of the Great Depression. Though critics of Mexican immigration had already received national attention in the years prior to the Great Depression, the economic crisis put Latinos in direct competition with Whites, both for the dwindling supply of jobs and for limited public relief funds. The belief that the government ought to secure employment for American citizens first was common, as was the fear that immigrants would deplete highly coveted relief funds. Most importantly, it was during this time that the term "illegal alien" and "Mexican" became ubiquitous and interchangeable terms in national discourse, charting for the foreseeable future an era where immigration enforcement was largely about disciplining, controlling, or expelling the Latino family.[28]

It was in this context that one national publication entitled its May 1931 issue "Mexicans in Our Midst." Noted anti-Mexican restrictionist Remsen Crawford labeled normal patterns of Mexican migration "the Mexican Invasion."[29] Accordingly, Crawford advocated that the Department of Labor embark on a nationwide deportation campaign against "illegal aliens—particularly Mexicans." Though noting that "[d]eportation has always been a word abhorrent to American sensibilities and traditional home spirit," Crawford postulated that the "Mexican invasion" made this police action a "necessity." Others called upon the State Department to begin decreasing the number of visas issued by its embassy in Mexico. Doing so, they believed, would adequately slow the influx of "undesirable" types from Mexico.[30] Whether the government issued fewer visas, imposed a quota on Mexican immigration, or increased deportation, there was broad public consensus that the federal government had a duty to halt the increase of the Mexican population in the United States.[31]

Prior to the Great Depression, the federal government reacted tentatively to this emerging consensus. The *Congressional Record*, for instance, documents efforts by the State Department to direct the American Embassy in Mexico to issue fewer visas.[32] A number of bills designed to impose quotas on Mexican immigration, such as those imposed against southern and eastern Europeans in the 1924 Immigration Act, were discussed before the Committee on Immigration. In the end, Congress did not pass any quotas restricting Mexican immigration. Instead, the government redoubled its efforts to enforce current immigration law, resulting in a significant decline of documented immigration from Mexico by 1930.[33]

The Great Depression put into sharp focus the nation's immigration law and policy as applied to Mexican workers. While unemployment "generally ranged from 20–33% of the working population," "it commonly reached 80 and 90 percent" among urban Latinos.[34] One reason for this was that unemployed Whites put incredible pressure on employers to hire only "citizens" in industries that previously had been limited largely to Mexican Americans and Mexicans. Racial designations "rather than strict definitions of citizenship" led to Latinos being replaced in large numbers by Whites.[35] And even where jobs were available, the economic crisis created perverse complications for the Latino working family. For example, although demand for sugar beet labor fell by more than 45%,[36] the number of beet workers rose sharply in the early years of the Great Depression.[37] The economic crisis allowed the sugar beet industry to "reduce wages so sharply that the work was not attractive even to unemployed Euro-Americans."[38]

Public assistance represented a much more compelling alternative to the back-breaking, low-wage, and racially charged labor of the beet fields. But public bureaucrats demonized Latino laborers for claiming public relief. The City and County of Denver's Bureau of Public Welfare, for instance, accused "Mexicans" of moving to Colorado in order to get on the state's welfare rolls, even though Latinos represented only 12% of those claiming relief.[39] As unemployment continued to skyrocket in the first few years of the Depression, "Mexican workers were singled out as scapegoats in virtually every locale in which they lived in substantial numbers."[40] Racialized sentiment against Latinos worked hand in hand with the labor demands of growers, who had long been lobbying local relief agencies to cut Latinos from public assistance at the start of the growing season. The most visible of the "undeserving poor" during the Great Depression, Latinos had little choice but to enter the beet economy, further depressing wages and pitting Latinos, yet again, in direct competition with Whites.[41]

The federal response to the "Mexican" problem during the early years of the Great Depression was fairly swift, and it had two far-reaching implications that greatly impacted Latinos, regardless of citizenship. First, for the only time in the history of the United States, in 1930 the United States Census Bureau declared Mexicans to be a separate race.[42] Because the 1924 Immigration Act required that "legal" immigrants could be only White or Black, the designation seemingly codified the restrictionists' sentiment that Mexicans were ineligible either for citizenship or for immigration.[43] Though the Supreme Court seemed to have settled the issue in the 1897 case, *In re Rodriguez*, by declaring Mexicans to be White and thus eligible for citizenship, subsequent Supreme Court cases regarding the racial classification of Asians and Asian Indians in the 1920s put the continued viability of that decision into doubt.[44] Indeed, the Supreme Court in a 1934 case, *Morrison v. California*, explicitly questioned whether *In Re Rodriguez* was still good law given that "not all that was there said is consistent with later decisions of this court."[45]

Second, beginning in 1931, the federal government under President Herbert Hoover and Secretary of Labor William N. Doak enlisted state and local governments, including local police departments, to remove Latinos through drives to deport and "repatriate" "Mexicans"—including many born in the United States and thus citizens—back to Mexico. Starting first in Los Angeles and then spreading to other locales, including Denver, Colorado, the federal government spearheaded what one contemporary writer called a "gladiatorial spectacle" to remove aliens from the United States.[46] Though there was no official policy to single out any specific ethnic group, the federal government's deportation campaign was tacitly aimed at the Mexican community, thereby encouraging state and local efforts to repatriate Mexicans (irrespective of their legal status) residing in the United States back to their "homeland." Understanding that deportation proceedings were often costly and time-consuming, local, state, federal, and Mexican bureaucrats colluded to create a "huge twilight zone between voluntary and forced migration" for many Latinos in the United States.[47] By the end of the decade, between 350,000 and 600,000 Mexicans and U.S. citizens of Mexican ancestry left the United States.[48]

III. "He Who Is Not Good to His Own Is Worse Than the Infidel"

It was against this backdrop that Colorado put forth its efforts to restrict Mexican migration. Though the state had never specifically targeted immigrants in legislative declarations,[49] it had an ambivalent history regarding the legal protections afforded those considered "foreign."[50] White supremacy drove riots against Chinese "coolies" during the 1880s; anti-Catholic sentiment contributed to the adoption of a constitutional prohibition against the sale of liquor in the 1910s; and antinativist and anti-Black sentiment contributed to the capture by the Ku Klux Klan of several prominent government posts. Indeed, the Klu Klux Klan arguably represented "the largest and most efficiently organized political force" in Colorado during the first half of the 1920s.[51] As an expression of specifically anti-Mexican sentiment in the state, the Denver chief of police, during the recession of 1921, rounded up and forced from the state hundreds of Mexicans—an action that federal immigration authorities deemed "beneficial" to larger federal immigration policy.[52]

It therefore was not surprising that Colorado would emerge in national debates regarding the "Mexican menace" in the 1930s. That it would not happen until 1935 spoke to the role of federal policy in shaping the immigrant debate, in particular section 4(c) of the Federal Emergency Relief Act, passed in 1933, providing financial relief to states burdened by migrants who had been displaced as a result of the Great Depression.[53] By 1935, however, the federal government ended its policy of extending grants to states for the support of transients. Critics at the time lamented that the "new national policy, combined with the devolution of relief upon the states and counties, has left the migrant population in almost helpless suspension between political units that cannot be expected to take responsibility for their plight."[54]

The federal policy came to a head in Colorado in 1935. Before the expiration of the government's support for transients and after the start of the beet season in April, Colorado's governor fixated on the issue of immigration as centrally connected to the state's problems stemming from the Great Depression. Johnson, an anti–New Deal Democrat "affectionately" known as "Big Ed," ascended to the governor's office in 1933. Opposed to almost all of the Roosevelt administration's efforts to use the federal government to respond to the economic crisis, Johnson devoted his administration to the creation of his own statewide reorganization and reform program.

A central piece of Johnson's efforts was immigration enforcement. In March 1935, Governor Johnson sent letters to the federal divisional director of immigration and the federal relief administrator detailing the new role he envisioned for the state, which was reeling from drought, recurrent dust storms, and the "complication of a steady flow of outsiders from southwestern states and from Mexico into Colorado."[55] In his plan to "aid distressed citizens in the state before extending further relief to aliens," Johnson specifically targeted Mexicans by restating what had emerged as "common wisdom" throughout the nation: "Hundreds of Mexicans are holding jobs which should be held by American citizens. Many of these Mexicans are employed during the crop season in the sugar beet fields. When fall comes, they go on relief."[56] Johnson asserted that "40,000 persons, approximately one-quarter of the Colorado relief load," were undeserving "aliens."[57] In order to respond to the "crisis," Johnson called for the federal government to deport all alien labor out of the state and the country.

While local and state governments had previously demanded that the federal government enforce the nation's immigration laws, what made Johnson's plan especially novel was his threat to use his powers as "commander-in-chief" of the National Guard to deport alien labor if the federal authorities did not take action.[58] Quoting the Bible as well as "several citizen organizations" that had urged him to act, Governor Johnson identified a "drastic" role for state government in the enforcement of the nation's immigration laws.[59]

Governor Johnson approved a plan to establish a "concentration camp" for "all aliens on relief" at the Colorado National Guard barracks.[60] Endorsed by the *Denver Post* as the only way to "meet the problems raised by the increasing horde of Mexicans coming into Colorado . . . from southwestern states and Old Mexico," the plan to populate the camp had several components.[61] First, the plan called for the state relief administrator to "round-up" all aliens in the state. Once this "task was accomplished," relief agents would be "authorized to refuse relief to any jobless alien and his family who refuses to transfer to the concentration camp." Relief officials would also be required to investigate the jobs held by "aliens which should be filled by American citizens." Finally, Johnson promised to call up the National Guard "to do the work, supervise the transfers and take charge of the camp" should local relief agencies refuse or fail in these tasks.[62] If there was any question as to whom this policy would apply, one account noted that "Johnson implied that the National Guard would be needed to preserve the peace in sections [of the state] where the proportion of Mexicans in the population was large."[63] The state would then institute deportation proceedings.

Though there seemed to be broad-based public support for Johnson's plan and though Johnson assured that "no person, regardless of race or nationality who has been naturalized or whose parents were American citizens would be disturbed in their rights,"[64] there was almost no legal precedent for such state action absent federal involvement. An editorial in the *New York Times*, for instance, stressed that Johnson lacked the authority to begin deportation proceedings and characterized Johnson's plan as a "political move" designed specifically to scapegoat the state's Latino population.[65] Nevertheless, Governor Johnson's local solution to the "Mexican Menace" in Colorado reflected that the rights of immigrants were in a state of flux, as was the precise degree of authority exercised by federal, state, and local agents over the "alien" problem in the United States.

As the repatriation campaigns in the American Southwest and Midwest during 1930 and 1931 demonstrated, there was an unprecedented degree of federal, state, and local coordination in immigration enforcement and policy. Nevertheless, Johnson's unilateral action went against the spirit, if not the law, of these collaborative efforts, and it thus put into sharp relief the importance of federal plenary authority over immigration law. The most salient issue was Governor Johnson's threat to deport all aliens. Federal law required the deportation of undocumented immigrants up to three years after their entry into the country. After three years, however, the Department of Immigration was not authorized to arrange for the deportation of an immigrant simply because he or she had once made an illegal entry into the United States.[66] Complicating this issue was the fact that it was unclear who had and had not made legal entry.

The political and legal questions of immigration emerging during the Great Depression had less to do with any particular immigrant than with larger questions of maintaining a docile and racialized labor supply.[67] American law recognized the rights of immigrants to work, though with some critically important limitations. As early as 1915 in *Truax v. Raich*, the Supreme Court examined the constitutionality of an Arizona law requiring at least 80% of the private-sector workforce to consist of native-born citizens or electors. Finding the statute unconstitutional, the Court held that the state's police power

> does not go so far as to make it possible for the State to deny to *lawful* inhabitants, because of their race or nationality, the ordinary means of earning a livelihood. It requires no argument to show that the right to work for a living in the common occupations of the community is of the very essence of the personal freedom and opportunity that it was the purpose of the Amendment to secure.[68]

Despite the holding in *Truax*, other courts held that local or state governments could determine where an immigrant could exercise his or her right to work. Particularly when it came to the employment that affected a public good, courts found that it was reasonable to exclude immigrants from certain professions.[69] In deciding such cases, courts typically required that the state demonstrate a reasonable relationship between regulation of the profession and citizens' health or morals, and courts gave broad judicial deference to anti-immigrant sentiments of local communities.[70] Implicit in this rationale was the underlying assumption that immigrants were predisposed to criminal behavior.[71]

Courts also found it reasonable for the state, as an employer, to discriminate against immigrants. By 1938, at least twelve states had passed legislation prohibiting or discouraging the employment of noncitizens

in public works jobs.[72] Many courts defended the states' right to prohibit the public employment of aliens on the grounds that employment
by the state was a privilege that could only permissibly be accessed by
citizens of the state. Courts argued that, "since the citizens of the state
constitute the state, *they* are entitled to the opportunities for work that
its common resources afford."[73]

In addition, statutes prohibiting noncitizens from owning land were
consistently upheld by the judiciary. As early as 1913, California passed
a statute barring "aliens" from land ownership.[74] In the following years
Washington, Texas, Arizona, Delaware, Nebraska, and New Mexico followed suit. The Supreme Court upheld such restrictions in *Terrace v.
Thompson* as a valid exercise of the state's police power.[75] According to
the Court, the state had a vested interest in assuring "[t]he quality and
allegiance" of property owners, especially those who "own, occupy, and
use farm lands" in a state, thereby perpetuating the second-class nature
of immigrant rights.[76]

As these statutes and cases demonstrate, distinct and exclusive
spheres of immigration authority existed among local, state, and federal
governments. While local ordinances or state statutes could truncate
the rights of immigrant labor, the authority to regulate immigration
belonged exclusively to the federal government.[77] The police power of
the states regarding the rights of aliens to practice certain professions
or become public employees ended where the federal government's
authority to regulate who was a lawful immigrant began.[78] Thus, there
was little question that "the sole power" to exclude and deport immigrants was vested in Congress.[79]

National immigration policy established the terms by which local
and state efforts to control "aliens" would be supported by the federal
government. Whereas the Hoover administration in 1931 explicitly
endorsed and provided tangible coordination and tactical support of
local solutions to the "Mexican Menace," by 1935, the Roosevelt administration had taken a more nuanced view. This is reflected in Governor
Johnson's own efforts to encourage citizen groups to pressure federal
bureaucrats to enforce federal law at the same time he was proposing
Colorado do so on its own.[80]

Two months after Johnson declared that Colorado was prepared to
go to war against aliens, Sheriff Ray Marty of Trinidad was specifically

asked by Governor Johnson to "halt Alien Mexicans enroute to the beet fields."[81] Sheriff Marty ultimately detained thirty-two Latino men, women, and children from Texas on their way to the sugar beet fields of northeastern Colorado when they stopped at the local relief office requesting gasoline because "their temporary labor passports are very old and probably have expired."[82] Pursuant to Johnson's order, relief administrators in Trinidad quickly notified the governor of the detention by its sheriff. Johnson telegraphed Marty with instructions to "hold these aliens until we can arrange for their disposition."[83] The next day, Johnson "pushed his vigorous drive against alien job seekers" by asking sheriffs throughout the state to help in his efforts to "keep aliens from taking jobs which Americans would be only too glad to have."[84]

When informed of the detention in Trinidad, Mexican consul H. E. Torres in Denver initiated his own investigation. Torres declared, "Only immigration officers and not the sheriff, have the right to arrest these people if they are suspected of being here illegally."[85] In response, the state argued that the "Mexicans" were not under arrest, were not in jail, and would be free to continue to the beet fields for work once their passports proved to be valid.[86] The next day, the federal government sent an agent to Trinidad for the purpose of inspecting the "papers" of the detained migrants. Despite the consul's objections, and before the federal immigration authorities could determine whether the laborers were eligible for deportation, Johnson sent orders to officers in all of Colorado's southern counties "to be on the lookout and hold all aliens entering the county who cannot show proper credentials and prove that they will not become charges on the state."[87] The governor's policy—"[a] s fast as they come in, put them out"—compelled local police authorities to make instant decisions about individuals' immigration status. Though Sheriff Marty himself conceded that he had no way of knowing whether the papers of the original detainees were valid or not, he utilized the authority vested in him by Governor Johnson to deny entry to another eight aliens before they entered the state.[88] Sheriff Marty then escorted the thirty-two original detainees to the New Mexico border and told them to "keep on going south" even though federal immigration officials had not taken any official action.[89]

In spite of the dragnet established by Johnson along the state's border, two of the thirty-two deported Latinos managed to make their way to Denver and enlist the help of the Mexican consul.[90] The consul telegraphed the Mexican ambassador when he learned that twenty of the deportees were U.S. citizens and that at least two members of the group not only were seeking work but also were returning to north-eastern Colorado to settle a debt on a truck.[91] The Mexican ambassador contacted Cordell Hull, secretary of state, to protest Johnson's actions. Hull then telegraphed Johnson and demanded to know the basis of his action. Johnson acknowledged that he had deported and refused entry to "forty destitute men, women, and children, mostly aliens without passports." Importantly, Johnson's communication with Hull high-lighted an important shift in his immigration policy: He did not question the legal status of those detained; rather, he noted that "[u]nem-ployment is very great in Colorado and there is no work for any of these people in our state."[92] Indigency, not illegality, emerged for Johnson as the basis of Colorado's enforcement of immigration law.

The next day the *Denver Post*'s headline claimed "Diplomacy Tri-umphed."[93] Diplomacy supposedly reigned when Johnson and Consul Torres reached a "gentlemen's agreement" whereby the consul would encourage all aliens to return to Mexico. The consul stated that the Mexican government would provide land grants to its repatriated citi-zens. The *Denver Post* interpreted this agreement as a sign that the con-sul "support[ed] . . . the movement to rid the Colorado relief rolls of Mexican aliens and give jobs held by aliens to Colorado citizens." In return, Johnson offered to use state funds to subsidize the costs of repa-triating Mexicans back to Mexico.[94]

News of the diplomatic breakthrough, however, was overshadowed by what should have been an unsurprising announcement. Deputy Commissioner of Immigration Edward Shaughnessy made a sweeping proclamation concerning the relationship between indigency and ille-gality for immigrants in the United States. According to Shaughnessy, the Department of Labor was

> without authority to direct the removal from the United States of aliens simply because they are receiving relief. Under the law, aliens are deport-able as public charges when it is shown that they have become pub-lic charges within five years of the date of their entry from causes not affirmatively shown to have arisen subsequent to such entry. . . . [T]he

predicament in which they now find themselves is a circumstance over which they had no control and which did not obtain at the time of their entry.

Though he recognized the legitimacy of various state governments assisting in "the voluntary repatriation of certain aliens who have been in this country too long to be removed voluntarily at the expense of the federal government," Shaughnessy pointedly rebuked the emerging rationale for Colorado's deportation efforts. Johnson deemphasized the ruling, pointing out that the state no longer needed to pursue deportation now that the Mexican government had agreed to encourage repatriation of aliens.[95]

Through the remainder of 1935, Johnson continued to lobby relief administrators for the exclusion of aliens. Federal bureaucrats, in response, however, chided the governor for the policies that he proposed. For instance, Johnson wrote Paul Shriver, the state WPA head, demanding "that no alien and no person not a citizen of this State be given employment in the Public Works Program under your direction, and that every person seeking Public Works employment be required by you to conclusively prove that he is a citizen of Colorado and the United States."[96] Shriver did not respond, and on August 14, an agitated Johnson wrote, "In the name of common decency you should not give the jobs that belong to our own citizens to aliens."[97] On August 15, Shriver tersely replied,

> Hunger, unfortunately is no respecter of persons or of citizenship. I cannot believe that your solution of the alien problem, even if it were to determine who are aliens and who are not, is that such unfortunate people are to be allowed to starve within the boundaries of a State which justly boasts of its friendliness and hospitality. If, on the other hand, you feel that all aliens should be deported, you should take that up with the immigration authorities. I prefer to stand with the president and err on the side of humanity.[98]

Johnson took umbrage at Shriver's letter and continued to argue the justice of his position. His reply stated, "We are keenly disappointed in your decision to employ aliens in your works program. . . . Colorado

stands ready to provide transportation to destitute aliens to their homeland. We have no thought of starving or abusing them, and I am surprised that you would insinuate that a great state like Colorado would
have such a purpose."[99] Shriver ultimately ended the correspondence
by citing the primacy of federal authority. He succinctly declared the
matter closed by referring to Executive Order Number 7046 of May 20,
1935, which ordered, "workers shall not be discriminated against on any
grounds whatsoever."[100] In a letter sent on September 19, the governor
conceded defeat.[101] Of questionable legality almost from its inception,
Johnson's ambitious plans to usurp federal control over deportation had
yielded him little.

IV. "Warning All Mexican and All Other Aliens to Leave the State of Colorado at Once"

Despite his failure in 1935, Johnson redoubled his efforts to protect the state from the "Mexican menace" at the start of the beet season in April of 1936.[102] Probably motivated by the introduction of the
Alien Deportation Bill submitted to the U.S. Congress by Representative Martin Dies of Texas earlier that year, as well as emboldened by
the "widespread praise . . . not only in Colorado but in other Western
States" that he received for his threat to use the National Guard, and his
soon-to-be-announced candidacy for the U.S. Senate, Johnson revived
the "alien" issue.[103]   In March of 1936, Johnson received a letter from
O. S. Wood, director of the state employment service, estimating that
nineteen thousand workers would be needed to provide labor for the
beet fields. He informed Johnson of his belief that the state employment
office could provide twenty thousand resident laborers needed for work
in the beet fields.[104] With this prediction in hand, Johnson announced
that this year there would be no need for importation of alien labor.[105]
As in the previous year's announcement of a "concentration camp" for
Mexicans, Johnson's declaration fed into the racism of his constituents.
One man wrote to Johnson, "You are to be highly commended in your
efforts to keep aliens out of this State. Particularly Mexicans. . . . [T]hey
are a blight to any country. Japs are infinitely better."[106] Another wrote to
the governor protesting the state's obligation to "feed, clothe, and shelter these dirty, lazy, shiftless, useless aliens whose very presence here is

an ever increasing danger to our civilization."[107] One concerned citizen suggested that the "one way to rid this state and country of them . . . is to pass a bill to sterilize every Mexican on relief who has more than two children."[108]

April 18, 1936, marked the official start of Colorado's military campaign to repel the invasion of Mexicans into the state. In contrast to his highly publicized efforts a year earlier, Johnson affirmatively exercised his authority as commander-in-chief and deployed the Colorado National Guard to the state's southern border. Arguing that "certain classes of individuals within the state of Colorado [who] are acting in conjunction with large numbers of persons outside of said state who are aliens and indigent persons *to effect an invasion* of said state," Johnson placed Colorado's border with New Mexico and Oklahoma under martial law.[109] Under its provisions, all travelers seeking to cross into the state via the southern border would be required to demonstrate their citizenship and financial stability. Fifty national guardsmen were ordered to the southern boundary of the state, where they were to stop and inspect every train, truck, and automobile seeking entry to the state; aliens and indigents were to be repelled. Particular attention was to be paid to attempted smugglers and vagrants entering the state *en masse* via trains.[110] The governor demanded the cooperation of all Coloradoans and attested that corporations seeking to subvert the blockade would be subject to prosecution by military tribunal.[111] The chairman of the board of the Great Western Sugar Co. responded, "We'll employ all of the beet labor available in Colorado and after that—well, if he doesn't want beets grown in Colorado—that's that."[112]

Armed with a new rationale, Johnson publicly claimed that the military action was designed to prevent indigent people from entering Colorado and competing directly with the laboring citizens of the state. In this regard, his action was on firmer legal ground. Though it was generally understood that states had no power to establish policies and procedures over the entry and deportation of immigrants from a state, state governments did have powerful authority to control the migration of indigents into their states. As early as the nineteenth century, states and localities continued "practices from the English poor law . . . [to exert] their power to exclude or at least require the removal of . . . newcomers whom they considered likely to become public charges."[113] Accordingly, the law made clear that a local and state government could "exclude from its limits paupers, vagabonds, and criminals, or sick, diseased, infirm and disabled persons who are likely to become a public charge."[114]

Following the federal government's withdrawal of relief for transients in 1935, states that traditionally attracted significant numbers of seasonal laborers (citizen and noncitizen alike) chose to close their borders to the indigent.[115] In a letter to Governor Johnson in February of 1936, Governor Dave Sholtz of Florida provided a model that Johnson would use in 1936:

> Florida was faced with a serious situation. Thousands of unemployed and hungry people were flocking into the State, which was already overburdened with the relief needs of our own people. Realizing that something had to be done quickly, I placed highway patrolmen at the main points along the state border to turn back persons who had no means of support and whose needs Florida could not meet.[116]

Such exclusion also occurred in California, whose resources had been particularly taxed by the vast migration of the Great Depression to the state. The Los Angeles Police Department established a blockade against vagrants in southern California;[117] 1,242 indigent migrants were refused entry and 972 vagrants already in the state were arrested and advised to either leave the state or face long jail sentences and forced labor. Los Angeles' chief of police defended the action as a crime-prevention measure that deterred all migrants who came to the state "to beg, steal, or throw themselves upon the already overburdened relief rolls."[118] In response to a request from the Los Angeles City Council, the city attorney issued his opinion on the legality of the blockade. Though the opinion questioned the authority of Los Angeles police to act in other counties, he nevertheless cited Supreme Court precedent to defend the principle of blockade.[119] The city attorney's office quoted extensively from the 1849 opinion of Justice Wayne in *Norris v. City of Boston*, arguing, in particular, that "[t]he States may meet such persons [paupers, vagabonds, and fugitives] upon their arrival in port and may put them under all proper restraints. They may prevent them from entering their territories, may carry them out or drive them off."[120] Lack of cooperation between counties eventually limited the success of the blockade. Nonetheless, no legal challenges were ever raised against what came to be known as the "bum blockade."

The actions of the state government in Florida and local government in California gave the Colorado governor the legal cover that he had lacked in 1935. Such cover, moreover, was bolstered by an unusual precedent in Colorado. Taking pains to distinguish the exercise of his powers as commander-in-chief, Johnson alluded to the infamous Ludlow Massacre: "The National Guard in the past has been called out against labor. I have called out the guard for the protection of labor."[121] Though the military zone was only imposed on Colorado's southern border,[122] Johnson was also careful to declare that this was not an exercise in immigration: "We're going to count their money. Our main object is to head off the destitute people from other States who would become public charges here." Yet, Johnson could not help adding that "if we catch a few aliens among them, so much the better."[123]

In spite of Johnson's statements, it was clear that the Colorado National Guard was going to war, in the words of the *Denver Post*, "against the [Mexican] alien."[124] Officers even considered establishing military courts for all lawbreakers.[125] April 20 saw the exclusion of the first travelers, Ramon Ruiz, his wife, and their five children. Ruiz carried only three dollars with him and was promptly ordered by the guardsmen to turn back. By the end of the first day, the guardsmen at Camp Johnson turned dozens of families away at Colorado's border. In reporting to Johnson, the adjutant general of the National Guard announced, "Approximately seventy Mexicans were turned back today."[126] Just as importantly, Coloradoans knew precisely who would bear the brunt of Johnson's border militarization. One couple wrote to Johnson of their support, "We are right behind you in your move to keep the Mexican race out of our state."[127] Another Coloradoan, writing in support of the military action, advocated that Johnson support legislation "to sterilize every Mexican on relief who has more than two children."[128] Even more inflammatory were bright orange placards publicly posted throughout the state: "warning all Mexican and all other aliens to leave the state of Colorado at once, by order of: Colorado state *vigilantes*."[129]

The federal government took an ambivalent public approach to Johnson's efforts. While federal relief officials continued to assert that the state could not deny immigrants relief and that "an unemployed alien gets just as hungry as a naturalized or other citizen of the country," officials also indicated that they were in "complete sympathy with the governor's objectives."[130] Indeed, about a week into the war, federal officials "moved to drop from the WPA and relief twenty-seven *Mexican* families which had refused to accept sugar beet labor jobs offered them," choosing instead to "live off the county welfare department."[131] The Department of Immigration took no public stance but did send an agent to the Colorado-New Mexico border.[132] There, the Department of Immigration found that of the five hundred turned away at the border during the operation, only two were eligible for deportation.[133]

Moreover, Colorado's Office of State Employment realized almost immediately that it could not find Colorado laborers willing to work for the depressingly low wages that migrant Latino laborers accepted. Out of three hundred men removed from the WPA rolls and offered jobs in the beet fields, only thirty accepted.[134] Not only was the state refusing entry to citizens and documented immigrants, but Colorado also soon faced an acute labor shortage as a result of the blockade. Johnson's predictions had been grossly wrong.

As the blockade continued, criticism of the governor's extraordinary use of his authority became more pronounced. The *Rocky Mountain News* called the blockade an "embargo against penniless humanity,"[135] while national pundits skewered the state.[136] Sustained and vocal opposition from the American Civil Liberties Union and the Catholic Church, as well as recognition by merchants, wholesalers, employers, and farmers about the impact of the ban on business, threatened a "collapse of the border blockade."[137] These "radical" leaders threatened to file an injunction against Johnson if he did not lift the blockade.[138] Perhaps most importantly, the militarization of Colorado's southern border raised the ire of its neighbor. New Mexico governor Clyde Tingley was skeptical of the blockade from the start and grew increasingly vexed against Governor Johnson's "private war" after Colorado guardsmen conducted reconnaissance missions on New Mexico's side of the border. Governor Tingley said, "We need no National Guard investigating this state or its people. Let Governor Johnson take care of his own state and we'll take care of ours. He can run his side of the border and we will run ours."[139] With its sizeable Latino population, New Mexico was also concerned at the overt discrimination faced by its citizens at the Colorado border.[140] According to Tingley, "you would think New Mexico had been cut off from the United States and was a foreign country."[141]

In turn, New Mexico's governor was threatening his own embargo against Colorado products "if the governor of Colorado wants to set up the National Guard as an immigration bureau."[142] Within the week, both of New Mexico's U.S. senators, Dennis Chavez and Carl Hatch, had condemned Colorado's actions and denounced them as a violation of the privileges and immunities clause.[143] Though Senator Robert Reynolds of North Carolina "lauded Governor Johnson's action" on the floor of the Senate, Senator Dennis Chavez argued that Reynolds "did not know the situation" because he believed that only "aliens are involved. . . . Even then, if [aliens] are in the country legally, it is a question of whether Colorado has a legal right to bar them."[144]

Nor did all of those caught up in the dragnet fit Johnson's profile of the individuals who were invading the state. Highly revealing was a "frontline" account in the *Rocky Mountain News*. In documenting the guardsmen's seizure of a freight train that had just crossed into Colorado, the *News* showed a compelling portrait of those who were taken off the train and marched back across the state line. On the one side were four Latinos—who spoke broken English. On the other was Roscoe Houghton, a one-armed former miner for whom "sympathetic newspapermen took up a collection" to help him get to his final destination.[145] According to one editorial that described the day with "Colorado's expeditionary forces," the four Latinos were "typical bums . . . the very kind that Governor Johnson wants to keep out of the state. But the fifth; well I watched him as he climbed painfully off a flat car. . . . He didn't have the face of a bum, even if it were covered with railroad soot and studded with the bristles of a gray beard."[146] Though Johnson's military action started as war against Mexicans, the collateral damage on Whites became untenable.

Less than two weeks after it started, and within days of New Mexico's public denouncement of Johnson's authority, the governor rescinded his order of martial law on April 29, 1936, and ordered Colorado's National Guard to stand down.[147] For ten days in April, Colorado's National Guard, "armed with pistols and clubs," was fully deployed to stop "Mexicans" and other indigents from entering the state.[148] Seventeen miles south of Trinidad, it established Camp Johnson as its base of operations as well as other support camps near Alamosa, Durango, and Cortez. The Guard posted soldiers at every major highway and railroad entering the state along its southern border, where guardsmen asked for and inspected car registration records, labor documents, rail passes, visas, and all forms of identification. It organized daily sorties of the Guard's 120th Air Squadron to patrol the southern half of the state. And, it exercised its authority far removed from the border by inspecting automobiles of suspected "invaders" hundreds of miles into the state.[149] Hundreds were turned back, some asked to leave in the cars they drove (with gasoline and money for their expenses paid by the Guard) while others were forced to march to the New Mexican border.[150]

Johnson explained that he was revoking the blockade because "martial law . . . cannot be invoked without working a distinct hardship upon the good citizens of other states."[151] He later confessed in a private letter that, even while he defended the blockade, "I knew that I would have to back up on martial law."[152] As in 1935, Johnson had seemingly overstepped his authority to control and deter "alien" labor from his state. Yet, emboldened by his decisive act, a few days after his revocation of martial law, Johnson announced his candidacy for the position of United States senator of Colorado.[153]

V. Conclusion

Less than half a year after his failed blockade of Colorado's southern border with New Mexico, Governor Johnson had a commanding lead for a seat to the United States Senate in the upcoming elections. While many of the state's leading citizens and institutions lined up to endorse him, many chose to ignore Colorado's failed foray into national immigration law and policy. One newspaper, however, wrote in its endorsement of Johnson, "[His] is a fair record, even if marked with some blunders, such as the recent abortive use of the National Guard to close Colorado's borders to 'indigent and alien workers.' Governor Johnson himself recognizes that move as a blunder."[154] Johnson's attempts to carve out a new role for state enforcement of immigration law were simply too bombastic by the legal and political standards of the time.

It is likely that Johnson would have been met with far less opprobrium if he had focused his efforts on lobbying for a law that prohibited the public employment of aliens. To be sure, as immigration law developed after 1924, federal bureaucrats, legislators, and jurists endorsed broad state controls over the form and scope of immigrant labor. Prohibited by state statute or local ordinance from engaging in a variety of private and public occupations, immigrants (most notably Mexicans) were funneled into segregated and racist labor markets. It was not that Mexicans were particularly well suited for beet and other types of labor; rather, state law and federal immigration jurisprudence gave Mexicans precious little choice. Such decisions, moreover, were magnified as local and state relief agencies developed practices, policies, and procedures that specifically singled out Mexicans—either for repatriation or for work in the fields.

Johnson's bombastic use of martial law might not have faced such national scrutiny if he had followed Florida's or California's example rather than publicly emphasizing the measure's specific application to immigrants. As a long line of common law precedent had made evident, a state had a legitimate and reasonable sovereign concern about the "invasion" of the indigent across its borders. While federal officials had been repeatedly called upon to mitigate the burdens placed upon a state as a result of a transient population, local and state governments nonetheless had broad authority to stop "undesirable" transients, vagabonds, and vagrants from threatening the health, safety, and welfare of the state. The problem for Johnson and his supporters was that they could not distinguish between "alien" and "vagrant." To him and scores of others, the two were one and the same.

That Johnson's "war," as well as much of national immigration law and policy, would ultimately fall hardest on Latinos is perhaps the greatest tragedy of Colorado's militarization of the border in the 1930s and the greatest lessons we can learn in the aftermath of the Supreme Court's opinion in *Arizona v. United States*.[155] Although the Court reaffirmed the "broad, undoubted power" of the federal government "over the subject of immigration and the status of aliens," it nevertheless upheld the right of the state to require its police officers to make a "reasonable attempt . . . to determine the immigration status" of any person its authorities stop, detain, or arrest if "reasonable suspicion exists that the person is an alien and is unlawfully present in the United States."[156] As Colorado's experience in the mid-1930s demonstrates, the question of "reasonability" is perversely entangled with particularly local anxieties of race, intractable structures of economic and political power, and patterns of social inequality regardless of one's citizenship.[157] Just as "Mexican" became synonymous with "vagrant" and "illegal" in the 1930s, so too did this era reinforce the racialization of Latinos as non-Americans and non-White. For proponents of Johnson's policy, it did not matter that most of those caught up in the dragnet were American citizens as long as they looked like the "alien bums" that his policies were designed to control. It was only at the point that such policies threatened the movement of White "citizens" that the policy came under its most sustained and durable public criticism. Even in an era where propriety of the law as it pertained to immigrants, especially Mexicans, was constantly debated, Colorado's efforts in 1935 and 1936 threatened to upset an emerging delicate balance between federal authorities and state control over Latino and other non-White, noncitizen labor.

In narrowing the scope of state-level immigration enforcement in 2012, the Supreme Court declared that "immigration policy [and law] shapes the destiny of the nation."[158] We ignore at our own peril this and similar histories in our understanding of immigration policy and law. Colorado's experience in 1935 and 1936 fits in seamlessly with a "U.S. immigration history that is not consistent with the nation's self-concept as the land of freedom, liberty, and equality."[159] At once desired and undesired, the "Mexican menace" refracted the constantly shifting federal goals of national immigration policy against often racist state and local rights rhetoric that would repeatedly animate immigration policy and law into the twenty-first century.

NOTES

1. John Farnham, *Colorado Aliens Face Deportation*, N.Y. Times, March 31, 1935, at E6; *Barricading Jobs: Troops Guard Colorado Borders to Keep Out the Indigent*, Literary Digest, May 2, 1936, at 5 (noting both of his parents as immigrants who naturalized). Edwin C. Johnson, March 2, 1936, Box 26916, Governor Edwin Carl Johnson Collection, Colorado State Archives (hereafter Johnson Collection at CSA) (lamenting the "evil of the alien menace").

2. Francis Wayne, *Colorado Aliens Will Be Deported*, Denv. Post, March 25, 1936, at 1, 3.

3. Francis Wayne, *Aliens on Relief to Be Put in Camp*, Denv. Post, March 27, 1935, at 1, 3; *Urges Deporting of Aliens*, N.Y. Times, March 28, 1935, at 7.

4. Wayne, *supra* note 3, at 1; Farnham, *supra* note 1, at E6.

5. I use the terms "color" and "color lines" throughout this article to describe legally enforced boundaries between Whiteness and non-Whiteness. These issues are explored in further detail in Tom I. Romero II, *¿La Raza Latina?: Multiracial Ambivalence, Color Denial, and the Emergence of a Tri-Ethnic Jurisprudence at the End of the Twentieth Century*, 37 N.M. L. Rev. 245, 249–55 (2007).

6. An Address by Thomas. F. Mahony, Problem of the Mexican Wage Earner, at the Catholic Conference on Industrial Problems, Denver, Colorado, May 12, 1930 (on file with author).

7. Dennis Nodín Valdés, Al Norte: Agricultural Workers in the Great Lakes Region, 1917–1970 5 (1991).

8. Mahony, *supra* note 6, at 1 and 4.

9. *Id.*, at 4.

10. Valdés, *supra* note 7, at 19.

11. Mahony, *supra* note 6, at 6.

12. Sarah Deutsch, No Separate Refuge: Culture, Class, and Gender on an Anglo-Hispanic Frontier in the American Southwest, 1880–1940 129 (1987).

13. Mahony, *supra* note 6, at 129.

14. *Id.*, at 3.

15. *Id.*, at 3. *See also* Valdés, *supra* note 7, at 12–15.

16. Mahony, *supra* note 6, at 5.

17. *Id.*, at 6.

18. Remsen Crawford, *The Deportation of Undesirable Aliens*, 30 Current Hist. 1075, 1080 (Sept. 1929).

19. Robert McLean, *Tightening the Mexican Border*, 64 Survey 28, 55 (April 1930).

20. Natalia Molina, *"In a Race All Their Own": The Quest to Make Mexicans Ineligible for U.S. Citizenship*, 79 Pac. Hist. Rev. 167, 171 (2010). *See also* David G. Gutiérrez, Walls and Mirrors: Mexican Americans, Mexican Immigrants, and the Politics of Ethnicity 39–68 (1995).

21. *See* Act of Mar. 26, 1790, ch. 3, 1 Stat. 103, 103 ("[A]ny alien, being a free white person, who shall have resided within the limits and under the jurisdiction of the United States for the term of two years, may be admitted to become a citizen."); and Naturalization Act of 1870, ch. 254, 16 Stat. 254, 256 (extending citizenship to persons of "African descent").

22. Section 13, Immigration Act of 1924, c. 190, 43 Stat. 153.

23. Kelly Lytle Hernández, Migra! A History of the U.S. Border Patrol 2, 19–69 (2010).

24. McLean, *supra* note 19, at 29.

25. *Id.*, at 28.

26. *Id.*, at 29. *See also*, Robert McLean, *The Mexican Return*, Nation 165–66 (1932); Paul Taylor, *More Bars against Mexicans*, 64 Survey 26–27 (April 1930).

27. Hernández, *supra* note 23, at 90.

28. Mai Ngai, Impossible Subjects: Illegal Aliens and the Making of Modern America 56–90 (2004).

29. Crawford, *supra* note 18, at 1075–80.

30. Taylor, *supra* note 26, at 26–27.

31. Ernesto Galarza, *Without Benefit of Lobby*, 66 Survey 181 (May 1931).

32. *Congressional Record*, 71st Congress, 1st Session, Part 3 (1929), p. 3368.

33. *Labor Immigration Halted at Hoover's Order*, N.Y. Times (September 10, 1930), at 1.

34. Valdés, *supra* note 7, at 32. *See also* George J. Sánchez, Becoming Mexican American: Ethnicity, Culture, and Identity in Chicano Los Angeles, 1900–1945 211 (1993).

35. Sánchez, *supra* note 34, at 211.

36. Deutsch, *supra* note 12, at 162.

37. Valdés, *supra* note 7, at 32.

38. *Id.*, at 32.

39. *Mexicans on Relief in Denver Found to Be Only 12 Percent of Total*, Rocky Mtn. News (Denver), October 26, 1937.

40. Gutiérrez, *supra* note 20, at 72.

41. Valdés, *supra* note 7, at 32–33; Deutsch, *supra* note 12, at 175–76.

42. *See* Clara E. Rodriguez, Changing Race: Latinos, the Census, and the History of Ethnicity in the United States 83–84 (2000).

43. *See* Molina, *supra* note 20, at 175–87; and David. A. Sandoval, *Recruitment, Rejection, and Reaction: Chicanos in the Twentieth Century* 240 in Enduring Legacies, Arturo Aldema, Elisa Facio, and Daryl Maeda, eds. (2010).

44. *See* Ozawa v. United States, 260 U.S. 178, 190–99 (1922); and United States v. Thind, 261 U.S. 204, 206–15 (1923). A particularly thorough examination of *Ozawa* is found in Devon W. Carbado, *Yellow by Law*, 97 Cal. L. Rev. 633 (2009). The history of the racial prerequisites for naturalization is documented fully in Ian F. Haney Lopez, White by Law: The Legal Construction of Race 37–109 (1996).

45. Morrison v. California, 291 U.S. 82, 96 (1934). At least one federal court in 1935 denied the naturalization petitions of three Mexican nationals. *See Indian Blood Bars Mexicans as Citizens*, N.Y. Times, Dec. 12, 1935. This case, *In the matter of Timoteo Andrade*, and the racial language as well as it implications for the naturalization of Latinos is documented in Molina, *supra* note 20, at 193–97; Patrick D. Lukens, A Quiet Victory for Latin Rights: FDR and the Controversy over "Whiteness" (2012); F. Arturo Rosales, *Shifting Self-Perceptions and Ethnic Consciousness among Mexicans in Houston, 1908–1946*, 16 Aztlán: A Journal of Chicano Studies 71–94 (1985); Francisco A. Rosales, ¡Pobre Raza! Violence, Justice, and Mobilization among México Lindo Immigrants, 1900–1936 (1999), Dara Orenstein, *Void for Vagueness: Mexicans and the Collapse of Miscegenation Law in California*, 74 Pac. Hist. Rev. 367, 367–408 (2005); and Michael Calderón-Zaks, *Debated Whiteness amid World Events: Mexican and Mexican American*

Subjectivity and the U.S.' Relationship with the Americas, 1924–1936, 27 Mexican Studies/Estudios Mexicanos 325–59 (2011). Original transcripts of the case as well as the strategy to escape the liability of "Indian blood" have been preserved by Professor Michael Olivas and can be downloaded at http://www.law.uh.edu/ihelg/andrade-files.

46. Roger W. Babson, Washington and the Depression: Including the Career of W. N. Doak 92–93 (1932). *See also* Gardner Jackson, *Doak the Deportation Chief*, Nation (March 18, 1931). The best and most extensive account of these efforts at the local level remains Francisco E. Balderrama, In Defense of La Raza: The Los Angeles Mexican Consulate and the Mexican Community, 1929 to 1936 (1982). *See also* Neil Betten and Raymond A. Mohl, *From Discrimination to Repatriation: Mexican Life in Gary, Indiana, during the Great Depression*, 42 Pac. Hist. Rev. 370, 377–85 (1973); Abraham Hoffman, Unwanted Mexican Americans in the Great Depression: Repatriation Pressures, 1929–1939 30–41 (1974); Mark Reisler, By the Sweat of Their Brow: Mexican Immigrant Labor in the United States: 1900–1940 59 (1976); Sánchez, *supra* note 34, at 57, 209–26; Gutiérrez, *supra* note 20, at 52–56, 71–74, and Eric Meeks, *Protecting the "White Citizen Worker": Race, Labor, and Citizenship in South-Central Arizona, 1929–1945*, 48 J. of the S.W. 91, 94–95 (2006).

47. Leo Grebler, Mexican Immigration to the United States: The Record and Its Implications 25 (1966).

48. Gutiérrez, *supra* note 20, at 72; Balderrama, *supra* note 46, at 16–20.

49. It should be noted that Colorado had never passed a blanket restriction on the employment of aliens. However, Colorado law required aliens to file declarations of intent before being employed as court reporters: Colo. Laws 1925, c. 159. Colorado also required that its pharmacists and coal mine inspectors be citizens: Colo. Stat. Ann. (Mills, 1930) § 5503 and Comp. Laws Supp. 1932, § 3455. Colorado also barred aliens from collecting relief benefits for the adult blind: Colo. Stat. Ann. (Mills, 1930) § 5046.

50. *See* Tom I. Romero II, *Wringing Rights out of the Mountains: Colorado's Centennial Constitution and the Ambivalent Promise of Human Rights and Social Equality*, 69 Albany L. Rev. 569, 570–74 (2006).

51. *Stapleton-Klan Alliance Assailed in State Democratic Resolution*, Denv. Post, Aug. 8, 1924, at 1. *See generally* Robert A. Goldberg, Hooded Empire: The Ku Klux Klan in Colorado (1981); James Davis, *Colorado under the Klan*, 42 Colo. Mag. 93 (1965); and Gerald L. Marriner, *Klan Politics in Colorado*, 15 J. of the West 76 (1976).

52. Reisler, *supra* note 46, at 54.

53. Federal Emergency Relief Act of 1933, Pub. L. No. 73-15 , ch. 30, 48 Stat. 57 (1933).

54. Eric Beecroft and Seymour Janow, *Toward a National Policy for Migration*, 16 Social Forces 475, 475–92 (1938).

55. Wayne, *supra* note 2, at 1 (emphasis mine).

56. *Id.,* at 8.
57. Farnham, *supra* note 1, at E6.
58. Wayne, *supra* note 2, at 1.
59. *Id.,* at 1, 8.
60. Wayne, *supra* note 3, at 1; and *Urges Deporting of Aliens, supra* note 3, at 7.
61. Wayne, *supra* note 3, at 3; and *That's That,* Denv. Post, March 26, 1935, at 2 (arguing that "[a]liens who have been in this country long enough to be naturalised [sic] but who have made no move to obtain citizenship should be deported without any delay").
62. Wayne, *supra* note 3, at 1, 3.
63. Farnham, *supra* note 1, at E6.
64. Wayne, *supra* note 2, at 3; Wayne, *supra* note 3, at 1 (noting the support of the Spanish-American Coronado club as well as a "host of overburdened taxpayers"); *Turning Back the Invasion,* Chronicle News (Trinidad, Colo.), May 10, 1935, at 5.
65. Farnham, *supra* note 1, at E6.
66. Act of March 3, 1903, Pub. L. No. 57-162 , ch. 1012, § 20–21, 32 Stat. 1213.
67. Not surprisingly, the deportation bills before Congress in 1935 tracked the larger national debate about the merits of a system that most agreed was broken. See Reuben Oppenheimer, *The Administration of the Deportation Laws of the United States,* Report to the National Commission on Law Observance and Enforcement (Washington, DC: U.S. Government Printing Office, 1931).
68. *Truax v. Raich,* 239 U.S. 33 (1915).
69. David Fellman, *The Aliens' Right to Work,* 22 Minn. L. Rev. 138, 155–61 (1937–38); Note, *Constitutionality of Legislative Discrimination against the Alien in His Right to Work,* 83 U. Penn. L. Rev. 75, 78–79 (1935).
70. Fellman, *supra* note 69, at 156–61. In some instances, lower courts disregarded this precedent and did find unconstitutional those statutes barring aliens from particular professions. *See e.g. George v. City of Portland,* 114 Ore. 418 (1925).
71. Fellman, *supra* note 69, at 160. *See, e.g., Clarke v. Deckenbach,* 274 U.S. 392, 394, 397 (1927).
72. Fellman, *supra* note 69, at 167 (arguing that "this discrimination is clearly the law of the land today").
73. Note, *supra* note 69, at 76.
74. Alien Land Law of 1913, California, Codes & Gen. Laws (1915), sec. 40.
75. *Terrace v. Thompson,* 263 U.S. 197 (1923).
76. *Id.,* at 221.
77. Ruben H. Klainer, *Deportation of Aliens,* 15 Bost. U. L. Rev. 663, 667 (1935). *See also Fong Yue Ting* v. *United States,* 149 U.S. 698 (1893).
78. Fellman, *supra* note 69, at 137–44; Note, *supra* 69, at 74–75.
79. Note, *supra* note 69, at 75.
80. Frances Wayne, *Officials Pass Buck on Moving Needy Families,* Denv. Post, May 1, 1935.

81. *Party of Aliens from Texas Is Being Held in Trinidad after Governor Wires Sheriff*, Chron. News (Trinidad, Colo.), May 7, 1935, at 1.

82. *Id.*, at 1. *See also, 27 under Arrest: Johnson Will Check Beet Laborers' Passports*, Denv. Post, May 7, 1935, at 1; *See also* Abraham Hoffman, *The Trinidad Incident*, 11 J. of Mex.-Amer. Hist, 143, 144 (1972).

83. *27 under Arrest, supra* note 82, at 1.

84. *Gov. Johnson Asks Sheriffs to Be on Lookout for Aliens*, Denv. Post, May 8, 1935, at 3.

85. *27 under Arrest, supra* note 82, at 1.

86. *Gov. Johnson Asks Sheriffs to Be on Lookout, supra* note 84, at 3.

87. Francis Wayne, *Johnson Orders Alien Beetfield Workers to Keep Out of State*, Denv. Post, May 9, 1935, at 1.

88. *Id.*, at 1; Hoffman, *supra* note 81, at 143.

89. *Influx of Migratory Labor Is Turned Back from Trinidad by Local Officers*, Chron. News (Trinidad, Colo.), May 9, 1935, at 1; *32 Aliens Put Out of State*, Rocky Mtn. News (Denver), May 9, 1936, at 1.

90. Francis Wayne, *Sec'y. Hull Wires for Facts in Case*, Denv. Post, May 11, 1935, at 1; *Gov. Johnson, Cordell Hull in Alien Row*, Rocky Mtn. News (Denver), May 11, 1935, at 1. *See also* Telegram from Consul Torres to Mexican Embassy, May 10, 1935, National Archives, RG 59, 311.1215/79; Telegram from Sec. Hull to Governor Johnson, May 10, 1935, National Archives, RG 59, 311.1215/79.

91. *See* Telegrams from Consul Torres to Mexican Embassy and Sec. Hull to Governor Johnson, *supra* note 90; Wayne, *supra* note 90, at 3.

92. *Gov. Johnson, Cordell Hull in Alien Row, supra* note 90, at 2.

93. *Diplomacy Triumphed*, Denv. Post, May 12, 1936, at 1.

94. *Mexico Backs Gov. Johnson in Drive on Aliens*, Denv. Post, May 13, 1935, at 1; *Trinidad Labor Deportation Case Smoothed Out by Agreement with Mexico Government*, Chronicle News (Trinidad, Colo.), May 13, 1935, at 1. *But see* Hoffman, *supra* note 82, at 148 (highlighting pointedly negative reaction to Governor Johnson by Mexican press).

95. Charles O. Gridley, *U.S. Will Not Help Johnson Deport Aliens*, Denv. Post, May 14, 1935, at 1.

96. Edwin C. Johnson to Paul Shriver, June 27, 1935, Box 26916, Johnson Collection at CSA.

97. Edwin C. Johnson to Paul Shriver, August 14, 1935, Box 26916, Johnson Collection at CSA.

98. Paul Shriver to Edwin C. Johnson, August 14, 1935, Box 26916, Johnson Collection at CSA.

99. Edwin C. Johnson to Paul Shriver, August 16, 1935, Box 26916, Johnson Collection at CSA.

100. Paul Shriver to Edwin C. Johnson, August 17, 1935, Box 26916, Johnson Collection at CSA.

101. Edwin C. Johnson to Louis Moya, September 19, 1935, Box 26916, Johnson Collection at CSA.

102. H. L. Robertson to Edwin C. Johnson, April 29, 1936, Box 26916, Johnson Collection at CSA.

103. *Deportation Talk Revived*, NY Times, February 16, 1911, at E11. *See generally*, William T. McCarthy, *Horse Sense: The Divided Politics of Edwin C. Johnson, 1923–1954*, University of Northern Colorado, unpublished master's thesis (1996).

104. O. S. Wood to Edwin C. Johnson, March 16, 1936, Box 26916, Johnson Collection at CSA.

105. Stephen Leonard, Trials and Triumphs: A Colorado Portrait of the Great Depression with FSA Photographs (1993).

106. C. W. Thuringer to Edwin C. Johnson, March 14, 1936, Box 26916, Johnson Collection at CSA.

107. C. W. Varnum to Edwin C. Johnson, March 17, 1936, Box 26916, Johnson Collection at CSA.

108. Robertson letter to Johnson, *supra* note 102.

109. *Proclamation Asks Citizens to Support Ban on Cheap Labor*, Denv. Post, April 19, 1936 (emphasis added).

110. Fred S. Warren, *Martial Law Saves Jobs for Citizens*, Denv. Post, April 19, 1936, at 1, 3; Barron B. Beschoar, *Governor Declares Martial Law and Mobilizes National Guard to Southern Border to Check Aliens*, Rocky Mtn. News (Denver), April 19, 1936, at 1–2.

111. *Proclamation Asks Citizens to Support Ban, supra* note 109, at 3.

112. *Barricading Jobs, supra* note 1, at 5.

113. Barbara Young Welke, Law and the Borders of Belonging in the Long Nineteenth Century (2010).

114. Klainer, *supra* note 77, at 667.

115. Beecroft and Janow, *supra* note 54, at 478–80.

116. David Sholtz to Edwin C. Johnson, February 29, 1936, Box 26915, Johnson Collection at CSA.

117. *California Border Closed to Vagrants*, N.Y. Times, February 5, 1936, at 2.

118. *Davis Seeks State Aid in Drive on Indigents*, L.A. Times, February 16, 1936, at A1.

119. *City Police Patrols Halt 1000 at State's Border*, L.A. Times, February 14, 1936.

120. *See* Norris v. City of Boston, 48 U.S. 283 (1849).

121. *Johnson Rejects Pleas to Call Off Patrol on Border*, Denv. Post, April 27, 1936. The last time the governor of Colorado had declared martial law had been in 1914 in response to labor unrest in the coal fields of southeastern Colorado. Atrocities committed by the National Guard culminated in the infamous "Ludlow Massacre." *See* Thomas G. Andrews, Killing for Coal: America's Deadliest Labor War (2008).

122. In the first few days of the order, Johnson was asked about an influx of workers that might occur from Kansas or Nebraska. The governor reserved his right to proclaim martial law on Colorado's eastern border, but never did so. *Continue Drive to Keep Needy from Colorado*, Chicago Times, April 21, 1936, at 11.

123. L.A. Times, April 20, 1936; N.Y. Times, April 20, 1936.

124. Jack Carberry, *Plane Watches for Alien Groups South of the Border*, Denv. Post, April 21, 1936, at 1.

125. *Id.*

126. Neil Kimball to Edwin C. Johnson, April 21, 1936, Box 26901, Johnson Collection at CSA. *See* Denv. Post, April 21–22, 1936, for extensive coverage of the first days of the deployment.

127. Mr. and Mrs. Williams to Edwin C. Johnson, April 20, 1936, Box 26916, Johnson Collection at CSA.

128. H. L. Robertson to Edwin C. Johnson, April 29, 1936, Box 26916, Johnson Collection at CSA.

129. Flyer, Box 26916, Johnson Collection at CSA.

130. *Border Patrolled by Aliens to Halt Needy*, Rocky Mtn. News (Denver), April 20, 1936, at 1, 2; *Many Aliens Enter State on Eve of Labor Blockade*, Denv. Post, April 20, 1936, at 1, 3; and Glen T. Neville, *Colorado Troops on Border Turn Back 70 Persons Who Have Neither Jobs Nor Cash*, Rocky Mtn. News (Denver), April 21, 1936, at 1, 2.

131. L. A. Chapin, *Families Rejecting Beet Field Jobs Will Be Cut off WPA Roll*, Denv. Post, April 27, 1936, at 1.

132. *U.S. Will Aid Colorado Ban on Alien Labor*, Denv. Post, April 20, 1936, at 1.

133. *Two Aliens Stopped by Guards Will Be Deported*, Rocky Mtn. News (Denver), April 28, 1936, at 1; Charles T. O'Brien, *Colorado Rejects Touring Indigents*, N.Y. Times, April 26, 1936, at E7.

134. *Colorado Workers Prefer to Stay with WPA, or Remain on Relief*, Rocky Mtn. News (Denver), April 28, at 1.

135. Glenn T. Neville, *Loopholes in Alien Patrol*, Rocky Mtn. News (Denver), April 22, 1936, at 1.

136. Westbook Pegler, *Colorado Keeping Out the Poor*, Rocky Mtn. News (Denver), April 23, 1936; *Aliens Not Wanted: Who Are They?* Catholic Register, April 23, 1936.

137. *Border Ban on Indigent Nearing End*, Rocky Mtn. News (Denver), April 26, 1936, at 1.

138. *Johnson Refuses Plea to Lift State Border Patrol*, Chronicle News (Trinidad, Colo.), April 27, 1936, at 1; *Johnson Rejects Pleas to Call Off Patrol on Border*, Denv. Post, April 27, 1936, at 3.

139. Jack Carberry, *Governor Orders Troops Kept on Colorado Side of Border*, Denv. Post, April 23, 1936, at 4.

140. *Tingley Warns Troops Not to Cross Border*, Rocky Mtn. News (Denver), April 23, 1936. *See also* David Chavez to Edwin C. Johnson, April 25, 1936, Box 26916, Johnson Collection at CSA (noting that "Spanish American people from New Mexico are American citizens" and not aliens subject to the blockade).

141. *Tingley Threatens Ban on Colorado Shipments*, Denv. Post, April 23, 1936, at 4.

142. *New Mexico May Bar Colorado Goods*, Rocky Mtn. News (Denver), April 24, 1936, at 1.

143. *Hatch Says Procedure Violates Constitution, Chaves Hints Reprisal*, Rocky Mtn. News (Denver), April 25, 1936, at 2.

144. *Id.*

145. *They Rode the Rods to the Border: They Walked Back*, Rocky Mtn. News (Denver), April 22, 1936.

146. *Just a Few Notes: By the Reporter Who Gets Around*, Rocky Mtn. News (Denver), April 22, 1936.

147. Executive Order, April 29, 1936, Box 26916, Johnson Collection at CSA.

148. Sandoval, *supra* note 43, at 245.

149. *Id.*, at 245–47.

150. *Troops Plug Loopholes in Alien Patrol*, Rocky Mtn. News (Denver), April 22, 1936, at 1, 3.

151. Statement of Edwin C. Johnson, April 29, 1936, Box 26916, Johnson Collection at CSA.

152. Edwin C. Johnson to Denver Methodist Ministerial Alliance, May 4, 1936, Box 26916, Johnson Collection at CSA.

153. *Governor Jonson Will Run for United States Senator*, Record J. of Douglas Cnty. (Castle Rock, Colo.), May 1, 1936.

154. Untitled, Littleton Independent, September 4, 1936, Box 26904, Johnson Collection at CSA.

155. 132 S. Ct. 2492 (2012).

156. *Id.*, at 2498, 2507.

157. A wonderful treatment of this as it applies to contemporary Arizona is found in George A. Martinez, *Arizona, Immigration, and Latinos: The Epistemology of Whiteness, the Geography of Race, Interest Convergence, and the View from the Perspective of Critical Theory*, 44 Ariz. St. L. J. 175 (2012).

158. Arizona v. United States, 132 S. Ct. 2492 (2012)

159. Kevin Johnson, Opening the Floodgates: Why America Needs to Rethink Its Borders and Immigration Laws 86 (2007).

PART III

A Defense of State and Local Efforts

4

Reinforcing the Rule of Law

What States Can and Should Do to Reduce Illegal Immigration

KRIS W. KOBACH

In the 2007 state legislative session, something truly extraordinary happened. For the first time ever, legislators in all fifty states introduced bills dealing with illegal immigration. A whopping 1,562 illegal immigration bills were submitted, up from 570 in 2006.[1] Of the bills submitted, 240 were enacted into law, up from 84 in 2006.[2] The vast majority were designed to discourage illegal immigration in one way or another. This legislative surge continued for several years thereafter.

It has been often said but seldom demonstrated so clearly: every state is a border state now. It is undeniable that the urge to reduce illegal immigration has become a powerful force in state legislatures across the country. In the following analysis, I ask and answer two questions about this phenomenon. First, why are they doing it? Second, what legislation can states (or cities) enact in the immigration arena without being preempted by federal law?

I. Forces Pushing the States to Act

Without question, the single largest factor motivating state governments to enact legislation discouraging illegal immigration is the fiscal burden that it imposes upon the states. As the Nobel Prize–winning economist Milton Friedman once famously observed, "It's just obviously you can't have free immigration and a welfare state."[3] The states have seen Friedman's principle confirmed, with crushing consequences for taxpayers. Although the state expenditures driven by illegal immigration do not all fit into the category of "welfare" expenditures—the consequences are the same. A massive influx of individuals who either pay very little in income taxes or evade income taxes entirely, but consume public services at a relatively high rate, is costly for any receiving state. Consequently, as the number of illegal aliens in a state increases, the financial burden becomes more and more difficult for taxpayers to bear.[4]

In 2007, economist Robert Rector conducted the most rigorous study to date on the *net* fiscal cost of illegal immigration (including any tax payments from illegal aliens). He concluded that the net fiscal cost imposed on all levels of government by illegal aliens was $89.1 billion a year.[5] The government expenditures attributable to illegal immigration range from law enforcement costs to public expenditures for emergency medical care. However, the biggest-ticket item is the cost of providing K-12 education to the children in illegal alien–headed households.[6] And that burden falls predominantly on the shoulders of the fifty state governments. For example, in Arizona, the total cost of providing public services to the state's estimated 475,000 illegal aliens is approximately $1.3 billion a year.[7] Of that total cost, approximately $748.3 million goes to providing free primary and secondary school education.[8] Because the numerous fiscal burdens associated with illegal immigration are so significant, there has been an extraordinary amount of activity at the state level to discourage illegal immigration. Although the fiscal burden at the federal level is significant—more than $10 billion annually—the lion's share hits state budgets.[9]

Similar forces have pushed dozens of municipalities to act. The burden on local communities is extremely high, particularly with respect to law enforcement costs resulting from crimes committed by illegal aliens and municipal services consumed by illegal aliens. The facts surrounding the case of Hazleton, Pennsylvania, which in 2006 enacted ordinances barring the employment of unauthorized aliens and the harboring of illegal aliens, illustrate the financial burden.[10] Hazleton's population exploded from approximately 22,000 in the 2000 census to

30,000–33,000 in the space of five years,[11] but the earned income tax receipts on which the city relied for its revenues stayed flat. This lack of additional revenues reflected the fact that much of the immigration was illegal, and the new arrivals were either working off the books or earning so little that they were paying little or nothing in taxes.[12] Meanwhile, expenditures for routine city services that reflect the size of the population, such as trash removal, increased by nearly 50%. Expenditures by the local school district for its English as a Second Language program skyrocketed from approximately $136,000 in 2002–03 school year to over $1.1 million in the 2006–07 school year.[13]

Other factors also impel local governments to act. Most notable among these factors are the overloading or closing of hospitals due to unpaid use of emergency rooms by illegal aliens, and crimes committed by illegal alien–dominated street gangs. Illegal immigration into a region often coincides with dramatic increases in patients visiting the emergency rooms of area hospitals, because the vast majority of illegal aliens do not possess health insurance, and federal law requires all hospitals to provide emergency medical care to all comers, regardless of immigration status and regardless of ability to pay.[14] Here again, Hazleton illustrates the problem. The Hazleton hospital's emergency room began losing millions of dollars annually, wait times in the emergency room increased to over five hours at times, and an expanded emergency room facility had to be built.[15] With respect to crimes, Hazleton witnessed a crime wave in narcotics and related violence due to the presence of gangs dominated by illegal aliens. Most noticeably, a small town that previously experienced murder once every seven or eight years saw a series of violent homicides involving illegal aliens in a two-year period.[16] In addition, members of the violent street gang Mara Salvatrucha-13 (MS-13) were arrested or identified in Hazleton.[17]

The criminal impact of illegal immigration has been noteworthy in other jurisdictions as well. I am referring to crimes over and above the numerous federal crimes that are part and parcel of simply residing and working unlawfully in the United States.[18] The concurrence of alien smuggling networks with drug smuggling networks often results in the same individuals engaging in various related criminal enterprises. In recent years, the emergence of MS-13 and related illegal alien–dominated gangs has resulted in unprecedented levels of gang violence in the more than thirty states in which MS-13 operates.[19] Approximately 90% of MS-13 gang members in the United States are illegal aliens.[20] While most MS-13 members join the gang prior to entering the United States illegally, other illegal-alien gang members join after entering the United States. For example, the illegal alien–dominated Latin Kings seek out and recruit young men who are unlawfully present in the United States, offering them social networks, money, and the illusion of security.[21] Not surprisingly, illegal aliens make up a disproportionate share of inmates in federal prisons.[22]

These latter two consequences of illegal immigration—health care costs and criminal costs—only exacerbate the fiscal burdens imposed by illegal immigration upon states and cities. And unlike the federal government, most states and cities must balance their budgets every year. Eventually, the overwhelming fiscal burdens resulting from illegal immigration force state and local legislators to act.

Legislators are not the only ones who have recognized the magnitude of the burden that illegal immigration imposes upon states and cities. Judges reviewing immigration-related state statutes have also observed this fact. As the U.S. District Court for the District of Arizona noted in 2008,

> If the authorized state and federal sanctions [of the Immigration Reform and Control Act of 1986] are disproportional in severity, that is because Congress recognized the disproportional harm to core state and federal responsibilities from unauthorized alien labor. The pervasive adverse effects of such employment fall directly on the states. Congress conspicuously did not take responsibility for those costs. In light of the disproportionate responsibilities and burdens on the states, Congress could reasonably conclude that states are better equipped than Congress to judge which licenses to sanction, and how much. It left the strong deterrence of licensing sanctions to individual states to implement in their own circumstances.[23]

This statement echoed an observation made thirty-two years earlier by the U.S. Supreme Court in *De Canas v. Bica*, when it sustained a state law prohibiting the employment of unauthorized aliens in California—a state that was already experiencing the fiscal burdens of illegal immigration in 1976:

These local problems are particularly acute in California in light of the significant influx into that State of illegal aliens from neighboring Mexico. In attempting to protect California's fiscal interests and lawfully resident labor force from the deleterious effects on its economy resulting from the employment of illegal aliens, [the state law] focuses directly on these essentially local problems. . . .[24]

Today the fiscal burdens imposed by illegal immigration are acute throughout the United States. As a result, many cities and states are for the first time exercising their authority to act.

II. Areas of Permissible State Lawmaking in the Field

It is clear from the fact that all fifty states have proposed bills affecting illegal immigration that there are ample forces pushing state legislators to stem the flow of illegal immigration into their respective jurisdictions. However, the will to act does not always coincide with the boundaries defined by Congress and the attendant principles of federal preemption doctrine. Not all of these state bills are permissible under federal law. Because immigration is a field in which the federal government enjoys plenary authority under Article I of the U.S. Constitution, state statutes must be carefully drafted to avoid federal preemption. And there are some things that states simply cannot do, no matter how well a statute is drafted. For example, a state may not create state-level criteria for determining which aliens are allowed to reside in the United States.[25] Nor may a state impose criminal penalties on the employers of unauthorized aliens.[26] A state statute of either sort would be clearly preempted by federal law.

That said, there is wide latitude for states and municipalities to act without being preempted, provided the statutes are drafted correctly. As the Supreme Court declared in the landmark immigration preemption case of *De Canas v. Bica*, "standing alone, the fact that aliens are the subject of a state statute does not render it a [prohibited] regulation of immigration, which is essentially a determination of who should or should not be admitted into the country, and the conditions under which a legal entrant may remain."[27] As the *De Canas* Court explained, states possess considerable authority to act in ways that affect immigration without being preempted by the Immigration and Nationality Act [INA]:

> Of course, even state regulation designed to protect vital state interests must give way to paramount federal legislation. But we will not presume that Congress, in enacting the INA, intended to oust state authority to regulate the employment relationship [concerning unauthorized aliens] in a manner consistent with pertinent federal laws. Only a demonstration that complete ouster of state power—including state power to promulgate laws not in conflict with federal laws—was "the clear and manifest purpose of Congress" would justify that conclusion. Respondents have not made that demonstration. They fail to point out, and an independent review does not reveal, any specific indication in either the wording or the legislative history of the INA that Congress intended to preclude even harmonious state regulation touching on aliens in general, or the employment of illegal aliens in particular.[28]

The *De Canas* Court expressly noted that Congress has never occupied the field of immigration so as to displace state laws in the area. Provided that a state statute is not expressly barred by federal law, that the state statute does not attempt to create state-level standards regarding which aliens may enter the United States, that the state statute does not pose an obstacle to the accomplishment of the manifest objectives of Congress, and that it is possible to simultaneously comply with state and federal law, preemption does not occur.

What follows is a summary of eight areas in which states or cities can constitutionally act in the field of immigration. Those eight areas are

A. denying public benefits to illegal aliens;

B. denying resident tuition rates to illegal aliens;

C. prohibiting the employment of unauthorized aliens;

D. enacting state-level crimes that mirror federal immigration crimes;

E. enacting state-level crimes against identity theft;

F. providing state and local law enforcement assistance to Immigration and Customs Enforcement (ICE);

G. presuming illegal aliens to be flight risks for bail purposes;

H. denying driver's licenses to illegal aliens.

In all of these areas, there are three important restrictions that must be built into any state statute if it is to conform to the requirements of federal law and avoid preemption: (1) the statute must not attempt to create any new categories of aliens not recognized by federal law; (2) the statute must use terms consistent with federal law; and (3) the statute must not attempt to authorize state or local officials to independently determine an alien's immigration status, without verification by the federal government.[29]

At the time of this writing, four states have enacted statutes that encompass all, or virtually all, of the eight areas listed above: Alabama, Arizona, Oklahoma, and Missouri. Arizona did so through a series of legislative bills and voter initiatives enacted between 2004 and 2007.[30] Oklahoma, Missouri, and Alabama did so through omnibus immigration bills enacted in 2007, 2008, and 2011, respectively.[31] The majority of the remaining states have enacted narrower bills covering one or more of the eight areas. In addition, dozens of municipalities and counties across the country have acted in at least one of the eight areas.[32] The following analysis offers examples in each area, as well as an explanation of the legal authority supporting such state or local enactments.

A. Denying Public Benefits to Illegal Aliens

One of the easiest and most obvious things a state, county, or municipality can do is deny public benefits to illegal aliens. The most well-known example of this is Arizona's Proposition 200, a popular initiative that was enacted with 56% of the vote in 2004.[33] Alabama, Colorado, Georgia, Missouri, Nebraska, and Oklahoma enacted similar statutes in the years thereafter; and more states are likely to follow.[34] Such statutes deny the vast majority of public benefits to illegal aliens, including Medicare, Medicaid, unemployment insurance, housing benefits, food assistance, commercial licenses, and numerous other public benefits.

It is important to understand that these statutes do no more than is already required by federal law. Indeed, the states that have not yet enacted statutes barring the provision of public benefits to illegal aliens are likely to be violating federal law, to the extent that any public benefits are currently flowing to illegal aliens. In 1996, Congress enacted the Personal Responsibility and Work Opportunity Reconciliation Act of 1996 (PRWORA). In that act, Congress included numerous provisions designed to ensure that illegal aliens do not receive public benefits at the federal, state, or local level. Those provisions are found at 8 U.S.C. § 1621. Specifically, Congress mandated that an illegal alien (who is not a "qualified" alien)[35] "is not eligible for any State or local public benefits."[36] Henceforth, states and localities were to deny the following broad array of benefits to illegal aliens:

A. any grant, contract, loan, professional license, or commercial license provided by an agency of a State or local government or by appropriated funds of a State or local government; and

B. any retirement, welfare, health, disability, public or assisted housing, postsecondary education, food assistance, unemployment benefit, or any other similar benefit for which payments or assistance are provided to an individual, household, or family eligibility unit by an agency of a State or local government or by appropriated funds of a State or local government.[37]

Exceptions are made for emergency medical assistance, emergency disaster relief, and immunizations.[38] In addition, since the 1982 decision of the U.S. Supreme Court in *Plyler v. Doe*, states have been required to provide free K-12 education to illegal alien children.[39]

These exceptions aside, states and municipalities are *required* by federal law to deny all public benefits to illegal aliens.[40] When enacting these provisions of federal law in 1996, Congress expressly spelled out its objectives. As stated in 8 U.S.C. § 1601(2),

It continues to be the immigration policy of the United States that (a) aliens within the Nation's borders not depend on public resources to meet their needs, but rather rely on their own capabilities and the resources of their families, their sponsors, and private organizations, and (b) the availability of public benefits not constitute an incentive for immigration to the United States.

A few subsections later in the U.S. Code, Congress reiterated its purpose: "It is a compelling government interest to remove the incentive for illegal immigration provided by the availability of public benefits."[41]

Congress was determined to remove the magnetic effect of public benefits in the illegal immigration crisis.

In order to implement these PRWORA provisions, the federal government expanded the Systematic Alien Verification for Entitlements (SAVE) Program, which was originally established in 1987, pursuant to the Immigration Reform and Control Act (IRCA). The SAVE Program utilizes a massive automated database that state and local government agencies can consult, via internet, to determine whether an alien is lawfully present in the United States and entitled to receive the benefits in question. Verification usually occurs in a matter of seconds. There are at least 205 participating government agencies across the country that are already using the SAVE program to verify aliens' immigration status.[42]

Congress was also careful to expressly pave the way for states to verify the status of aliens seeking public benefits. Congress gave the states explicit authorization to do so in 8 U.S.C. § 1625: "A State or political subdivision of a State is authorized to require an applicant for State and local public benefits . . . to provide proof of eligibility." Congress also provided that states would have a clear legal avenue for reporting to federal authorities illegal aliens who seek public benefits. Indeed, Congress prohibited states from concealing this information if they discover it. According to 8 U.S.C. § 1644, no government entity may be "in any way restricted, from sending to or receiving from [federal immigration officials] information regarding the immigration status, lawful or unlawful, of an alien in the United States."

The authority of a state to comply with the express requirements of federal law is beyond serious dispute. Nevertheless, legal challenges have been brought against such laws; and two U.S. district courts have confirmed the authority of states to enact statutes that deny public benefits to illegal aliens. The most recent decision came out of the District of Arizona in the case of *Friendly House v. Napolitano* in 2005. In that case, the Court sustained Arizona's Proposition 200 against a preemption challenge. The Court concluded that Congress clearly intended that states should verify the status of aliens seeking public benefits and that Proposition 200 was not preempted by federal law.[43] Eight years earlier, in the case of *LULAC v. Wilson*, the District Court for the Central District of California had articulated the same principle. Although the Court struck down certain provisions of Proposition 187, which had been enacted via popular initiative in 1994 two years prior to PRWORA, the Court found that benefits-denial provisions were not an impermissible regulation of immigration and therefore withstood scrutiny under the first *De Canas* test.[44] The Court also noted that "[t]he benefits denial provisions of Proposition 187 may therefore be implemented without impermissibly regulating immigration if state agencies, in verifying for services and benefits, rely on federal determinations made by the INS and accessible through SAVE."[45] These judicial decisions confirmed what was already clear: states are on solid legal ground if they follow the requirements of federal law and deny public benefits to illegal aliens, using the SAVE program to verify with the federal government the legal status of any alien applicant. Numerous states, counties, and cities have already done so. This is perhaps the easiest step that can be taken to remove an incentive for continued unlawful presence and further illegal immigration.[46]

B. Denying Resident Tuition Rates to Illegal Aliens

One subset of public benefits that has received a great deal of attention with respect to illegal aliens is access to in-state tuition rates (or "resident" tuition rates).[47] In September 1996, Congress passed the landmark Illegal Immigration Reform and Immigrant Responsibility Act (IIRIRA).[48] Advocates for illegal aliens in some states—most notably California—had already raised the possibility of making in-state tuition rates available to illegal aliens who attend public universities.[49] Illegal aliens had been eligible for in-state tuition rates at the California State University System prior to the passage of Proposition 187 by California voters in 1994.[50] To prevent states from extending in-state tuition eligibility to illegal aliens, IIRIRA's sponsors inserted a section that prohibited any state from doing so, unless the state also provided the same discounted tuition to all U.S. citizens:

> Notwithstanding any other provision of law, an alien who is not lawfully present in the United States shall not be eligible on the basis of residence within a State (or a political subdivision) for any postsecondary education benefit unless a citizen or national of the United States is eligible for such a benefit (in no less an amount, duration, and scope) without regard to whether the citizen or national is such a resident.[51]

Congress's intent was clear. If a state wished to make in-state tuition rates available to any illegal aliens, it would have to make the benefit available to *all* nonresident U.S. citizens and nationals. Fifteen states have brazenly violated this provision of federal law, rewarding illegal aliens with the valuable benefit of a taxpayer-subsidized college education. Those fifteen states are California, Texas, New York, Illinois, Washington, Utah, Oklahoma, Kansas, New Mexico, Nebraska, Connecticut, Maryland, Oregon, Minnesota, and Colorado.[52] Four of those states—California, Kansas, Texas, and Nebraska—have seen their laws challenged in state or federal court.[53]

However, some states have taken action to make sure that they adhere to 8 U.S.C. § 1623. They have expressly barred their public universities from offering in-state tuition rates to illegal aliens. The most notable is Arizona, which did so with the passage of Proposition 300 in 2006. The Arizona legislature approved a legislative resolution (S.C.R. 1031) that was placed on the November 7, 2006, election ballot.[54] Arizona voters approved Proposition 300 overwhelmingly, with 71.4% voting in favor.[55] Had the question been put to a popular vote in the ten states that offer in-state tuition rates to illegal aliens, it is not unreasonable to suggest that the outcome would have been similar in most of them. Scientific polls consistently show that overwhelming majorities of the public oppose making in-state tuition rates available to illegal aliens.[56]

Of course a state legislature need not place the issue on a referendum ballot in order to comply with federal law. A normal statute will suffice. South Carolina enacted such a statute in 2007.[57] Missouri did so in 2008.[58] Given the unequivocal congressional statement on the matter in 8 U.S.C. § 1623, it should come as no surprise that laws or policies denying in-state tuition rates to illegal aliens have also survived legal challenge. In 2004, the U.S. District Court for the Eastern District of Virginia found that a Virginia policy denying postsecondary education benefits to illegal aliens was permissible under federal law. Importantly, the Virginia policy adopted federal standards for classifying aliens and deferred to federal determinations of alien status. It was therefore on secure constitutional ground.[59]

C. Prohibiting the Employment of Unauthorized Aliens

The employment of unauthorized aliens is one area in which states can make a huge difference. Indeed, if there is a silver bullet in addressing the problem of illegal immigration, this is it. Jobs are the primary magnet that draws illegal aliens to the United States. Removing this magnet can significantly reduce illegal immigration and can encourage many illegal aliens to leave the United States on their own. It has been a crime to knowingly employ an unauthorized alien since the passage of IRCA in 1986.[60] However, the federal government has found it difficult to keep illegal labor out of the workplace. Worksite enforcement of immigration laws has ebbed and flowed for more than two decades,[61] but the central flaw of the I-9 process described in IRCA has been the proliferation of false identification cards and other documents that suffice to fool employers who have no background or knowledge in the detection of counterfeit documents.

Nonetheless, states can transform worksite enforcement of federal immigration laws. In 2007, the Arizona legislature made it a violation of state law to knowingly hire an unauthorized alien and made Arizona the first state in the country to require all employers to verify the employment authorization of newly hired workers through the federal government's "E-Verify" system.[62] On January 1, 2008, the law went into effect. The internet-based E-Verify system is free of charge and easy to use. The employer simply enters the employee's name, date of birth, and Social Security number or other work authorization number. He gets an answer back from the federal government in seconds. Over twenty thousand businesses across the country were already using E-Verify voluntarily before January 1, 2008.[63] Thereafter, Arizona's 145,000 were obliged to join their ranks. When employers verify every new employee with the federal government, it becomes very difficult to violate the law. Illegal aliens know that E-Verify makes it impossible for them to fabricate Social Security numbers or use counterfeit identity cards to obtain jobs. And when the jobs dry up, they leave.

Arizona's statute had immediate and profound effects. Newspapers in the state reported in January 2008 that illegal aliens were already *self*-deporting by the thousands.[64] Apartment complexes in Phoenix and Tucson confirmed that high numbers of alien tenants had departed their apartments.[65] The Arizona public school system immediately began to experience some relief, with a $48.6 million surplus suddenly appearing in FY 2008.[66] Although some illegal aliens undoubtedly moved to neighboring states, many returned across the border to

Mexico. In January 2008, the leaders of the neighboring Mexican state of Sonora sent a delegation of nine state legislators from Sonora to Arizona to criticize the new law. Strangely, they complained that Sonora could not handle the burden that the influx of returning Mexican citizens was imposing on Sonoran schools and housing.[67] Evidently, they thought that Arizona's taxpayers were obligated to bear that burden.

Arizona's success offers empirical proof that attrition through enforcement works. The premise is a straightforward one—the way to solve America's illegal immigration problem is to make it more difficult for unauthorized aliens to work illegally in the United States, while incrementally stepping up the enforcement of other laws discouraging illegal immigration. The result is that many illegal aliens self-deport. Illegal aliens are rational decision makers. If the probability of successfully obtaining a job goes down, then at some point the only rational decision is to return to one's country of origin.[68]

Others have followed Arizona's lead. In the 2008 legislative session, Mississippi enacted a similar law requiring all private employers to utilize the E-Verify system when hiring new employees. The requirements were phased in gradually over a three-year period, beginning in July 2008 with employers of more than 250 employees and extending to all employers by July 2011.[69] South Carolina, Georgia, and Alabama followed in 2011.[70]

Municipalities have also acted in this area. Most notably, Hazleton, Pennsylvania, and Valley Park, Missouri, enacted similar ordinances prohibiting local employers from knowingly employing unauthorized aliens, and giving employers safe harbor if they used the E-Verify system to verify the work authorization of new employees. The only consequence imposed upon an employer who violates the ordinance is the suspension of the employer's business license. The same is true of Arizona's statute: the only consequence is suspension of a business license.

The statutes were drafted this way because, when enacting IRCA in 1986, Congress expressly preempted states from imposing criminal penalties on the employers of unauthorized aliens, but expressly *allowed* states to impose the consequence of a suspension or loss of business license. The relevant federal law states, "Preemption. The provisions of this section preempt any State or local law imposing civil or criminal sanctions (*other than through licensing and similar laws*) upon those who employ, or recruit or refer for a fee for employment, unauthorized aliens."[71] Accordingly, a state statute or local ordinance that only suspends the business license of an offending employer, and that relies on the federal government's determination of any alien's employment authorization, will not be preempted.

Statutes of this nature have already been tested and upheld in federal courts. In 2011, the United States Supreme Court sustained against a preemption challenge Arizona's law requiring E-Verify participation and prohibiting the knowing employment of unauthorized aliens.[72] The Court found that the state was completely within its authority to require the use of E-Verify: "Arizona's use of E-Verify does not conflict with the federal scheme."[73] Similarly, the Eastern District of Missouri sustained the City of Valley Park's ordinance suspending the business licenses of employers who knowingly employ unauthorized aliens.[74] The Court was unequivocal in concluding that "[t]he plain meaning of the [federal] statute clearly provides for state and local governments to pass licensing laws which touch upon the subject of illegal immigration. The [local] statute at issue is such a licensing law, and therefore is not expressly preempted by federal law."[75] These decisions have paved the way for other states and cities to follow.[76]

Because it is possible to combine a requirement that employers use E-Verify, a process for the suspension of licenses held by employers of unauthorized aliens, with rules governing state income taxes, there are many approaches that a state or municipality can take in preventing the employment of unauthorized aliens. A state can

1. require all private employers in the state to participate in E-Verify;
2. suspend the business licenses of employers who knowingly employ unauthorized aliens;
3. require all government agencies to participate in E-Verify;
4. require recipients of government contracts to participate in E-Verify;
5. prohibit employers from deducting wages paid to unauthorized aliens from their income, when paying state income taxes; and
6. create a private cause of action allowing any U.S. citizen who is fired by an employer who is knowingly employing unauthorized aliens to sue the employer for damages in state court.

Numerous states have already enacted various combinations of these provisions. For example, Arizona, Oklahoma, and Missouri require governmental agencies to utilize the E-Verify system when hiring new employees and require all recipients of public contracts to participate in the E-Verify program.[77] Arizona and Missouri prohibit employers from knowingly employing unauthorized aliens and provide for the suspension of business licenses held by those employers who violate the statutes.[78] Georgia and Missouri prohibit employers from deducting wages or other compensation paid to unauthorized alien employees from their income for tax purposes.[79] And Oklahoma, Mississippi, and Utah recognize a private cause of action against an employer for any U.S. citizen or lawful permanent resident alien who is discharged from employment while the employer is knowingly employing an unauthorized alien.[80] It is likely that the number of states taking some combination of the six actions listed above to discourage the employment of unauthorized aliens will only increase in the years ahead.[81]

D. Enacting State-Level Crimes That Mirror Federal Crimes

State governments possess the authority to criminalize particular conduct concerning illegal immigration, provided that they do so in a way that mirrors the terms of federal law. In this way, state governments can utilize state and local law enforcement agencies to enforce these state crimes, thereby reinforcing the efforts of federal law enforcement agencies. The federal crimes that are most suited to duplication at the state level are alien smuggling and alien harboring.

For example, in 2007, Oklahoma carefully duplicated federal law to prohibit the transportation or harboring of illegal aliens within the state. The Oklahoma statute applied the precise terms of federal law in the state context:

A. It shall be unlawful for any person to transport, move, or attempt to transport in the State of Oklahoma any alien knowing or in reckless disregard of the fact that the alien has come to, entered, or remained in the United States in violation of law, in furtherance of the illegal presence of the alien in the United States.

B. It shall be unlawful for any person to conceal, harbor, or shelter from detection any alien in any place within the State of Oklahoma, including any building or means of transportation, knowing or in reckless disregard of the fact that the alien has come to, entered, or remained in the United States in violation of law.[82]

Utah enacted similar language in 2008.[83] Such concurrent enforcement is clearly within a state's authority. As the Ninth Circuit has opined, "Where state enforcement activities do not impair federal regulatory interests *concurrent enforcement activity is authorized*."[84] Where "[f]ederal and local enforcement have identical purposes," preemption does not occur.[85] In the words of Judge Learned Hand, "it would be unreasonable to suppose that [the federal government's] purpose was to deny itself any help that the states may allow."[86]

Recent examples of such state criminal statutes have already been tested and sustained in court. For example, the Arizona Human Smuggling Statute of 2005 created a state crime prohibiting the smuggling of illegal aliens.[87] The Arizona statute was upheld against a preemption challenge because it represented concurrent enforcement against substantially the same activity prohibited by federal immigration law:

[C]oncurrent state and federal enforcement of illegal alien smuggling and conspiracy to smuggle illegal alien laws serves both federal and state law enforcement purposes and is highly compatible. In fact, concurrent enforcement enhances rather than impairs federal enforcement objectives. Thus, *because federal and State enforcement have compatible purposes, and Congress has not expressly preempted state prosecution of such conduct, preemption does not exist.*[88]

Georgia has established a similar state offense—that of trafficking a person for labor servitude.[89] As long as such state statutes mirror federal statutory language and defer to the federal government's determination of the legal status of any alien in question, they will be on secure constitutional footing.[90] It should be noted that since 1996, the federal government has been under a statutory obligation to respond to any inquiry from a state or local government about the immigration status of any alien.[91] Thus, the federal government must provide an answer, whenever any state or local official acting under color of law inquires as to a particular alien's immigration status.[92]

One variation of this concept of concurrently prohibiting the same conduct at the federal level and the state or local level is seen in local ordinances that prevent landlords from harboring illegal aliens in apartments. Several federal courts have confirmed that the provision of an apartment or other housing to an illegal alien fits squarely within the federal crime of harboring under 8 U.S.C. § 1324(a)(1)(A) or its precursor, 8 U.S.C. § 1324(a)(3).[93] A city may therefore prohibit the harboring of an illegal alien, where the harboring individual acts knowing, or in reckless disregard of the fact, that the alien is unlawfully present in the United States.[94] Challenges to several local ordinances that prohibit the harboring of illegal aliens by landlords are being litigated at the time of this writing.[95] However, it is clear that the doctrine of concurrent enforcement allows state or local jurisdictions to act without being preempted.[96]

E. Enacting State Laws That Prohibit Identity Theft and the Use of False Documents in the Employment Context

Identity theft is both a facilitator and a consequence of mass illegal immigration. As long as unauthorized aliens seek jobs in the United States, many will attempt to do so by stealing or inventing a false identity. A 2002 General Accounting Office study reported that identity theft is an integral part of illegal entry by aliens through U.S. ports of entry, obtaining unauthorized employment in the United States, and concealing the commission of serious crimes by aliens, including narcotics trafficking.[97] The number of incidents of identity theft was estimated to be between one quarter of a million and three quarters of a million per year, and growing.[98] The study also noted that more than eight thousand state and local government offices issue birth certificates, driver's licenses, or other identity documents, virtually all of which may be counterfeited or used fraudulently by illegal aliens.[99]

Forty-eight of the fifty states already have some version of an identity theft offense on their statute books. However, those state crimes vary widely.[100] Recognizing the crucial role that identity theft plays in illegal immigration, some states have enacted new laws to broaden existing definitions of identity theft. For example, Arizona in 2007 defined the crime of "aggravated taking of identity of another person or entity" to include "taking the identity of another person or entity if the person knowingly takes, purchases, manufactures, records, possesses or uses any personal identifying information or entity identifying information of . . . another person, including a real or fictitious person, with the intent to obtain employment."[101]

Because defining and prosecuting the crime of identity theft is clearly within a state's police powers, there is little dispute that a state may define that crime so as to apply within the employment context. A preemption challenge to a state statute on this subject would be difficult, if not impossible, to mount successfully. Broadening the crime of identity theft offers yet another avenue for states that wish to discourage illegal aliens from residing, and to discourage unauthorized aliens from seeking employment, in the United States.

F. Providing State and Local Law Enforcement Assistance to ICE

In recent years, many states and cities have sought to maximize cooperation between their law enforcement agencies and the Bureau of Immigration and Customs Enforcement (ICE). There are three principal ways in which states and cities have accomplished this objective: (1) by directing their law enforcement agencies to utilize their inherent arrest authority more frequently, (2) by entering into so-called Section 287(g) agreements with ICE so that their officers can exercise the delegated authority of federal immigration officers, and (3) by prohibiting sanctuary cities. It must be noted at the outset that inherent arrest authority and Section 287(g) authority are two very different authorities.[102] The inherent arrest authority of states and localities is simply the power to arrest an illegal alien who is removable, detain the alien temporarily, and then transfer the alien to the custody of the ICE. That authority has been recognized by numerous federal courts of appeals, as well as by the Office of Legal Counsel of the U.S. Department of Justice.[103] The Supreme Court sustained a provision of Arizona law compelling state and local police to exercise that inherent arrest authority in *Arizona v. United States* in 2012.[104]

In contrast, Section 287(g) delegates authority that is considerably broader than the power to merely arrest an illegal alien and transfer him to ICE custody. Any state or municipality can enter into a formal Memorandum of Understanding (MOU) with ICE, which effectively deputizes officers of the state or local law enforcement agency to perform the "function[s] of an immigration officer," under Section 287(g) of the Immigration and Nationality Act (INA).[105] Section 287(g) encompasses the full spectrum of enforcement powers, including not only the power to arrest and transfer but also the power to investigate immigration violations, the power to collect evidence and assemble an immigration case for prosecution or removal, the power to take custody of aliens on behalf of the federal government, and other general powers involved in the routine enforcement of immigration laws.

The first two states that signed Section 287(g) agreements with the federal government were Florida and Alabama. The Florida MOU became effective on July 7, 2002. Under that agreement, thirty-five Florida law enforcement officers were trained for six weeks and were delegated specific immigration enforcement powers, including the power to interrogate, the power to collect evidence, and the power to conduct broad immigration investigations. The Alabama MOU was signed on September 10, 2003. Under the agreement, the first group of twenty-one Alabama state troopers undertook five weeks of immigration enforcement training, which they completed in October 2003. A second class of twenty-five troopers received training in October 2005. Since then, Colorado, Arizona, Georgia, and numerous counties have entered into similar Section 287(g) agreements.[106] At the end of 2005, the federal government appropriated $5 million to pay for the training and associated expenses of new states that enter into Section 287(g) agreements.[107] However, after 2009, the Obama Administration took steps to circumscribe the scope of such agreements, reducing their value to participating jurisdictions.

In contrast to the formality, negotiation, and delays involved in entering into a 287(g) MOU with the federal government, inherent arrest authority can be maximized quickly if a jurisdiction chooses to do so. For example, in 2007, the governor of Missouri issued an executive order directing Missouri state troopers to verify with the federal government the immigration status of all aliens arrested.[108] Aliens found to be unlawfully present in the United States would be delivered to ICE custody. In 2008, the Missouri legislature etched this policy into statute and extended it to all state and local law enforcement agencies, with respect to individuals charged with a crime and confined to jail.[109] The same year, the state of Utah enacted a law requiring all sheriffs to determine the immigration status of any alien arrested for a felony or for driving under the influence. Both states directed law enforcement officers to rely upon verifications of status given by the Law Enforcement Support Center—a 24/7 communications center located in Williston, Vermont, and operated by ICE.[110]

States may also enact legislation to ensure that their municipalities do not become so-called sanctuary cities, which refuse to communicate any illegal alien's immigration status to the federal government. Despite the fact that Congress outlawed sanctuary policies in 1996,[111] more than seventy municipalities have adopted such policies. In response, some states have enacted state legislation prohibiting their municipalities from adopting sanctuary policies. For example, Oklahoma did so in 2007.[112] Such statutes need only reiterate the terms of federal law, found at 8 U.S.C. §§ 1373(a)–(b) and 1644, and provide disincentives for municipalities that violate the state statutes. The most obvious disincentive is to make sanctuary cities ineligible to receive any state funding. That is precisely what the Missouri legislature did in 2008, denying state funding to sanctuary cities and allowing any state legislator to request an attorney general's opinion as to whether a particular city has adopted a sanctuary policy.[113] In this way, the proliferation of sanctuary cities in a state can be brought to a stop; or a state can prevent sanctuary cities from emerging in the first place.

G. Presuming Illegal Aliens to Be Flight Risks for Bail Purposes

Another law enforcement measure that is being adopted by some states concerns the presumption of flight risk for the purposes of setting bail and determining whether or not to release a defendant prior to trial. These statutes direct state courts to presume that an illegal alien is a flight risk when making bail determinations. For example, in 2008 Utah and Missouri made it a rebuttal presumption in the grant or issuance of bond that such an individual is at risk of flight.[114]

Such statutes not only serve the purpose of reinforcing federal immigration law; they also serve the state's independent law enforcement objectives. It is a well-documented fact that an extraordinary number of illegal aliens either do not show up for their hearings before immigration courts or do not present themselves for removal upon the issuance of a removal order. As the Inspector General of the U.S. Department of Justice reported in 2003, a stunning 87% of those aliens who are not detained during removal proceedings become absconders—they fail to show up for their removal hearings or disappear once a removal order is issued.[115] At the time of this writing, there are an estimated 585,000 absconders at large in the United States.[116] The reality of such a high absconding rate drives up the probability that any given illegal alien charged with a state offense may flee. Regardless of whether the alien is convicted of the state offense, the state is likely to attempt to transfer him to ICE for removal, either immediately after trial if he is acquitted, or after he serves any prison sentence if he is convicted. By directing state judges to presume that illegal aliens pose a flight risk, the state can ensure that any illegal aliens charged with a crime are present for trial and can ensure that they are eventually transferred to ICE for removal.

H. Denying Driver's Licenses to Illegal Aliens

The final area in which states possess clear authority to act concerns the issuance of driver's licenses to aliens. Because driver's licenses serve as de facto, all-purpose identification cards in the United States, and the possession of one greatly facilitates remaining in the country, both Congress and individual states have taken action to deny driver's licenses to illegal aliens. In particular, Congress in 2005 enacted the "REAL ID" Act, which denies the use of a state's driver's licenses for access to commercial airplanes and access to federal buildings, if that state issues its licenses to illegal aliens.[117] The REAL ID Act also encourages states to cause driver's licenses that are issued to aliens lawfully present in the United States to expire when the aliens' authorized periods of stay expire.[118]

Many states had already enacted statutes denying driver's licenses to illegal aliens. Others did so after the passage of the REAL ID Act.[119] As of January 2008, forty-two states denied driver's licenses to illegal aliens.[120] However, many more than the eight states that allow illegal aliens to obtain driver's licenses have yet to adjust their state laws to require that a license for a legal alien must expire on the date that the alien's authorized period of stay in the United States ends. In addition, some states that prohibit illegal aliens from receiving driver's licenses nevertheless do not require their agencies to verify an alien applicant's immigration status with the federal government through the SAVE program, prior to issuance of the license. As a result, those states may be inadvertently issuing driver's licenses to illegal aliens. Accordingly, in many states there is room to further tighten restrictions on the issuance of driver's licenses.

In addition to the federal statutory provisions of the REAL-ID Act that encourage states to deny driver's licenses to illegal aliens, there is a more fundamental problem that occurs whenever a state's laws require a recipient of a driver's license to be a permanent or long-term resident of the state. If the state tacitly recognizes the "residence" of an illegal alien by granting him a driver's license, then the state impermissibly attempts to confer residency on the alien—something only the federal government can do. The Attorney General of Michigan recognized this conflict in a December 2007 opinion and correctly concluded that providing a driver's license to an illegal alien would conflict with federal law: "Michigan law must be interpreted against that background of federal law when considering questions involving aliens. It would be inconsistent with that body of law to find that a person in this country illegally, who has not secured permanent alien status from the federal government, can be regarded as a permanent resident in Michigan."[121] Thus, not only are there explicit inducements in federal law that encourage states to deny driver's licenses to illegal aliens; there are also implicit requirements in federal law that compel states to deny driver's licenses to illegal aliens, in states where issuance of a driver's license entails recognition of the holder's residency.

III. Conclusion

Whenever a state has taken a major step to restore the rule of law in immigration, there has been an immediate effect on the level of illegal immigration in that state. Arizona's 2007 employer verification law has had the most dramatic effect to date. Illegal aliens self-deported by the tens of thousands immediately before, and for months after, the law took effect on January 1, 2008. A similar, but somewhat smaller, exodus of illegal aliens occurred when Oklahoma passed its omnibus immigration act in 2007.[122] These successful state laws have caused illegal aliens to self-deport to their countries of origin, as well as increased the burdens imposed by illegal immigration on neighboring states. It is therefore reasonable to expect that other states will follow suit and duplicate the most effective state laws in deterring illegal immigration.

This progression of state laws promises to be much more than simply an expression of competition between the states. Nor is it likely to be a temporary trend that fades as quickly as it emerged. It is a predictable and positive development in a federalist system in which the federal government has been unable to effectively curtail an unrelenting influx of illegal aliens for more than two decades. Those who claim that the states have no role in addressing the problem of illegal immigration are evidently unaware of the substantial body of legal authority that exists to the contrary, or blind to the financial burdens borne by the states. Those financial burdens translate into political realities. States will continue to exercise their authority to act in this field, absent a sweeping enactment by Congress to preempt such state laws and erase existing federal statutes that invite states to act. Such extraordinary congressional preemption is unlikely to occur.

Other opponents of state activity in the field of illegal immigration have warned that it will create a patchwork of divergent laws. This argument is voiced most loudly by organizations that profit from continued violations of federal immigration laws.[123] What this criticism fails to recognize is that the states are only permitted to act in ways that are in harmony with federal law and consistent with congressional objectives. Far from creating a patchwork quilt, the states are providing the fibers that strengthen the rule of law throughout the country and fill in the gaps created by inconsistent federal enforcement. Arizona, Alabama, South Carolina, Oklahoma, Missouri, and a growing number of other states have demonstrated that they are the best allies the federal government has in the battle to restore the rule of law in immigration.

NOTES

1. National Conference of State Legislators, Immigrant Policy Project, *2007 Enacted State Legislation Related to Immigrants and Immigration* 1 (2008), *available at* http://www.ncsl.org/programs/immig/2007immigrationfinal.htm.

2. *Id. See also* Julia Preston, *In Reversal, Courts Uphold Local Immigration Laws*, N.Y. Times, Feb 10, 2008, at A16.

3. Robert Rector, *Look to Milton*, National Review, June 20, 2007.

4. I use the term "illegal alien" because it is a legally accurate term used repeatedly in the immigration laws of the United States. *See, e.g.*, 8 U.S.C. § 1356(r)(3)(ii) (West 2008) ("expenses associated with the detention of illegal aliens"); 8 U.S.C. § 1366(1) (West 2008) ("the number of illegal aliens incarcerated in Federal and State prisons").

5. Robert Rector, "The Fiscal Cost of Low-Skill Immigrants to State and Local Taxpayers," Heritage Foundation Study (testimony before the Subcommittee on Immigration Committee on the Judiciary, U.S. House of Rep., May 17, 2007), at 10, *available at* judiciary.house.gov/media/pdfs/rector070517.pdf.

6. *Id.* at 3. States have been required to provide free public K-12 education to all children, regardless of immigration status, since the decision of the United States Supreme Court in *Plyler v. Doe*, 457 U.S. 202 (1982).

7. "Arizona: Illegal Aliens," Federation for American Immigration Reform Report (2007), *available at* http://www.fairus.org/site/PageServer? pagename=research_research82b2.

8. The $748.3 million figure is from the year 2005. Jack Martin, "Breaking the Piggy Bank: How Illegal Immigration Is Sending Schools into the Red," Federation for American Immigration Reform Report (2007).

9. The net cost of illegal immigration to the federal government is $10.4 billion per year. Steven A. Camarota, "The High Cost of Cheap Labor: Illegal Immigration and the Federal Budget," Center for Immigration Studies Report, Aug. 2004, at 5. The total cost is $26.3 billion, minus approximately $16 billion in federal taxes and Social Security contributions paid. *Id.*

10. The author was the lead attorney representing Hazleton in the case decided by the Third Circuit U.S. Court of Appeals, Lozano v. Hazleton, 2013 U.S. App. LEXIS 15256 (3rd Cir. 2013) *cert. pending*, at the time of this writing.

11. Lozano v. Hazleton, Case No. 07-3531 (3d Cir.), Appx. A2291–93.

12. *Id.* at A1647, A1399–1400, A2290–91.

13. Stipulated Testimony of Sean Shamany, School Board Director of Hazleton Area School District, Lozano v. Hazleton, Case No. 3:06-CV-01586-JMM (M.D. Pa.), Doc. No. 219-2 (March 21, 2007), at 4.

14. 42 U.S.C. § 1395dd (West 2008). *See also* Lozano v. Hazleton, Case No. 07-3531 (3d Cir.), Appx. A2296–98.

15. Uncompensated emergency and urgent care cost the facility more than $8.7 million in 2006. Stipulated Testimony of James D. Edwards, President and Chief

Executive Officer of the Greater Hazleton Health Alliance, Lozano v. Hazleton, Case No. 3:06-CV-01586-JMM (M.D. Pa.), Doc. No. 219-3 (Mar. 21, 2007), at 4.

16. *Id.* at A1382–83, A1674.

17. *Id.* at A2482–83.

18. For example, it is a federal crime to enter the United States without inspection, 8 U.S.C. § 1325(a) (West 2008); it is a crime to use a false immigration document, 18 U.S.C. § 1546(b) (West 2008); it is a crime to misuse or fabricate a Social Security number when seeking employment, 42 U.S.C. § 408(a)(7) (West 2008); it is a crime to open a bank account with false identity information, 18 U.S.C. § 1014 (West 2008); and it is a crime to present false identification documents to any federal, state, or local law enforcement official, 18 U.S.C. §§ 1001, 1512 (b)(3) (West 2008).

19. Kris W. Kobach, Testimony before the U.S. House of Representatives, Judiciary Committee, Subcommittee on Immigration, Border Security, and Claims, regarding H.R. 2933, June 28, 2005.

20. Lozano v. Hazleton, Case No. 07-3531 (3d Cir.), Appx. at A2483–84.

21. *Id.* at A2490–91.

22. *See* Federal Bureau of Prison "Quick Facts," *available at* http:// www.bop.gov/ news/quick.jsp#1 (last visited Apr. 8, 2008).

23. Ariz. Contractors Ass'n v. Candelaria, 534 F. Supp. 2d 1036, at *35–*36 (D. Ariz. 2008).

24. DeCanas v. Bica, 424 U.S. 351, 357 (1976).

25. *Id.* at 355.

26. 8 U.S.C. § 1324a(h)(2) (West 2008).

27. *De Canas,* 424 U.S. at 355.

28. *Id.* at 357–58 (internal citations omitted).

29. It is essential that such ordinances be carefully drafted, in order to avoid federal preemption and satisfy the requirements that courts of the United States have applied in relevant preemption cases. Examples of well-drafted state and local statutes in these areas are posted by the Immigration Reform Law Institute and may be found at www.irli.org.

30. Specifically, Arizona Proposition 200 (2004), Ariz. Rev. Stat. § 13-2319 (West 2008) (enacted 2005), Arizona Proposition 300 (2006), and Arizona H.B. 2779 (2007), described in detail in the relevant sections below.

31. Oklahoma H.B. 1804 (2007); Missouri Conf. Comm. Subst. for H.B. 1549, 1771, 1395, and 2366 (2008); Alabama H.B. 56 (2011).

32. The authority of municipalities and counties to act is defined not only by the principles of federal preemption described in this article but also by the powers granted to such governments under the applicable state constitutions. Four of the eight areas have seen significant activity by municipal and county governments: providing law enforcement assistance to ICE, denying public benefits to illegal aliens, prohibiting the employment of unauthorized aliens, and enacting

ordinances that reflect federal immigration crimes (e.g., ordinances prohibiting landlords from harboring illegal aliens).

33. *See, e.g.*, Susan Carroll & Yvonne Wingett, *Immigration Federal Ruling: Prop. 200 Now Law in Arizona*, Arizona Republic, Dec. 23, 2004, at 1A.

34. Colorado enacted the Colorado Restrictions on Public Benefits Act in 2006; Colo. Rev. Stat. 24-76.5-103 (West 2008). Georgia enacted the Georgia Security and Immigration Compliance Act in 2006; O.G.C.A. 50-36-1 (West 2008). Oklahoma enacted the Oklahoma Taxpayer and Citizen Protection Act in 2007; 56 Okla. Stat. Ann. 71 (West 2008). Missouri enacted Conf. Comm. Subst. for H.B. 1549, 1771, 1395, and 2366 in 2008; Rev. Stat. Mo. 208.009. Nebraska enacted L.B. 403 in 2009. Alabama enacted H.B. 56 in 2011.

35. Illegal aliens are generally not "qualified aliens," with a few exceptions. See 8 U.S.C. § 1641 (West 2008).

36. 8 U.S.C. § 1621(a) (West 2008).

37. 8 U.S.C. § 1621(c) (West 2008).

38. 8 U.S.C. § 1621(b) (West 2008).

39. Plyler v. Doe, 457 U.S. 202 (1982).

40. There is a safe harbor provision in 8 U.S.C. § 1621, allowing a state to provide a public benefit to an alien unlawfully present in the United States by enacting a state law that "affirmatively provides for such eligibility." 8 U.S.C. § 1621(d) (West 2008). In order to meet the requirements of this safe harbor, the state must expressly indicate that illegal aliens are provided the public benefit in question, and must expressly refer to 8 U.S.C. § 1621. 104th Cong., 2d Sess., Conference Report No. 104-725 on H.R. 3734 (July 31, 1996), at 383.

41. 8 U.S.C. 1601(6) (West 2008).

42. Department of Homeland Security, *Privacy Impact Assessment for the Verification Information System Supporting Verification Programs*, Apr. 1, 2007, at 18.

43. Friendly House v. Napolitano, D.C. No. CV-04-00649-DCB (Dist. of AZ). This case ended in the Ninth Circuit, which held that the plaintiffs lacked standing to bring the suit in the first place. Accordingly, the Ninth Circuit vacated the decision on the merits by the Court below. Friendly House v. Napolitano, 419 F.3d 930 (9th Cir. 2005).

44. League of United Latin American Citizens v. Wilson, 908 F.Supp. 755, 770 (C.D. Cal. 1995).

45. *Id.* at 770.

46. For an example of a well-drafted law that denies public benefits to illegal aliens, *see* 56 Okla. Stat. 71.

47. For a comprehensive discussion of this issue, see Kris W. Kobach, *Immigration Nullification: In-State Tuition and Lawmakers Who Disregard the Law*, 10 N.Y.U. J. Legis. & Pub. Pol'y 473 (2007).

48. Illegal Immigration Reform and Immigrant Responsibility Act (IIRIRA) of 1996, Pub. L. No. 104-208, Div. C. 110 Stat. 3009-546 (1996) (codified as amended in scattered sections of 8 U.S.C.).

49. Linda Chavez, *What to Do about Immigration*, Commentary, Mar. 1995, at 29.

50. *Id.*

51. 8 U.S.C. § 1623 (West 2008).

52. *See* Cal. Educ. Code § 68130.5 (West 2008) (enacted 2002); 110 Ill. Comp. Stat. Ann. § 305/7e-5 (West 2008) (enacted 2003); Colorado S.B. 33 (enacted 2013); Connecticut Subst. H.B. 6390 (enacted 2011); Kan. Stat. Ann. § 76-731a (West 2008) (enacted 2004); Maryland S.B. 167 (enacted 2011); Minnesota SF 723 HF 875 (enacted 2013); Neb. Rev. Stat. § 85-502 (West 208) (enacted 2006); N.M. Stat. Ann. § 21-1-4.6 (West 2008) (enacted 2005); N.Y. Educ. Law.§ 6301.5 (West 2008) (enacted 2002); 70 Okl. Stat. Ann. 3242 (West 2008) (enacted 2003) (as amended by H.B. 1804, 51st Leg., 1st Sess. (Okl. 2007)); Oregon H.B. 2787 (enacted 2013); Tex. Educ. Code Ann. §§ 54.051-54.060 (West 2008) (enacted 2001); Utah Code Ann. § 53B-8-106 (West 2008) (enacted 2002); Wash. Rev. Code Ann. § 28B.15.012 (West 2008) (enacted 2003).

53. *See, e.g.,* Day v. Bond, 500 F.3d 1127 (10th Cir. 2007) (decided solely on standing grounds, with no discussion of the merits); Martinez v. Regents of the Univ. of Calif., 50 Cal. 4th 1277 (2010).

54. Christian Palmer, *Arizona Voters OK 4 Immigration Measures*, Ariz. Capitol Times, Nov. 7, 2006, at 1.

55. Ariz. Sec'y of State, 2006 General Election—Ballot Measures, http://www.azsos.gov/results/2006/general/BM300.htm (last visited Apr. 8, 2008).

56. Seventy-one percent of Utah residents thought that the law offering resident tuition rates to illegal aliens should be repealed, according to a June 2006 poll of 625 Utah residents commissioned by the *Salt Lake Tribune*. Jennifer W. Sanchez, *Immigration Worries: A Cold Welcome*, Salt Lake Trib., June 22, 2006. An October 2005 poll of New Mexico residents by Research & Polling, Inc., found that 72% opposed allowing some illegal alien students to pay in-state college tuition. Leslie Linthicum, *Immigration Divide*, Albuquerque J., Oct. 30, 2005, at A1. However, in 2012 Maryland voters in a statewide referendum approved a bill giving in-state tuition to illegal aliens at community colleges, with 58% in favor and 42% opposed. David Gutman, *Motivated by Referendums, Maryland Voters Turn Out on Election Day*, Capital News Service, Nov. 6, 2012.

57. South Carolina enacted the following statutory provision in 2007: "No state or other appropriated funds authorized in this act or authorized in any state law may be used to provide illegal aliens tuition assistance, scholarships, or any form of reimbursement of student expenses for enrolling in or attending an institution of higher learning in this State." 117th Sess. H. 3620, § 5A.24 (2007).

58. Missouri Conf. Comm. Subst. for H.B. 1549, 1771, 1395, and 2366 (2008); Rev. Stat. Mo. 208.009 (denying aliens unlawfully present in the United States any "postsecondary education . . . benefit under which . . . reduced rates or fees are provided.").

59. Equal Access Education v. Merten, 305 F. Supp.2d 585, 603 (2004).

60. *See* 8 U.S.C. § 1324a (West 2008).

61. *Secretaries Chertoff, Gutierrez Speak on Border Security, Administrative Immigration Reforms at Press Conference*, U.S. FED. NEWS, Aug. 10, 2007.

62. Ariz. H.B. 2779 (2007), codified at Ariz. Rev. Stat. 23-212 to 214. E-Verify was formerly called the "Basic Pilot Program."

63. Theo Milonopoulos, *Worker Status Checks' Errors Called "Severe": E-Verify Often Wrongly Flags Foreign-Born Hires as Illegal, a Report Says, Raising Fears the System Could Lead to Bias*, L.A. Times, Nov. 28, 2007, at A21.

64. *See, e.g.*, Daniel González, *Apartments Going Empty as Hiring Law Hits Migrants*, Arizona Republic, Jan. 31, 2008, at 1.

65. *Id.*; *see also* Randal C. Archibold, *Arizona Seeing Signs of Flight by Immigrants*, N.Y. Times, Feb. 12, 2008, at A13.

66. JLBC Monthly Fiscal Highlights: December 2007, at 2, *available at* http://www. azleg.gov/jlbc/mfh-dec-07.pdf. See also Jacques Billeaud, *Employer-Sanctions Law Forces Illegal Immigrants to Move On*, Sierra Vista Herald, Mar. 3, 2008, *available at* http:// www.svherald.com/articles/2008/03/03/news/doc47cb-9f7c14db5486886624.txt.

67. Sheryl Kornman, *Sonoran Officials Slam Sanctions Law in Tucson Visit*, Tucson Citizen, Jan. 16, 2008, at 4A.

68. *See* Kris W. Kobach, *The Immigration Answer*, N.Y. Post, Feb. 13, 2008.

69. Mississippi Employment Protection Act, S.B. 2988 (enacted Mar. 17, 2008).

70. South Carolina S. 20 (2011); Georgia H.B. 87 (2011); Alabama H.B. 56 (2011).

71. 8 U.S.C. § 1324a(h)(2) (West 2008) (emphasis added).

72. Chamber of Commerce v. Whiting, 131 S. Ct. 1968 (2011).

73. *Id.* at 1985.

74. Gray v. Valley Park, Case No. 4:07-cv-881-ERW, 2008 U.S. Dist. LEXIS 7238 (E.D. Mo. Jan. 31, 2008).

75. *Id.* slip op. at 21.

76. The only federal court to reach a different holding in a final order is the U.S. District Court for the Middle District of Pennsylvania, which came to the strained conclusion that the same federal law that authorizes such licensing laws somehow prohibits such licensing laws. *Lozano*, 496 F.Supp. 2d 477, 519–20. The Middle District of Pennsylvania also set aside the binding Supreme Court precedent of *De Canas*, 496 F. Supp. 2d at 524.

77. Ariz. H.B. 2779 (2007), codified at Ariz. Rev. Stat. 23-212 to 214; Oklahoma H.B. 1804 (2007), codified at 25 Okla. Stat. 1313; Missouri Conf. Comm. Subst. for H.B. 1549, 1771, 1395, and 2366 (2008), codified at Rev. Stat. Mo. 285.530.

78. Ariz. H.B. 2779 (2007), codified at Ariz. Rev. Stat. 23-212 to 214; Missouri Conf. Comm. Subst. for H.B. 1549, 1771, 1395, and 2366 (2008), codified at Rev. Stat. Mo. 285.530, 285.535.

79. O.C.G.A. § 48-7-21.1 (2007); Missouri Conf. Comm. Subst. for H.B. 1549, 1771, 1395, and 2366 (2008), codified at Rev. Stat. Mo. 285.535.

80. Oklahoma H.B. 1804 (2007), codified at 25 Okla. Stat. 1313; Mississippi S.B. 2988 (2008); Utah S.B. 81 (2008).

81. For examples of well-drafted laws that discourage the employment of unauthorized aliens, see Arizona's H.B. 2779 (2007), which was sustained against a preemption challenge in *Chamber of Commerce v. Whiting*, 131 S. Ct. 1968 (2011), and Valley Park, Missouri, Ordinance 1722, which was sustained against a preemption challenge in *Gray v. Valley Park*, Case No. 4:07-cv-00881-ERW, 2008 U.S. Dist. LEXIS 7238.

82. Oklahoma H.B. 1804 (2007), codified at 21 Okla. Stat. 446. These provisions mimic the terms of federal law found at 8 U.S.C. § 1324(a)(1)(A).

83. Utah S.B. 81 (2008), codified at Utah Stat. Ann. 76-10-2701.

84. Gonzales v. Peoria, 722 F.2d 468, 474 (9th Cir. 1983) (citing Florida Avocado Growers v. Paul, 373 U.S. 132, 142 (1963)) (emphasis added).

85. *Id.*

86. Marsh v. United States, 29 F.2d 172, 174 (2d Cir. 1928).

87. Ariz. Rev. Stat. §13-2319 (West 2008).

88. Arizona v. Salazar, C.R. 2006-005932-003DT, Slip Op. at 9 (Ariz. Super. Ct., June 9, 2006) (emphasis added) (quoting *Gonzales*, 722 F. 2d at 474).

89. O.C.G.A. § 16-5-46 (West 2008).

90. For examples of bills that are consistent with federal law and drafted in a manner to survive legal challenge, see www.irli.org.

91. 8 U.S.C. § 1373(c) (West 2008).

92. *Ariz. Contractors Ass'n*, 534 F. Supp. 1036, at *13 ("USCIS has an affirmative obligation to provide 'verification or status information' requested by state and local entities 'for any purpose authorized by law.' § 1373(c).").

93. *See, e.g.*, United States v. Aguilar, 883 F.2d 662, 669–70 (9th Cir. 1989) (providing apartment to illegal aliens found to constitute harboring).

94. Two variations of such local anti-harboring laws may be seen in the Illegal Immigration Relief Act Ordinance of Hazelton, Pennsylvania, at issue in *Lozano, supra*, and in Ordinance 2952, enacted by Farmers Branch, Texas. Villas at Parkside Partners v. Farmers Branch, 2013 U.S. App LEXIS 14953 (5th Cir. 2013), *cert. pending. See* Stephanie Sandoval, *Farmers Branch Bans Illegal Immigrants from Renting Houses*, Dallas Morning News, Jan. 23, 2008.

95. *See Lozano, Farmers Branch, supra,* and Keller v. Fremont, Case Nos. 12-1702, 12-1705, 12-1708 (8th Cir. 2013), *cert. pending.*

96. For examples of statutory language that can survive a legal challenge based on federal preemption, see www.irli.org.

97. U.S. Gen. Accounting Office, GAO-02-830T, *Identity Fraud: Prevalence and Links to Alien Illegal Activities* (2002) (statement of Richard M. Stana).

98. *Id.* at 3–4.

99. *Id.* at 6.

100. Tara Alexandra Rainson, *Identity Theft Laws: State Penalties and Remedies and Pending Federal Bills*, CRS Report for Congress, June 1, 2007, at 2–3, *available at* www.opencrs.com/rpts/RL34028_20070601.pdf.

101. Ariz. Rev. Stat. §13-2009(A) (West 2008).

102. For a comprehensive discussion of these two forms of local authority to make immigration arrests, *see* Kris W. Kobach, *The Quintessential Force Multiplier: The Inherent Authority of Local Police to Make Immigration Arrests*, 69 Albany L. Rev. 179 (2005).

103. United States v. Salinas-Calderon, 728 F.2d 1298, 1301 n.3 (10th Cir. 1984); United States v. Vasquez-Alvarez, 176 F.3d 1294, 1295–96 (10th Cir. 1999); Lynch v. Cannatella, 810 F.2d 1363, 1367 (5th Cir. 1987); United States v. Rodriguez-Arreola, 270 F.3d 611, 617, 619 (8th Cir. 2001); *see* Memorandum, Non-Preemption of the Authority of State and Local Law Enforcement Officials to Arrest Aliens for Immigration Violations, from Jay S. Bybee, Ass't Att'y Gen., Office of Legal Counsel, U.S. Dep't of Justice, to U.S. Att'y Gen. 13 (Apr. 3, 2002) *available at* http:// www.fairus.org/site/DocServer/OLC_Opinion_2002.pdf?docID=1041.

104. 132 S. Ct. 2492 (2012).

105. 8 U.S.C. § 1357(g) (West 2008).

106. *State Immigration Law Training and Enforcement Programs Enhance Homeland Security and Public Safety*, State News Service, Dec. 7, 2007; Seth Blomeley, *Just Learned of Law on Aliens, Beebe Says Act Lets State Police Aid Federal Authorities*, Arkansas Democrat-Gazette, Sept. 20, 2007.

107. Janice Francis-Smith, *U.S. Rep. Istook Questions Lengthy Process for ICE Application*, Journal Record, Sept. 14, 2006.

108. *Gov. Blunt Outlines Law Enforcement Directives to Fight Illegal Immigration*, State News Service, Oct. 30, 2007.

109. Missouri Conf. Comm. Subst. for H.B. 1549, 1771, 1395, and 2366 (2008), codified at Rev. Stat. Mo. 577.900.

110. *Id.*; Utah S.B. 81 (1988), codified at Utah Code Ann. 17-22-9.5 (West 2008).

111. 8 U.S.C. § 1373(a)–(b) (West 2008); 8 U.S.C. § 1644 (West 2008).

112. Oklahoma H.B. 1804 (2007), codified at 74 Okla. Stat. 20j (West 2008).

113. Missouri Conf. Comm. Subst. for H.B. 1549, 1771, 1395, and 2366 (2008), codified at Rev. Stat. Mo. 67.307.

114. Utah S.B. 81, codified at Utah Code Ann. 17-22-9.5 (West 2008); Missouri Conf. Comm. Subst. for H.B. 1549, 1771, 1395, and 2366 (2008), codified at Rev. Stat. Mo. 544.470.

115. U.S. Department of Justice Office of the Inspector General, The Immigration and Naturalization Service's Removal of Aliens Issued Final Orders, Report Number 1-2003-004 (February 2003), ii, *available at* http:// www.usdoj.gov/oig/reports/INS/e0304/final.pdf.

116. Bureau of Immigration and Customs Enforcement, Press Release, *Local ICE Fugitive Operations Team Arrests 24 in 4-Day Operation*, Feb. 26, 2008, *available at* http:// www.ice.gov/pi/news/newsreleases/articles/080226madison.htm.

117. REAL ID Act of 2005, Pub. L. No. 109-13, Div. B, 119 Stat. 231 (West 2008).

118. *Id.* § 202(c)(2)(C).

119. For example, Missouri in its omnibus illegal immigration statute of 2008 clarified that illegal aliens were ineligible to receive Missouri driver's licenses.

Missouri Conf. Comm. Subst. for H.B. 1549, 1771, 1395, and 2366 (2008), codified at Rev. Stat. Mo. 302.063.

120. Tom LoBianco, *O'Malley Says State Will Use Real ID*, Wash. Times, Jan. 16, 2008,
at B1. The eight states are Hawaii, Maine, Maryland, Michigan, New Mexico,
Oregon, Utah, and Washington. Gregory Lopes, *New York Mulls Licenses for
Illegals*, Wash. Times, Oct. 30, 2007.

121. Opinion of Michael Cox, Attorney General of Michigan, "Permanent Residency
Requirement for Driver's Licenses," Dec. 27, 2007, *available at* http://www.
ag.state.mi.us/opinion/datafiles/2000s/op10286.htm.

122. Devona Walker, *Immigration: Construction Industry Sees Fewer Undocumented
Workers Applying for Jobs: Housing Decline Offsets Shortage*, Oklahoman, Feb. 9,
2008, at 1A.

123. For example, an organization of employers and other associations calling itself
the Human Resource Initiative for a Legal Workforce sent a letter in February 2008 to numerous state legislatures considering bills to discourage illegal
immigration and urging them to reject such bills. *Human Resource Experts Urge
Wisconsin Legislators to Reject "No-Match" Employment Verification Penalties*, PR
Newswire, Feb. 11, 2008. The letter reportedly stated, "Wisconsin would only
add to a confusing and ineffective patchwork of federal and state laws that are
proving impossible for employers to follow." *Id.*

5

The States Enter the Illegal Immigration Fray

Introduction

"Give me your tired, your poor, your huddled masses yearning to breathe free." These iconic words from Emma Lazarus's famous poem, penned to help raise funds for the construction of the Statue of Liberty's pedestal in the 1880s, are widely believed to reflect the purpose of the Statue of Liberty, beckoning an open-borders U.S. immigration policy to the world. Yet that version of the Statue of Liberty story is anachronistic, driven more by Lazarus's poem and the chance location of the Statue near the immigrant processing center that opened on Ellis Island in 1892 than by the Statue's original purpose. Contrary to popular belief, the words are not engraved on the tablet Lady Liberty holds in her left arm—the inscription there is "July 4, 1776"—but were engraved on a bronze plaque and affixed to the base of the Statue in 1903 (and now housed inside in the museum), thirty years after the Statue was built and seventeen years after it was dedicated.

Instead, the Statue was intended to commemorate the success of the American Revolution and the vindication of the Revolution's ideals in the recently ended Civil War. It was originally supposed to be dedicated in 1876 to mark the centennial anniversary of the Declaration of Independence. It was a gift from the people of France, who had helped make military success in the American Revolution possible, but Edouard de

Laboulay, who proposed the Statue, also hoped that the Statue would inspire the French people to revive their own democracy in the face of what had again become a repressive monarchy. The famous torch that Lady Liberty holds above her head, like the Statue's original name, "Liberty Enlightening the World," was not a beacon lighting the way for immigrants but rather a reflection of the "shining city on the hill" metaphor of America as enlightened example of how to organize governmental institutions elsewhere in the world to secure the blessings of liberty for other nations' own peoples.

These two dramatically different views of the Statue of Liberty story are playing out today in our national debate over immigration policy. Have borders themselves become anachronistic, a throwback to a nation-state mentality that developed as Europe was emerging from the "Dark Ages"? Do the developing norms of human rights guarantee to every human being unfettered access to territory and resources anywhere on the globe? Or do notions of national sovereignty still matter? Does the idea that "peoples" form governments in order to best secure the inalienable rights of their own members, so eloquently described in our Declaration of Independence, still prevail? And if the latter, does the delegation to Congress of the plenary power over naturalization, conveyed in a constitution that institutionalizes a federal system of parallel sovereigns (state and federal) deprive the states of authority to act when illegal immigration imposes burdens on the states' own citizens?

In this chapter, I assume that sovereignty still matters, and therefore that our national government may still define the terms on which peoples from other parts of the globe may become part of our body politic. Whether that *ought* to be the rule (and here, I am unapologetically a defender of the Declaration's views on that subject), it clearly is the rule recognized by our existing Constitution. In the exercise of its delegated authority "to establish an uniform Rule of Naturalization," therefore, Congress can impose restrictions on immigration and make it unlawful to immigrate to this country in violation of those restrictions. That means that there can be "illegal immigration," and therefore "illegal immigrants." The phrase, "undocumented immigrant," which has come into vogue of late, does not seem to accurately reflect the legal status of those who have entered, and remain in, the country illegally. Much more is at issue than whether someone has the right "documents." But neither do I countenance the word "alien," which is used in the federal statutes, because I think the meaning of the word as simply "foreign" has, since the advent of the Space Age, been altered to include "not human." I nevertheless use the word on occasion here, when quoting from the federal statutes or when referring to historical materials.

One last bit of preliminary matter. I do not seek to address, in this chapter, the controversy over whether illegal immigration is economically beneficial or harmful, or even whether *legal* immigration is economically beneficial or harmful. The latter is a policy judgment delegated to Congress, and the former inquiry should, in a nation of laws, be foreclosed by the policy judgment that is currently in effect. Nevertheless, I will make this brief observation: If illegal immigration were such an economic boon, we would expect to see states and local jurisdictions clamoring to facilitate it; instead, with some notable exceptions that seem more ideologically than economically driven, we tend to see just the opposite.

So the question becomes, just what can the states do to discourage *illegal* immigration in order to avoid what they apparently believe are adverse impacts within their individual borders? And in addressing that question, I want to focus on what I consider to be the three principal magnets for illegal immigration: (1) better employment prospects than exist in the immigrant's country of origin; (2) access to better social welfare benefits (education, health care, infrastructure, poverty-support programs, etc.); and (3) citizenship for one's children and, perhaps, for oneself.

Because the pull of these magnets is enhanced by lackluster enforcement (or even deliberate nonenforcement) by the federal government, efforts to reduce the pull of all three have recently been under consideration in the states. Arizona's efforts have gained the most attention. The state legislature adopted the Legal Arizona Workers Act of 2007, which revokes the license to do business in the state of any business knowingly hiring illegal immigrants. While the constitutional challenge to that law was pending in the courts, Arizona adopted S.B. 1070, a more comprehensive bill making "attrition through enforcement the public policy of all state and local government agencies in Arizona."[1] The bill was enacted, according to the district court that considered the constitutional challenge to it, "[a]gainst a backdrop of rampant illegal immigration, escalating drug and human trafficking crimes, and serious public safety concerns."[2]

But Arizona is not alone. Two decades earlier, California voters famously (or infamously) approved Proposition 187, an initiative that prohibited illegal immigrants from receiving government benefits (other than those mandated by the Constitution). Alabama recently added a new immigration law to its books, the Taxpayer and Citizen Protection Act,[3] Section 28 of which requires every public elementary and secondary school in the state to determine whether an enrolling student is lawfully present in the United States. And in January 2011, a coalition of state legislators announced plans to introduce in a number of states proposals dealing with birthright citizenship, with the explicit goal of clarifying that the Fourteenth Amendment's Citizenship Clause does not confer automatic citizenship on everyone merely by virtue of birth on U.S. soil.

Are the state efforts constitutional? Several Supreme Court decisions help frame the constitutional inquiry. In the 1941 case of *Hines v. Davidowitz*,[4] the Supreme Court held that the states cannot interfere with federal immigration laws. At issue was an alien registration law passed by Pennsylvania in 1939, which required all aliens over the age of eighteen to register annually with the state, pay a one-dollar annual registration fee, and carry their registration card with them at all times.[5] A three-judge district court enjoined the law as unconstitutional, holding that the law denied aliens the equal protection of the laws and encroached upon legislative powers constitutionally vested in the federal government.[6] But before the Supreme Court could hear the state's appeal, Congress adopted its own alien registration act, requiring that all aliens over the age of fourteen register a single time (rather than annually) with federal immigration officials.[7] In addition to requiring less frequent filing, the federal law did not require aliens to carry a registration card, and only *willful* failure (as opposed to Pennsylvania's *any* failure) to register was made a criminal offense.[8] Federal penalties, however, were more stringent. Violation of the federal statute was punishable by a fine of up to $1,000, imprisonment of not more than six months, or both, while violation of the Pennsylvania law was punishable by a fine of up to $100, or sixty days in jail, or both.[9]

Although those challenging the Pennsylvania law argued that the law was unconstitutional even before adoption of the federal law, the Supreme Court declined to rule on those claims, "expressly leaving open" "the argument that the federal power in this field, whether exercised or unexercised, is exclusive."[10] Instead, the Supreme Court held that "[w]hen the national government by treaty or statute has established rules and regulations touching the rights, privileges, obligations or burdens of aliens as such, the treaty is the supreme law of the land. *No state can add to or take from the force and effect of such treaty or statute.*"[11] After explaining the importance of leaving federal power in fields affecting foreign affairs "entirely free from local interference," lest the actions of one state create international repercussions that affect the entire nation,[12] the Court elaborated that "where the federal government, in the exercise of its superior authority in this field, has enacted a complete scheme of regulation and has therein provided a standard for the registration of aliens, states cannot, inconsistently with the purpose of Congress, conflict or interfere with, curtail or complement, the federal law, or enforce additional or auxiliary regulations."[13]

At the other end of the spectrum of Supreme Court jurisprudence dealing with immigration-related state law is *De Canas v. Bica,*[14] decided thirty-five years after *Hines,* in which the Court takes a more nuanced view, recognizing that the states are not without authority to exercise core state police powers even in matters that touch federal immigration policy. *De Canas* presented a challenge to a state statute prohibiting employers from knowingly employing unlawful aliens on the grounds that it amounted to state regulation of immigration and thus was preempted by federal law.[15] The Court held that federal immigration law did not prevent the states from regulating the employment of illegal aliens because states possess broad authority under their police powers to regulate employment and protect workers within the state.[16] "[T]he fact that aliens are the subject of a state statute does not alone render it a regulation of immigration,"[17] held the Court, thus apparently rejecting the challenge left unaddressed in *Hines,* namely, whether "the federal power in this field, whether exercised or unexercised, is exclusive."[18]

That principle was applied in *Chamber of Commerce v. Whiting,*[19] in which the Supreme Court upheld the Legal Arizona Workers Act against challenges based on federal immigration law preemption.[20] The Court held that the state law, which penalized employers of illegal aliens by withdrawing permission to do business in the state, a penalty much harsher than the fines imposed under federal immigration law, was not expressly preempted by federal law,[21] nor was it preempted by implication.[22] On the contrary, the federal statute's preemption clause had an explicit exemption for state licensing laws, and the Court rejected the argument that the exemption should be read narrowly, in part because the state was operating in an area of traditional state concern.[23] As these and other cases demonstrate, the states retain significant power to police their internal affairs in order to protect their citizens and lawful residents, but that principle must now be tempered in the wake of *Arizona v. United States*,[24] in which the Court affirmed a preliminary injunction against three of the four provisions of Arizona's Support Our Law Enforcement and Safe Neighborhoods Act, S.B. 1070 .

The leading Supreme Court case addressing restrictions on delivery of government services to illegal immigrants is *Plyler v. Doe*, which held unconstitutional a Texas statute withholding state funding from local school districts for the education of children not legally admitted into the United States and authorizing local school districts to deny enrollment to such children.[25] Congress has, however, through the Personal Responsibility and Work Opportunity Reconciliation Act of 1996, adopted as official immigration policy of the United States that "the availability of public benefits not constitute an incentive for immigration to the United States" and that there is "a compelling government interest to remove the incentive for illegal immigration provided by the availability of public benefits."[26]

Finally, there are two principal cases that help frame the question of birthright citizenship. In *Elk v. Wilkins*, the Supreme Court held in 1884 that the children of Native Americans were not citizens by birth because they owed allegiance to a separate sovereign, their tribal government. On the other end of the spectrum, the Supreme Court held in the 1898 case, *Wong Kim Ark*, that children born on U.S. soil to lawful, permanent residents were automatically citizens by virtue of the Fourteenth Amendment's Citizenship Clause.

With those cases in mind, let us explore the constitutionality of recent efforts by the states to address what they perceive to be the negative consequences of illegal immigration.

I. Arizona's S.B. 1070

As the Ninth Circuit Court of Appeals noted when it considered the constitutionality of the law, Arizona adopted S.B. 1070 "in response to a serious problem of unauthorized immigration along the Arizona-Mexico border." But the Ninth Circuit went further, claiming that "the State of Arizona had enacted its *own* immigration law enforcement policy," placing a thumb on the scale against Arizona when the very point in contention is whether Arizona is creating its own immigration law, or merely pursuing, as it noted in the law's preamble, its "compelling interest in the cooperative enforcement of *federal* immigration laws."[27] The former is unconstitutional under *Hines*, but the latter would seem to be perfectly constitutional under *De Canas*, a point bolstered by the fact that the law expressly provides that its terms "shall be construed to have the meanings given to them under federal immigration law"[28] and that the "act shall be implemented in a manner consistent with federal laws regulating immigration."[29] Such language rebuts the notion that Arizona has somehow embarked upon a maverick course to develop its own rules regarding immigration into the state.

A full section-by-section analysis of S.B. 1070 and an assessment of the Supreme Court's decision in *Arizona v. United States* is not the purpose of this chapter, but there are some salient points worth making. A brief review of those provisions is therefore necessary.

The Arizona statute, officially called the "Support Our Law Enforcement and Safe Neighborhoods Act,"[30] contains ten operative sections. Section 2, which in turn is broken down into ten subparts, prohibits Arizona officials, agencies, and political subdivisions from limiting enforcement of federal immigration laws, requires that they work with federal officials regarding unlawfully present aliens, and authorizes suits by lawful Arizona residents against any Arizona official, agency, or political subdivision that adopts a policy of restricting enforcement of federal immigration laws.[31] Subsection (L) specifically provides that the Section "shall be implemented in a manner consistent with federal laws regulating immigration, protecting the civil rights of all persons and respecting the privileges and immunities of United States citizens."[32]

The remaining subdivision of Section 2 has been the most controversial. With the amendments that were adopted seven days after passage of the original bill, that provision requires Arizona law enforcement officials to make a "reasonable attempt" "to determine the immigration status" of any person lawfully stopped, detained, or arrested on other grounds, whenever "reasonable suspicion exists that the person is an alien and is unlawfully present in the United States." It also provides that "[a]ny person who is arrested shall have the person's immigration status determined before the person is released" and that that status "shall be verified with the federal government." Although many, including President Obama and the Attorney General of the United States, have claimed that the law would lead to racial profiling of Americans who look Hispanic, the law specifically prohibits law enforcement from considering "race, color or national origin in implementing the requirements of this subsection except to the extent permitted by the United States or Arizona Constitution."[33]

Another provision of S.B. 1070, Section 3, creates a new state crime for conduct that is already a crime under federal law: failure to carry immigration papers.[34] The provision imposes the identical punishment provided by federal law[35] and expressly "does not apply to a person who maintains authorization from the federal government to remain in the United States."[36]

Other provisions make it illegal to hire workers from a motor vehicle (or to be so hired) if the motor vehicle blocks or impedes the normal flow of traffic;[37] for unauthorized aliens (as defined by federal law) to seek employment;[38] and to transport, conceal, or harbor illegal aliens in furtherance of the illegal presence of the alien in the United States (with vehicles used for the purpose subject to impoundment, per Section 10 of the act).[39]

In response to a lawsuit filed by the United States Department of Justice (DOJ) against Arizona, the United States District Court for the District of Arizona preliminarily enjoined four provisions of the law before it went into effect,[40] rejected DOJ's request to enjoin two other provisions that, on the district court's own reasoning, seemed equally problematic,[41] and rejected DOJ's broader request to enjoin enforcement of the entire act beyond the six specific provisions that it had challenged.[42] On appeal by Arizona,[43] the United States Court of Appeals for the Ninth Circuit affirmed the district court's preliminary injunction.[44] The Supreme Court granted the state's petition for writ of certiorari in December 2011,[45] and on June 25, 2012, affirmed the preliminary injunction with respect to three of the provisions but reversed the Ninth Circuit's holding with respect to the most controversial provision, Section 2b.

The Supreme Court's decision thus leaves most of S.B. 1070 intact. Analyzing the constitutional line drawn by the Supreme Court in *Hines* and *De Canas*, it seemed pretty clear that most of the Arizona statute would be upheld. The district court correctly upheld a number of the provisions of S.B. 1070 that clearly fit within police-power authority of the states that was reaffirmed in *De Canas*, for example. Indeed, the Department of Justice did not even explicitly challenge many of the provisions. But the district court, in a decision later affirmed by the Ninth Circuit and then largely by the Supreme Court, preliminarily enjoined four provisions of S.B. 1070:[46] Subsection B of Section 2 (requiring local law enforcement to verify immigration status upon reasonable suspicion); Section 3 (creating state law crime for failure to carry immigration papers as required by federal law); part of Section 5 (making it illegal for an illegal immigrant to solicit, apply for, or perform work); and Section 6 (authorizing warrantless arrest where police have probable cause that the alien has committed a removable offense). Oddly, these provisions also involve an exercise of the state's police powers to deal with the collateral health, safety, and welfare impacts of illegal immigration that is virtually indistinguishable from the police power authority that undergird the provisions that were upheld. The district court enjoined Section 5(C), for example, which prohibited illegal immigrants from seeking work,[47] even though the Supreme Court in *Whiting* already has upheld parallel provisions of Arizona state law that prohibit employers from hiring illegal immigrants.[48] And the district court enjoined Section 3, making it a state law crime for nonnaturalized immigrants to fail to carry the immigration papers that federal law requires them to carry,[49] while declining DOJ's specific request to enjoin Section 4, making it a state law crime to transport or harbor illegal immigrants,[50] or DOJ's generalized request to enjoin Section 5(A) and (B), making it a state law crime to hire or be hired from a vehicle that in stopping impedes traffic.[51]

More significantly, Judge Bolton, who presided over the case in the district court, made several egregious factual and legal errors en route to her decision preliminarily enjoining Sections 2(B), 3, 5(C), and 6 of the act. For example, two sentences in the middle of Section 2(B), when read in isolation, seem to require submission of an overwhelming volume of immigration status requests to the federal government:

"Any person who is arrested shall have the person's immigration status determined before the person is released. The person's immigration status shall be verified with the federal government pursuant to 8 United States Code § 1373(c)."[52] Judge Bolton relied on the contention that the requirement would impose undue burdens on lawful residents as well as overwhelm federal resources in invalidating the provision,[53] but in doing so, she refused to credit a narrowing construction of the provision, derived from its context, advanced by the state. Immediately before the relevant sentences, for example, is the requirement that law enforcement shall make a *"reasonable attempt . . . when practicable*, to determine the immigration status" of any person stopped, detained, or arrested by law enforcement and "where *reasonable suspicion* exists that the person is an alien."[54] And immediately after the offending sentences, Section 2(B) sets out four ways in which an alien will be "presumed to not be an alien who is unlawfully present in the United States"—by providing a valid Arizona driver's license or three other forms of government-issued identification that require proof of lawful presence in the United States before issuance.[55] Not unreasonably, the state argued that the two sentences should be read *in pari material* with the rest of the paragraph, such that the reasonableness caveat in the preceding sentences, or the presumptions in the following sentences, or both would modify and therefore limit the volume of requests that would be transmitted to the federal government,[56] thereby alleviating the concern that led Judge Bolden to enjoin enforcement of the law. Accepting such a narrowing construction by the state, when the language is "fairly susceptible" to the proffered construction, is not only the norm but is compelled by the constitutional avoidance doctrine, "[t]he elementary rule . . . that every reasonable construction must be resorted to, in order to save a statute from unconstitutionality."[57] "So far as statutes fairly may be construed in such a way as to avoid doubtful constitutional questions," the Supreme Court noted nearly a century ago, "they should be so construed; and it is to be presumed that state laws will be construed in that way by the state courts."[58]

To provide another example: Judge Bolton also found that the first sentence of subsection 2(B)—the requirement to ascertain immigration status during any stop or arrest upon reasonable suspicion—was probably unconstitutional, accepting the Department of Justice's claim that "the federal government has long rejected a system by which aliens' papers are routinely demanded and checked."[59] That claim is manifestly untrue. Federal law, which Judge Bolton herself quotes later in the opinion when discussing a different provision of S.B. 1070, is quite explicit: "Every alien, eighteen years of age and over, shall at all times carry with him and have in his personal possession any certificate of alien registration or alien registration receipt card issued to him pursuant to subsection (d) of this section."[60] Failure to comply is a misdemeanor, subjecting the offender to a fine of up to $100, imprisonment of up to thirty days, or both.[61] And failure to apply for the required registration card in the first place carries a fine of up to $1,000, imprisonment of up to six months, or both.[62]

Yet another example: After erroneously failing to credit Arizona's narrowing construction of Section 2(B), Judge Bolton used the resulting burden on the federal government that DOJ claimed would flow from the increased number of immigration status inquiries mandated by the section to hold, without citation of any authority, that the burden created an "inference of preemption."[63] The law, of course, is generally the opposite. There is a presumption *against* preemption, not an inference in favor of it. As the Court stated in *DeCanas v. Bica,*

[W]e will not presume that Congress, in enacting the INA, intended to oust state authority to regulate . . . in a manner consistent with pertinent federal laws. Only a demonstration that complete ouster of state power including state power to promulgate laws not in conflict with federal laws was "the clear and manifest purpose of Congress" would justify that conclusion.[64]

Moreover, the Supreme Court's recent preemption decisions demonstrate an increasing suspicion of implied preemption claims. As the Court reminded us just last year in *Chamber of Commerce v. Whiting,* "Implied preemption analysis does not justify a 'freewheeling judicial inquiry into whether a state statute is in tension with federal objectives'; such an endeavor 'would undercut the principle that it is Congress rather than the courts that preempts state law.'"[65] The injunction against Section 2B was affirmed by the Ninth Circuit, but reversed by the Supreme Court, which upheld the provision against the facial attack, albeit with cautionary language expressing concerns lest the provision be implemented in an unconstitutional manner.

Judge Bolton's struggle with the law and facts did not improve when she turned to Section 3, the provision making it a state law crime to fail to carry immigration papers, which federal law requires be carried at all times. Judge Bolton held that the provision was "an impermissible attempt by Arizona to regulate alien registration" because "[a]lthough the alien registration requirements remain uniform [a point that could not be contested, since Arizona's provision incorporates by reference the federal requirement], Section 3 *alters the penalties* established by Congress under the federal registration scheme" and for that reason "stands as an obstacle to the uniform, federal registration scheme."[66] The penalty for violating the federal law is a fine of up to $100 and up to thirty days' imprisonment.[67] The penalty for violating Section 3 is a maximum fine of $100 and a maximum of twenty days in jail for a first violation and up to thirty days in jail for any subsequent violation.[68] These penalties are virtually identical; the only difference is that Arizona has capped the discretionary imprisonment for first offenders at twenty days rather than thirty, a cap that is encompassed within the federal "up to thirty days" language.[69]

It is hard to fathom how that minor difference qualifies as an "obstacle to the uniform, federal registration scheme," yet by her material exaggeration, Judge Bolton avoided the more difficult inquiry that actually makes the validity of Section 3 a close call. As anyone old enough to remember the 1992 race riots in Los Angeles that followed the state court acquittal of the police officers charged in the beating of Rodney King will remember, Sgt. Stacey Koon and his fellow police officers were subsequently prosecuted in federal court and convicted.[70] The second prosecution did not violate the Double Jeopardy Clause of the Fifth Amendment because of the controversial doctrine of dual sovereignty, in which a second prosecution brought by a different sovereign (state followed by federal, or federal followed by state), though based on the same conduct, is permitted.

By creating a separate state law crime, Arizona could be exposing illegal aliens to double prosecution, with the possibility of double convictions (and double the penalties), or conviction after an acquittal, or at the very least the burden of defending against two separate court actions. That would certainly provide a more serious challenge to Section 3 under a *Hines v. Davidowitz* analysis than the specious grounds relied upon by Judge Bolton, but even that is an open question, one for which the state would not be without significant defenses. Does the doctrine of dual sovereignty even apply when both the state and federal crimes are defined by reference to the same federal statute, for example? The so-called *Bartkus* exception to the dual sovereignty doctrine, though limited, seems close to point. Relying on *dicta* in *Bartkus v. Illinois*,[71] a number of circuit courts have recognized that the dual sovereignty doctrine does not apply, and the Double Jeopardy Clause may be violated despite single prosecutions by separate sovereigns, when one prosecuting sovereign can be said to be acting as a tool of the other, or where the second prosecution is merely pursued as a sham on behalf of the first sovereign.[72] And even if the dual sovereignty doctrine might apply, should that possibility invalidate the state statute *ab initio*, on a facial challenge, or simply be grounds for subsequent "as applied" consideration in the event a second prosecution is ever brought? Thus, while Section 3 is, in my view, the provision of S.B. 1070 that is most susceptible to challenge under the *Hines* analysis, its constitutionality was much closer than Judge Bolton acknowledged.

The Ninth Circuit's decision affirming the district court's issuance of a preliminary injunction repeats these errors and adds some new ones of its own. That court refused to accept Arizona's narrowing interpretation of its own statute (Section 2(B)) to avoid a constitutional problem, for example, instead adopting an interpretation that created a constitutional problem.[73] It refused to read sentences in Section 2(B) in context with the rest of the provision (although it later insisted on doing that with respect to a federal statute that might otherwise have suffered a similar, taken-out-of-context interpretive fate).[74] It made the nonsensical point that Arizona's decision to assist with the enforcement of federal immigration law would somehow "interfer[e] with the federal government's authority to implement its priorities"[75]—one would have thought that by providing additional resources to the enforcement effort, the federal government would be more able to implement its own priorities, not less. It claimed that "*the record* unmistakably demonstrates that S.B. 1070 has a deleterious effect on the United States' foreign relations,"[76] despite the fact that there was no evidentiary "record"[77] and despite the fact that the injunction was issued before S.B. 1070 even took effect.[78]

But by far the most glaring error is a broad conceptual one. The Ninth Circuit appears to have adopted the view that the states not only are bound by prohibitions in the U.S. Constitution but derive their positive authority exclusively from that document as well. For example, it notes early in the opinion that "Congress has instructed under what conditions state officials are permitted to assist the Executive in the enforcement of immigration laws."[79] Later, it holds that "Subsection (g)(10) [of 8 U.S.C. § 1357] does not operate as a broad alternative grant of authority for state officers to systematically enforce the INA outside of the restrictions set forth in subsections (g)(1)-(9)."[80] And it contends that its restrictive interpretation of the derivation of state authority is bolstered by 8 U.S.C. § 1103(a)(10), which authorizes the Attorney General to deputize state and local law enforcement officers "[i]n the event the Attorney General determines that an actual or imminent mass influx of aliens arriving off the coast of the United States, or near a land border, presents urgent circumstances requiring an immediate Federal response."[81] "If subsection (g)(10) meant that state and local officers could routinely perform the functions of DHS officers outside the supervision of the Attorney General," the court asserts, "there would be no need for Congress to give the Attorney General the ability, in § 1103(a)(10), to declare an 'actual or imminent mass influx of aliens,' and to authorize 'any State or local law enforcement officer' to perform the functions of a DHS officer."[82]

These statements reveal a fundamental conceptual misunderstanding of federalism. States do not derive their authority to act from the federal Constitution, nor do they require the approval of federal officials or an act of Congress to exercise police powers in their own states. The federal Constitution serves only to limit state authority where specified.[83] Conversely, the federal government both derives its authority from the federal Constitution and is limited by it. It is no surprise, then, that in each of the statutes that the Ninth Circuit cites dealing with federal-state enforcement cooperation, authorization is given to federal officials to enter into such agreements.[84] No such authorization is given to the states, because none was needed. Indeed, quite the opposite is true. For example, as 8 U.S.C. § 1103(a)(10) makes clear, the Attorney General's ability to enlist officials in *federal* enforcement efforts is contingent on "the consent of the head of the department, agency, or establishment under whose jurisdiction the individual is serving."[85] To hold otherwise, as the Ninth Circuit did, is to answer the question left open by the Supreme Court in *Hines* in the negative and to repudiate the Supreme Court's holding in *De Canas*.

A lengthy discussion in the Supreme Court's *Chamber of Commerce v. Whiting* decision seems apropos. Granted, the Court decided *Whiting* on rather technical preemption and statutory interpretation grounds, but the reasoning from a section of Chief Justice Roberts's opinion joined by three other justices would seem to have put a rather heavy thumb on Arizona's side of the scale in the S.B. 1070 case:

> And here Arizona went the extra mile in ensuring that its law closely tracks IRCA's provisions in all material respects. The Arizona law begins by adopting the federal definition of who qualifies as an "unauthorized alien." Compare 8 U.S.C. § 1324a(h)(3) (an "unauthorized alien" is an alien not "lawfully admitted for permanent residence" or not otherwise authorized by federal law to be employed) with Ariz. Rev. Stat. Ann. § 23-211(11) (adopting the federal definition of "unauthorized alien"); see *De Canas*, 424 U.S., at 363, 96 S.Ct. 933 (finding no preemption of state law that operates "only with respect to individuals whom the Federal Government has already declared cannot work in this country").
>
> Not only that, the Arizona law expressly provides that state investigators must verify the work authorization of an allegedly unauthorized alien with the Federal Government, and "shall not attempt to independently make a final determination on whether an alien is authorized to work in the United States." § 23-212(B). What is more, a state court "shall consider *only* the federal government's determination" when deciding "whether an employee is an unauthorized alien." § 23-212(H) (emphasis added). As a result, there can by definition be no conflict between state and federal law as to worker authorization, either at the investigatory or adjudicatory stage.
>
> The federal determination on which the State must rely is provided under 8 U.S.C. § 1373(c). That provision requires the Federal Government to "verify or ascertain" an individual's "citizenship or immigration status" in response to a state request. . . .

From this basic starting point, the Arizona law continues to trace the federal law. Both the state and federal law prohibit "knowingly" employing an unauthorized alien. Compare 8 U.S.C. § 1324a(a)(1)(A) with Ariz. Rev. Stat. Ann. § 23–212(A). But the state law does not stop there in guarding against any conflict with the federal law. The Arizona law provides that "'[k]nowingly employ an unauthorized alien' means the actions described in 8 United States Code § 1324a," and that the "term shall be interpreted consistently with 8 United States Code § 1324a and any applicable federal rules and regulations." § 23–211(8).

The Arizona law provides employers with the same affirmative defense for good-faith compliance with the I–9 process as does the federal law. Compare 8 U.S.C. § 1324a(a)(3) ("A person or entity that establishes that it has complied in good faith with the [employment verification] requirements of [§ 1324a(b)] with respect to hiring . . . an alien . . . has established an affirmative defense that the person or entity has not violated" the law) with Ariz. Rev. Stat. Ann. § 23–212(J) ("an employer that establishes that it has complied in good faith with the requirements of 8 United States Code section 1324a(b) establishes an affirmative defense that the employer did not knowingly employ an unauthorized alien"). And both the federal and Arizona law accord employers a rebuttable presumption of compliance with the law when they use E–Verify to validate a finding of employment eligibility. Compare IIRIRA § 402(b), 110 Stat. 3009–656 to 3009–657 with Ariz. Rev. Stat. Ann. § 23–212(I).[86]

S.B. 1070 bears similar indicia of conformity with federal law. Section 1, for example, describes the state's "compelling interest in the cooperative enforcement of *federal* immigration laws."[87] Section 2(A) prohibits local government from "restrict[ing] the enforcement of *federal* immigration laws."[88] Section 2(B) requires that immigration status "be verified with the federal government pursuant to 8 United States code section 1373(c)."[89] Section 2(K) requires that Section 2 "be implemented in a manner consistent with federal laws regulating immigration, protecting the civil rights of all persons and respecting the privileges and immunities of United States citizens."[90] Section 3 defines the state law crime of failure to comply with alien registration requirements by incorporating the federal criminal statutes.[91] Section 5(C)'s prohibition on unauthorized aliens applying for work in the state incorporates, in subsection (G)(2), the federal statutory definition of "unauthorized alien."[92] Sections 6 and 7 amend existing provisions of Arizona law dealing with employment of unauthorized aliens from the employer's side, provisions that already incorporated determinations made pursuant to *federal* law.[93] Section 8 requires employers to participate in the *federal* e-verify program.[94] And, lest the point still be lost, Section 12(B) provides that "[t]he terms of this act regarding immigration shall be construed to have the meanings given to them under federal immigration law,"[95] and Section 11(C) provides that "[t]his act shall be implemented in a manner consistent with federal laws regulating immigration, protecting the civil rights of all persons and respecting the privileges and immunities of United States citizens."[96]

In sum, with the possible (and only *possible*) exception of Section 3, Arizona's S.B. 1070 seemed well within the bounds of state authority, as recognized by the Supreme Court in *De Canas* and as the tea leaves from *Whiting* suggested. As Judge Bolton herself recognized in rejecting the Department of Justice's alternative argument that Section 5 violated the Dormant Commerce Clause, S.B. 1070 only "criminalizes specific conduct already prohibited by federal law"[97] by creating "parallel state statutory provisions."[98] Indeed, the entire statute was designed to parallel, not supplement or detract from, existing federal law, a circumstance that seemed to weigh heavily in the high Court's holding in *Whiting*.

Nevertheless, the Supreme Court affirmed the preliminary injunction against three of the four provisions before it. Although Justice Kennedy, who wrote for Court, recognized that "there is an 'epidemic of crime, safety risks, serious property damage, and environmental problems' associated with the influx of illegal migration across private land near the Mexican border," he reverted to a more robust "field" and "obstacle" preemption analysis than had been applied by the Court in recent years. This led him to affirm the preliminary injunction against Sections 3, 5(C), and 6.

On Section 3, the Court held that immigrant registration is an area over which Congress has occupied the entire field and that, as a result, under *Hines*, states could not "'curtail or complement' federal law or . . . 'enforce additional or auxiliary regulations.'"[99] In response to Arizona's contention that the *Hines* rule was not violated because Arizona's provision "has the same aim as federal law and adopts its substantive standards," Justice Kennedy asserted that there was an "inconsistency between §3 and federal law with respect to penalties." Federal law permits a term of probation, he claimed, but Arizona law "rules out probation as a possible sentence." But as noted above, the relevant federal immigration statute and Section 3 of Arizona's S.B. 1070 impose virtually identical penalties. Justice Kennedy's claim is grounded not in the penalty imposed by the federal immigration statute, 8 U.S.C. §1304(e), but in an unrelated, generic provision of the federal criminal code, 18 U.S.C. §3561, which allows for probation in most federal misdemeanors. That, he held, "creates a conflict with the plan Congress put into place." Nowhere does Justice Kennedy discuss the savings clause of Arizona's S.B. 1070, Section 11(C), which provides, "This Act shall be implemented in a manner consistent with federal laws regulating immigration, protecting the civil rights of all persons and respecting the privileges and immunities of United States citizens." Particularly in light of the requirement, recognized earlier in Justice Kennedy's opinion for the Court, that in "preemption analysis, courts should assume that 'the historic police powers of the States' are not superseded 'unless that was the clear and manifest purpose of Congress,'"[100] this savings clause should have been more than adequate to save Section 3 from the "conflict" that Justice Kennedy found debilitating.

That was not the only basis on which Justice Kennedy found Section 3 to be preempted, but the other basis is even more troubling. "Were §3 to come into force," he wrote, "the State would have the power to bring criminal charges against individuals for violating a federal law even in circumstances where federal officials in charge of the comprehensive scheme determine that prosecution would frustrate federal policies." This shifts the preemption analysis from what *Congress* intended to what federal executive officials unilaterally choose to adopt by way of enforcement policies. That really is a broad new step in field preemption analysis.

With respect to Section 5(C), the Court used "obstacle" preemption rather than field preemption. Section 5(C) imposed state criminal penalties on *employees* who seek work they are not authorized to seek under federal law, whereas federal law only imposes penalties on *employers*. Although Justice Kennedy recognized that this provision of the Arizona law was not expressly preempted by Congress, he ascertained from parts of the legislative history "that Congress made a deliberate choice not to impose criminal penalties on aliens who seek, or engage in, unauthorized employment." As a result, he held that Arizona's provision "stands as an obstacle to the accomplishment and execution of the full purposes and objectives of Congress," even while acknowledging that Section 5(c) "attempts to achieve one of the same goals as federal law." Of course, as one commentator favorable to the United States' position in the case has noted, Congress may well have chosen not to impose criminal sanctions because of the added costs involved (due process protections; provision of an attorney; etc.). If this is true, Arizona's efforts would further rather than undermine Congress's objectives, incurring for itself the costs that Congress felt constrained not to incur at the national level. That possibility, and what it would mean for the "obstacle" preemption analysis, is not addressed.

Section 2—the most controversial provision of S.B. 1070—fared differently. It was upheld, albeit with some caveats that all but guarantee further litigation. Section 2 is the provision requiring Arizona law enforcement officials to ascertain the immigration status of individuals who are lawfully stopped for other reasons, when practical to do so and when the officer has reasonable suspicion, apart from race or national origin, to believe that the individual may be in the country unlawfully. Largely because federal law[101] already requires federal immigration officials to respond to immigration status inquiries made by state and local law enforcement, the Court reversed the lower courts' preliminary injunction against this provision. Most significantly, the Court left open the important question "whether reasonable suspicion [by state officials] of illegal entry or another immigration crime would be a legitimate basis for prolonging a detention, or whether this too would be preempted by federal law." But by citing only two cases, both of which upheld the authority of state officials to make arrests for federal crimes, the Court strongly suggested that such local law enforcement activity would not be preempted. The Court cited *United States v. Di Re*[102] for the proposition that the "authority of state officers to make arrests for federal crimes is, absent federal statutory instruction, a matter of state law," and *Gonzales v. Peoria*[103] for the conclusion that state officers "have authority to enforce the criminal provisions of federal immigration law."

Given the Court's interesting split decision—upholding Section 2 (with caveats) while affirming the preliminary injunctions against Sections 3, 5(C), and 6—one thing is clear: more litigation on this subject awaits!

II. Alabama's Taxpayer and Citizen Protection Act

Section 28 of Alabama's new "Taxpayer and Citizen Protection Act,"[104] which requires every public elementary and secondary school in the state to determine whether an enrolling student is lawfully present in the United States,[105] has gained much notoriety. It is said to run afoul of *Plyler v. Doe*, in which the Supreme Court held that denying free public school education to illegal immigrants violates the Fourteenth Amendment's requirement of equal protection. The district court quite properly disagreed, as even a cursory reading of *Plyler* will confirm. Alabama's law does not bar illegal immigrant children from its public schools, but rather identifies them, gathers statistics about the scope of the educational services provided to them, and, most importantly, analyzes the impact of providing free educational services to illegal immigrants on the quality and cost of education being provided to U.S. citizens.[106]

Far from violating the holding of *Plyler v. Doe*, this is the very information lacking from the record that supported the Court's ruling in that case. Acknowledging the district court's finding that Texas had "failed to offer any 'credible supporting evidence that a proportionately small diminution of the funds spent on each child [which might result from devoting some state funds to the education of the excluded group] will have a grave impact on the quality of education,'" the Supreme Court concluded that "the record in no way supports the claim that exclusion of undocumented children is likely to improve the overall quality of education in the State."[107]

Alabama's law seeks to collect the data necessary to conduct the analysis the Supreme Court found missing in *Plyler*. If the data show that providing free education to students unlawfully present in the United States has no significant effect on education or its costs, this provision of the Alabama law probably will not alter the status quo that has existed since *Plyler*. But the data might show that providing a free public education to illegal immigrants severely undermines the quality or drastically increases the cost of education for those who are lawful residents and citizens. Alabama's effort to collect the data necessary for the analysis that Justice Brennan was unable to undertake in *Plyler* seems not only permissible but also eminently sensible. We should not let our public policy, much less our constitutional understanding, be developed behind the veil of ignorance that has heretofore prevailed on this subject.

Plyler was and remains an extremely controversial decision, issued by a bare majority of the Court over a strong and persuasive dissenting opinion by Chief Justice Warren Burger.[108] It has turned an incidental benefit of illegal immigration—Justice Brennan's opinion for the Court even noted that "few if any illegal immigrants come to this country, or presumably to the State of Texas, in order to avail themselves of a free education"[109]—into one of the three great magnets for illegal immigration.

Moreover, it is fair to say that the Court has shifted significantly toward the states in questions of federal-state balance since *Plyler* was decided in 1982. Justice Anthony Kennedy replaced Justice Lewis Powell in 1988, and Justice Clarence Thomas replaced Justice Thurgood Marshall in 1991. Both have been more attentive to questions of federalism and of state authority (Justice Kennedy marginally so; Justice Thomas quite significantly) than their respective members-of-the-*Plyler*-majority predecessors.[110] The balance shifted back a bit in 1993 when Justice Ruth Bader Ginsburg replaced Justice Byron White, who had dissented in *Plyler*, but the pendulum had still swung enough to give us such pro-federalism decisions as *United States v. Lopez* in 1995,[111] *United States v. Morrison* in 2000,[112] and *Chamber of Commerce v. Whiting* in 2011.[113] Given that *Plyler* is still controversial thirty years after it was decided, that the balance on the Court appears to have shifted in an outcome-determinative way, and that the Alabama law seeks to collect the very information that the Court in *Plyler* specifically said Texas had failed to produce in that case, it is certainly not beyond the realm of possibility that the Alabama case will prove to be the vehicle for a reconsideration of *Plyler v. Doe*.

III. Birthright Citizenship

Finally, there is the issue of birthright citizenship. Because the prospect of citizenship for one's children who are born on U.S. soil is a significant magnet for illegal immigration, several states recently have turned their attention to whether the Fourteenth Amendment's Citizenship Clause actually mandates automatic citizenship in such circumstances. Although the common understanding is that mere birth on U.S. soil is sufficient, the language of the Fourteenth Amendment actually contains two requirements: "All persons born . . . in the United States, *and subject to its jurisdiction*, are citizens of the United States and of the state wherein they reside."[114] Modern parlance interprets the phrase "subject to its jurisdiction" to mean simply subject to our laws, rendering it almost entirely redundant to the first phrase. The debates in Congress during the adoption of the Fourteenth Amendment suggest a different interpretation, however, one that distinguishes between mere territorial jurisdiction and a broader, more complete, allegiance-owing jurisdiction. Think of it this way: A foreign tourist visiting the United States is subject to the laws of the United States while here. An English man must drive on the right side of the road rather than the left, for example, when visiting here. But he cannot be prosecuted for treason if he takes up arms against the United States, because he owes no allegiance to the United States. He is subject to the partial, territorial jurisdiction while here, but not to the broader jurisdiction that would follow him beyond the borders.

The issue whether the children of illegal immigrants are "subject to the jurisdiction" of the United States in the way intended by this language has never been definitively addressed by the Supreme Court. Because the meaning of that phrase defines the constitutional floor for both U.S. and state citizenship, the states have an interest in determining how broadly the grant of automatic citizenship reaches.

In January of 2011, a coalition of state legislators, State Legislators for Legal Immigration, announced a new initiative designed to resolve that open question, with a multipronged legislative proposal. First, participating state legislators would introduce legislation that would simply provide a definition of state citizenship consistent with their understanding of the original meaning of the Fourteenth Amendment's Citizenship Clause. Section A of the model bill would declare that "a person is a citizen of the state of —— if (1) the person is born in the United States and subject to the jurisdiction thereof, and (2) the person is a resident of the state of ——, as defined by [state law]." Section B of the model legislation then proposed to clarify that the definition of the critical constitutional phrase requires something more than mere territorial jurisdiction, as follows:

(B) For the purposes of this statute, subject to the jurisdiction of the United States has the meaning that it bears in Section 1 of the Fourteenth Amendment to the United States Constitution, namely that the person is a child of at least one parent who owes no allegiance to any foreign sovereignty, or a child without citizenship or nationality in any foreign country. For the purposes of this statute, a person who owes no allegiance to any foreign sovereignty is a United States citizen or national, or an immigrant accorded the privilege of residing permanently in the United States, or a person without citizenship or nationality in any foreign country.

A second part of the state legislative strategy would build on the first, with the states availing themselves of the constitutional authority to enter into multistate compacts. Through a compact, participating states would agree to designate on the birth certificates issued in their state whether the child was born "subject to the jurisdiction" of the United States, according to the definition outlined above. Birth certificates with that designation would then be accepted in other states participating in the compact as proof of citizenship, while birth certificates without that designation would merely confirm the fact of birth on U.S. soil.

Finally, the legislators would urge their respective state congressional delegations to support national legislation similarly clarifying the meaning of the Fourteenth Amendment's "subject to the jurisdiction" phrase, consistent with the above definition.

Some have claimed that these efforts are unconstitutional, that the Supreme Court has already held that the Fourteenth Amendment compels birthright citizenship, and therefore that only a constitutional amendment can alter the guarantee of automatic citizenship upon birth. Truth be told, there is no such *holding* by the Supreme Court, only *dicta* in three cases: *United States v. Wong Kim Ark*;[115] *INS v. Rios-Pineda*,[116] and *Plyler v. Doe*.[117] In *Wong Kim Ark* the Court *held* that the children of lawful, permanent residents were automatic citizens by virtue of their birth; but it also *held* in *Elk v. Wilkins*[118] that the children of

Native Americans were *not* automatic citizens by birth because, owing primary allegiance to their tribe, a separate sovereign, they were not subject to the full and complete jurisdiction of the United States.

So what exactly does the Citizenship Clause of the Fourteenth Amendment mean? Historically, the language of the 1866 Civil Rights Act, from which the Citizenship Clause of the Fourteenth Amendment (like the rest of Section 1 of the Fourteenth Amendment) was derived so as to provide a more certain constitutional foundation for the 1866 act, strongly suggests that Congress did *not* intend to provide for a broad and absolute birthright citizenship. The 1866 act provides, "All persons born in the United States, *and not subject to any foreign power*, excluding Indians not taxed, are hereby declared to be citizens of the United States."[119] As this formulation makes clear, any child born on U.S. soil to parents who were temporary visitors to this country and who, as a result of the foreign citizenship of the child's parents, remained a citizen or subject of the parents' home country, was not entitled to claim the birthright citizenship provided in the 1866 act.

Of course, the Jurisdiction Clause of the Fourteenth Amendment is somewhat different from the jurisdiction clause of the 1866 act. The positively phrased "subject to the jurisdiction" of the United States might easily have been intended to describe a broader grant of citizenship than the negatively phrased language from the 1866 act, one more in line with the contemporary understanding that birth on U.S. soil is alone sufficient for citizenship. But the relatively sparse debate we have regarding this provision of the Fourteenth Amendment does not support such a reading. For example, when pressed about whether Indians living on reservations would be covered by the Clause because they were "most clearly subject to our jurisdiction, both civil and military," Senator Lyman Trumbull, a key figure in the drafting and adoption of the Fourteenth Amendment, responded that "subject to the jurisdiction" of the United States meant subject to its "complete" jurisdiction: "[n]ot owing allegiance to anybody else." And Senator Jacob Howard, who introduced the language of the Jurisdiction Clause on the floor of the Senate, contended that it should be construed to mean "a full and complete jurisdiction," "the same jurisdiction in extent and quality as applies to every citizen of the United States now" (i.e., under the 1866 act). That meant that the children of Indians who still "belong[ed] to a tribal relation," and hence owed allegiance to another sovereign (however dependent the sovereign was), would not qualify for citizenship under the Clause. Because of this interpretative gloss provided by the authors of the provision, an amendment offered by Senator James Doolittle of Wisconsin to explicitly exclude "Indians not taxed," as the 1866 act had done, was rejected as redundant.[120]

The interpretative gloss offered by Senators Trumbull and Howard was also accepted by the Supreme Court—by both the majority and the dissenting justices—in *The Slaughter-House Cases*. The majority correctly noted that the "main purpose" of the Clause "was to establish the citizenship of the negro" and that "[t]he phrase, 'subject to its jurisdiction' was intended to exclude from its operation children of ministers, consuls, and citizens or subjects of foreign States born within the United States."[121] Justice Steven Field, joined by Chief Justice Chase and Justices Swayne and Bradley in dissent from the principal holding of the case, likewise acknowledged that the Clause was designed to remove any doubts about the constitutionality of the 1866 Civil Rights Act, which provided that all persons born in the United States were as a result citizens both of the United States and of the state in which they resided, provided they were not at the time subjects of any foreign power.[122]

Although the statement by the majority in *Slaughter-House* was *dicta*, the position regarding the "subject to the jurisdiction" language advanced there was subsequently adopted by the Supreme Court in the 1884 case addressing a claim of Indian citizenship, *Elk v. Wilkins*.[123] The claimaint in that case was an Indian who had been born on a reservation, subsequently moved to nonreservation U.S. territory, and renounced his former tribal allegiance. The Court held that the claimant was not "subject to the jurisdiction" of the United States at birth, which required that he be "not merely subject in some respect or degree to the jurisdiction of the United States, but completely subject to their political jurisdiction, and owing them direct and immediate allegiance."[124] John Elk did not meet the jurisdictional test because, as a member of an Indian tribe at his birth, he "owed immediate allegiance to" his tribe and not to the United States. Although "Indian tribes, being within the territorial limits of the United States, were not, strictly speaking, foreign states," "they were alien nations, distinct political communities," according to the Court.[125] Drawing explicitly on the language of the 1866 Civil Rights Act, the Court continued,

Indians born within the territorial limits of the United States, members
of, and owing immediate allegiance to, one of the Indian tribes, (an alien
though dependent power,) although in a geographical sense born in the
United States, are no more "born in the United States and subject to the
jurisdiction thereof," within the meaning of the first section of the fourteenth amendment, than the children of subjects of any foreign government born within the domain of that government, or the children born
within the United States, of ambassadors or other public ministers of foreign nations.[126]

Indeed, if anything, Indians, as members of tribes that were themselves dependent to the United States (and hence themselves subject
to its jurisdiction), had a stronger claim to citizenship under the Fourteenth Amendment merely by virtue of their birth within the territorial
jurisdiction of the United States than did children of foreign nationals.
But the Court in *Elk* rejected that claim, and in the process necessarily rejected the claim that the phrase "subject to the jurisdiction" of the
United States meant merely territorial jurisdiction as opposed to complete, political jurisdiction.

Such was the interpretation of the Citizenship Clause initially given
by the Supreme Court. As Thomas Cooley noted in his treatise, *The
General Principles of Constitutional Law in America*, "subject to the
jurisdiction" of the United States "meant full and complete jurisdiction to which citizens are generally subject, and not any qualified and
partial jurisdiction, such as may consist with allegiance to some other
government."

The clear (and as I contend, correct) holding of *Elk v. Wilkins* was
distinguished by the Supreme Court in 1898, thirty years after the adoption of the Fourteenth Amendment, in the case of *United States v. Won
Kim Ark*.[127] In that case, the Supreme Court held that "a child born in the
United States, of parents of Chinese descent, who at the time of his birth
were subjects of the emperor of China, but have a permanent domicile
and residence in the United States," was, merely by virtue of his birth in
the United States, a citizen of the United States as a result of the Citizenship Clause of the Fourteenth Amendment. Justice Horace Gray, writing for the Court, correctly noted that the language to the contrary in
The Slaughter-House Cases was merely *dicta* and therefore not binding

precedent.[128] He found the *Slaughter-House dicta* unpersuasive because of a subsequent decision, in which the author of the majority opinion in *Slaughter-House* had concurred, holding that foreign consuls (unlike ambassadors) were "subject to the jurisdiction, civil and criminal, of the courts of the country in which they reside."[129] Justice Gray appears not to have appreciated the distinction between partial, territorial jurisdiction, which subjects all who are present within the territory of a sovereign to the jurisdiction of its laws, and complete, political jurisdiction, which requires as well allegiance to the sovereign.

More troubling than his rejection of the persuasive dicta from *Slaugher-House* was the fact that Justice Gray also declined to apply the actual holding in *Elk v. Wilkins*, which he himself had authored, to the case at hand. After quoting extensively from the opinion, including the portion reprinted above, Justice Gray simply held, without any analysis, that *Elk* "concerned only members of the Indian tribes within the United States, and had no tendency to deny citizenship to children born in the United States of foreign parents of Caucasian, African, or Mongolian descent, not in the diplomatic service of a foreign country."[130]

By limiting the "subject to the jurisdiction" clause to the children of diplomats, who neither owed allegiance to the United States nor were (at least at the ambassadorial level) subject to its laws merely by virtue of their residence in the United States as the result of the long-established international-law fiction of extraterritoriality by which the sovereignty of a diplomat is said to follow him wherever he goes, Justice Gray simply failed to appreciate what he seemed to have understood in *Elk*, namely, that there is a difference between territorial jurisdiction and the more complete, allegiance-obliging jurisdiction that the Fourteenth Amendment codified.

Justice Gray's failure even to address, much less appreciate, the distinction between territorial jurisdiction and complete, political jurisdiction was taken to task by Justice Fuller, joined by Justice Harlan, in dissent. Drawing on an impressive array of legal scholars, from Vattel to Blackstone, Justice Fuller correctly noted that there was a distinction between two sorts of allegiance—"the one, natural and perpetual; the other, local and temporary." The Citizenship Clause of the Fourteenth Amendment referred only to the former, he contended. Furthermore, the absolute birthright citizenship urged by Justice Gray was really a lingering vestige of a feudalism that the Americans had rejected, implicitly at the time of the Revolution and explicitly with the 1866 Civil Rights Act and the Fourteenth Amendment.

Quite apart from the fact that Justice Fuller's dissent was logically compelled by the text and history of the Citizenship Clause, Justice Gray's broad interpretation led him to make some astoundingly incorrect assertions. He claimed, for example, that "a stranger born, for so long as he continues within the dominions of a foreign government, owes obedience to the laws of that government, *and may be punished for treason.*"[131] And he had to recognize dual citizenship as a necessary implication of his position,[132] despite the fact that, ever since the Naturalization Act of 1795, "applicants for naturalization were required to take, not simply an oath to support the constitution of the United States, but of absolute renunciation and abjuration of all allegiance and fidelity to every foreign prince or state, and particularly to the prince or state of which they were before the citizens or subjects."[133] That requirement still exists though it no longer seems to be taken seriously.

Finally, Justice Gray's position is simply at odds with the notion of consent that underlay the sovereign's power over naturalization. What it meant, fundamentally, was that foreign nationals could secure American citizenship for their children unilaterally, merely by giving birth on American soil, whether or not their arrival on America's shores was legal or illegal, temporary or permanent.

In *dicta*, Justice Gray contended that the children of two classes of foreigners were not entitled to the birthright citizenship he thought guaranteed by the Fourteenth Amendment: first were the children of ambassadors and other foreign diplomats who, as the result of the fiction of extraterritoriality, were not even considered subject to the territorial jurisdiction of the United States; second were the children of invading armies born on U.S. soil while it was occupied by the foreign army. But apart from that, all children of foreign nationals who managed to be born on U.S. soil were, in his formulation, citizens of the United States. Children born of parents who had been offered permanent residence but were not yet citizens and who, as a result, had not yet renounced their allegiance to their prior sovereign would become citizens by birth on U.S. soil. This was true even if, as was the case in *Wong Kim Ark* itself, the parents were, by treaty, unable ever to become citizens. This was the extent of the actual holding of the case.

The dictum was much broader, of course. Children of parents residing only temporarily in the United States on a work or student visa would also become U.S. citizens, if the *dicta* were to become binding precedent. Children of parents who had overstayed their temporary visa would also become U.S. citizens, even though born of parents who were now here illegally. And, perhaps most troubling from the standpoint of the "consent" rationale, children of parents who never were in the United States legally would also become citizens as the direct result of the illegal action by their parents. This would be true even if the parents were nationals of a regime at war with the United States and even if the parents were here to commit acts of sabotage against the United States, at least so long as the sabotage did not actually involve occupying a portion of the territory of the United States. The notion that the framers of the Fourteenth Amendment, when seeking to guarantee the right of citizenship to former slaves, also sought to guarantee citizenship to the children of enemies of the United States who were in our territory illegally is simply too absurd to be a credible interpretation of the Citizenship Clause.

This is not to say that Congress could not, pursuant to its naturalization power, choose to grant citizenship to the children of foreign nationals. But thus far it has not done so. Instead, the language of the current naturalization statute simply tracks the minimum constitutional guarantee—anyone born in the United States, *and subject to its jurisdiction*, is a citizen. Understanding that constitutional phrase is therefore as necessary now as it was in 1884 and 1898. Recent efforts in the states to force the issue are therefore not just welcome, but long overdue.

Conclusion

States are increasingly feeling the negative effects of illegal immigration, and have recently taken a series of steps designed to reduce the inducements for illegal immigration. Those who dismiss these efforts as patently unconstitutional fail to appreciate that the Supreme Court's decisions in this area leave much more room for state action than is commonly believed. Many of the state efforts are likely to be upheld by the Supreme Court, and when they are, the "States as Laboratories" aspect of "our federalism" will come into play, allowing us to assess, on the basis of actual experience in the different states, some of the very difficult policy concerns that are implicated by illegal immigration. That can only facilitate our journey toward a more coherent national immigration policy.

NOTES

Dr. Eastman participated as *amicus curiae* before the Supreme Court in *Arizona v. United States*, addressing the constitutionality of Arizona's SB 1070. The portions of this chapter dealing with that statute and the Alabama Taxpayer and Citizen Protection Act are drawn from an article by Dr. Eastman pending publication in the *Harvard Journal of Law and Public Policy*. The portions of this chapter dealing with birthright citizenship are drawn from testimony Dr. Eastman delivered in 2005 to the House Judiciary Subcommittee on Immigration, Border Security, and Claims, which was subsequently published in 2008 in both the *Texas Review of Law and Politics* and the *Richmond Law Review*.

1. United States v. Arizona, 641 F.3d 339, 343 (9th Cir. 2011).
2. United States v. Arizona, 703 F. Supp. 2d 980, 985 (D. Ariz. 2010).
3. Beason-Hammon Alabama Taxpayer and Citizen Protection Act, H.B. 56, 2011 Leg., Reg. Sess. (2011).
4. 312 U.S. 52 (1941).
5. *Id.* at 59.
6. *Id.* at 60.
7. *Id.*
8. *Id.* at 60–61.
9. *Id.* at 59–61.
10. *Id.* at 62.
11. *Id.* at 62–63 (emphasis added).
12. *Id.* at 63.
13. *Id.* at 67–68.
14. 424 U.S. 351 (1976).
15. *Id.* at 352–53.
16. *See id.* at 356–58.
17. *Id.* at 355.
18. Hines v. Davidowitz, 312 U.S. 52, 62 (1941).
19. 131 S. Ct. 1968 (2011).
20. *Id.* at 1981, 1985.
21. 8 U.S.C. § 1324a(h)(2)
22. *Whiting*, 131 S. Ct. at 1985.
23. *Id.* at 1987.

24. 132 S.Ct. 2492 (2012).

25. 457 U.S. 202, 205 (1982) (citing Tex. Educ. Code Ann. § 21.031).

26. 8 U.S.C. § 1601.

27. Ariz. S.B. 1070 § 1 (2010) (emphasis added).

28. *Id.* § 12(B).

29. *Id.* § 12(C).

30. *Id.* § 13.

31. *See id.* § 2. These provisions, which might collectively be called the anti–sanctuary city provisions, are codified at Arizona Revised Statutes §§ 11-1051(A), (C)–(K). *See id.*

32. *Id.* (codified at Ariz. Rev. Stat. § 11-1051(L)).

33. *Id.* § 2(B) (codified at Ariz. Rev. Stat. § 13-1051(B)).

34. *See id.* § 3 (codified at Ariz. Rev. Stat. § 13-1509).

35. *Id.* § 3(F) (2010) (codified at Ariz. Rev. Stat. § 13-1509).

36. *Id.* § 3 (codified at Ariz. Rev. Stat. §§ 13-1509(A), (F), (H)).

37. *Id.* § 5(A)–(B) (codified at Ariz. Rev. Stat. §§ 13-2928).

38. *Id.* § 5(C) (codified at Ariz. Rev. Stat. §§ 13-2928).

39. Ariz. Rev. Stat. §§ 13-2928, 13-2929, 28-3511(A)(4)–(5).

40. United States v. Arizona, 703 F. Supp. 2d 980, 987 (D. Ariz. 2010).

41. *Id.*

42. *Id.* at 986.

43. DOJ did not appeal the denial of its request to enjoin two of the provisions or, more broadly, the entire statute. United States v. Arizona, 641 F.3d 339, 344 (9th Cir. 2011).

44. *Id.*

45. Arizona v. United States, 132 S. Ct. 845, 845 (2011).

46. *Arizona*, 703 F. Supp.2d at 1008.

47. *Id.* at 1000–1002.

48. 131 S. Ct. 1968, 1987 (2011).

49. *Arizona*, 703 F. Supp. 2d. at 998–99.

50. *Id.* at 999–1000.

51. *Id.* at 986, 1008.

52. Ariz. S.B. 1070, § 2(B) (2010) (codified at Ariz. Rev. Stat. § 11-1051(B)).

53. *Arizona*, 703 F. Supp. at 993–96.

54. Ariz. S.B. 1070, § 2(B) (2010) (codified at Ariz. Rev. Stat. § 11-1051(B)). (emphasis added).

55. *Id.*

56. Defendants' Response to Plaintiff's Motion for Preliminary Injunction at 9, United States v. Arizona, 703 F. Supp. 980 (D. Ariz. 2010) (No. 210CV01413), 2010 WL 3154413.

57. Edward J. DeBartolo Corp. v. Florida Gulf Coast Bldg. & Const. Trades Council, 485 U.S. 568, 575 (1988) (quoting Hooper v. California, 155 U.S. 648, 657 (1895)).

58. Fox v. Washington, 236 U.S. 273, 277 (1915) (citing United States *ex rel.* Atty. Gen. v. Delaware & Hudson Co., 213 U. S. 366, 407, 408 (1909)).

59. United States v. Arizona, 703 F.Supp.2d 980, 997 (D. Ariz. 2010), *aff'd*, 641 F.3d 339 (9th Cir. 2011), *aff'd*, 132 S. Ct. 2492 (2012).

60. 8 U.S.C. § 1304(e) (2006).

61. *Id.*

62. 8 U.S.C. § 1306(a).

63. She acknowledged, and apparently did not have any concern about, the fact that law enforcement officials in Arizona already had the *discretion* to direct immigration status inquiries to the federal government, or that the federal government, by law, has an "obligation" to respond to such inquiries. *See* 8 U.S.C. § 1373(c). Just how a decision by the state to define in advance how its own state officials should exercise that discretion alters the legal calculus so much that a different preemption presumption should prevail, Judge Bolton does not say.

64. De Canas v. Bica, 424 U.S. 351, 357 (1976) (quoting Florida Lime & Avocado Growers v. Paul, 373 U.S. 132, 146 (1963)).

65. Chamber of Commerce v. Whiting, 131 S. Ct. 1968, 1985 (2011) (quoting Gade v. National Solid Wastes Management Assn., 505 U.S. 88, 111 (1992) (Kennedy, J., concurring in part and concurring in judgment), and citing Silkwood v. Kerr–McGee Corp., 464 U.S. 238, 256 (1984)).

66. *Arizona*, 703 F. Supp. 2d at 999 (emphasis added).

67. 8 U.S.C. § 1304(e).

68. Ariz. S.B. 1070, § 3 (2010) (codified at Ariz. Rev. Stat. § 13-1509(H)).

69. Judge Bolton also descriptively notes that "Section 3 also limits violators' eligibility for suspension of sentence, probation, pardon, and commutation of a sentence and requires violators to pay jail costs." 703 F. Supp.2d at 998 (citing Ariz. S.B. 1070, § 3 (2010) (codified at Ariz. Rev. Stat. § 13-1509(D), (E))). But she does not address whether those provisions differ from federal law or, if they do, how limiting *a priori* the sentencing discretion available to any judge could stand as an obstacle to the uniform federal registration scheme.

70. Seth Mydans, *Verdict in Los Angeles: 2 of 4 Officers Found Guilty in Los Angeles Beating*, N.Y. Times, Apr. 18, 1993, at A1.

71. Bartkus v. Illinois, 359 U.S. 121, 123–24 (1959).

72. United States v. All Assets of G.P.S. Auto. Corp., 66 F.3d 483, 494 (2d Cir. 1995) (citing United States v. Certain Real Prop. & Premises Known as 38 Whalers Cove Drive, Babylon, N.Y., 954 F.2d 29, 38 (2d Cir. 1992) (quoting United States v. Aboumoussallem, 726 F.2d 906, 910 (2d Cir.1984)); United States v. Davis, 906 F.2d 829, 832–34 (2d Cir.1990); United States v. Guy, 903 F.2d 1240, 1242 (9th Cir.1990); *In re* Kunstler, 914 F.2d 505, 517 (4th Cir.1990); United States v. Moore, 822 F.2d 35, 38 (8th Cir.1987); United States v. Aleman, 609 F.2d 298, 309 (7th Cir.1979); United States v. Liddy, 542 F.2d 76, 79–80 (D.C. Cir.1976)).

73. United States v. Arizona, 641 F.3d 339, 347–48 (9th Cir. 2011), *aff'd*, 132 S. Ct. 2492 (2012).

74. *Id.* at 351 ("Because our task is to interpret the meaning of many INA provisions as a whole, not § 1373(c) and § 1357(g)(10) at the expense of all others, we are

not persuaded by the dissent's argument, which considers these provisions in stark isolation from the rest of the statute). If anything, the interpretive distinction should cut the other way. In interpreting Arizona's Section 2(B), the Ninth Circuit (following the District Court), read two sentences "in stark isolation" from the other sentences in the same paragraph of the same section, but with respect to the federal statute, it refused to read entirely separate statutory sections as distinct provisions of the law.

75. *Id.*

76. *Id.* at 352 (emphasis added).

77. As with most preliminary injunction decisions, the district court issued an injunction before any evidence was taken.

78. The Ninth Circuit did have the benefit of briefing by the United Mexican States, the nation from which the largest number of illegal immigrants to the United States hail. In the brief, Mexico strongly intimated that U.S. officials had secretly made "commitments" to give a low priority to enforcement of U.S. immigration laws, Brief of *Amicus Curiae* United Mexican States, at 2, and conclusorily claimed, parroting the position of the Department of Justice, "that SB 1070 encourages an unacceptable risk of unfair and disproportionate targeting of Latinos," *id.* at 15.

79. *United States v. Arizona*, 641 F.3d 339, 348 (9th Cir. 2011), *aff'd*, 132 S. Ct. 2492 (2012).

80. *Id.* at 349.

81. *Id.* at 350 n.9.

82. *Id.*

83. As originally written, the Constitution's restrictions on state authority are found in Article I, Section 10. The list of restrictions was broadened rather dramatically with the Civil War Amendments and the subsequent incorporation of the Bill of Rights, but neither of those developments altered the fact that the states do not derive their authority to act from the federal Constitution.

84. *Id.*

85. *Id.*

86. Chamber of Commerce v. Whiting, 131 S. Ct. 1968, 1981–83 (2011) (plurality) (internal footnotes omitted).

87. Ariz. S.B. 1070, § 1 (2010).

88. *Id.* § 2 (codified at Ariz. Rev. Stat. § 11-1051).

89. *Id.*

90. *Id.*

91. *Id.* § 3 (codified at Ariz. Rev. Stat. § 13-1509).

92. *Id.* § 5(E)(2) (2010) (codified at Ariz. Rev. Stat. § 13-2928).

93. *Id.* §§ 6, 7 (codified at Ariz. Rev. Stat. §§ 13-3883, 23-212).

94. *Id.* § 8 (codified at Ariz. Rev. Stat. § 23-212.01).

95. *Id.* § 12(B).

96. *Id.* § 12(C).

97. United States v. Arizona, 703 F. Supp. 2d 980, 1004 n.19 (D. Ariz. 2010).

98. *Id.* at 1003.
99. Arizona .v United States, 132 S. Ct. 2492, 2502 (2012) (quoting *Hines*, 312 U.S. at 66–67).
100. *Id.* at 2501.
101. 8 U.S.C. §1373(c).
102. 332 U.S. 581, 589 (1948).
103. 722 F.3d 468, 475–76 (9th Cir. 1983).
104. Ala. H.B. 56 (2011).
105. *Id.* § 28(a)(1).
106. 457 U.S. 202 (1982).
107. H.B. 56 § 2.
108. 457 U.S. at 242 (Burger, C.J., dissenting).
109. *Id.* at 228 (majority opinion).
110. *See, e.g.*, New York v. United States, 505 U.S. 144 (1992).
111. 514 U.S. 549 (1995).
112. 529 U.S. 598 (2000).
113. 131 S. Ct. 1968 (2011). The record is not entirely in this direction, of course. Justice Kennedy sided with the *Plyler*-leaning members of the Court to reject the state's position in *U.S. Term Limits, Inc. v. Thornton*, 514 U.S. 779 (1995), and both he and Justice Scalia sided with federal preemption in the medical marijuana case out of California in 2005, *Gonzales v. Raich*, 545 U.S. 1 (2005).
114. U.S. Const. Amend. XIV, § 1 (emphasis added).
115. 169 U.S. 649 (1898).
116. 471 U.S. 444 (1985).
117. 457 U.S. 202 (1982).
118. 112 U.S. 94 (1884).
119. Chapter 31, 14 Stat. 27 (April 9, 1866).
120. Cong. Globe, 39th Cong., 1st Sess., 2892–97 (May 30, 1866). For a more thorough discussion of the debate, see Peter H. Schuck & Rogers M. Smith, Citizenship without Consent: Illegal Aliens in the American Polity 72–89 (1985).
121. 83 U.S. (16 Wall.) 36, 73 (1872).
122. *Id.* at 92–93.
123. 112 U.S. 94 (1884).
124. *Id.* at 102.
125. *Id.* at 99.
126. *Id.* at 102.
127. 169 U.S. 649 (1898).
128. *Id.* at 678.
129. *Id.* at 679 (citing, e.g., 1 Kent, Comm. 44; *In re* Baiz, 135 U.S. 403, 424 (1890)).
130. *Id.* at 681–82.
131. *Id.* at 693.
132. *Id.* at 691.
133. *Id.* at 711 (Fuller, J., dissenting) (citing Act of Jan. 29, 1795, 1 Stat. 414, c. 20).

PART IV

A Critical Evaluation of the New State Regulation

6

Broken Mirror

The Unconstitutional Foundations of New State Immigration Enforcement

GABRIEL J. CHIN AND MARC L. MILLER

The mirror-image theory of cooperative state enforcement of federal immigration law proposes that states can help carry out federal immigration policy by enacting and enforcing state laws that mirror federal statutes. The mirror-image theory provided the legal foundation for Arizona's controversial and sweeping Support Our Law Enforcement and Safe Neighborhoods Act—better known as SB 1070.[1]

The rejection in *Arizona v. United States*[2] by the United States Supreme Court of all of the Arizona provisions that were claimed to mirror federal law sets the stage for challenges and further policy twists in other states that enacted similar and in some cases even more aggressive state immigration laws. This includes Alabama's harsh law enacted in June 2011, Georgia and Indiana statutes enacted in May 2011, and a more moderate state law ("the Utah compromise") enacted in March 2011.

All of these statutes are called into question by the Supreme Court's decision. However, *Arizona v. United States* may not drive the stake all the way through the coffin. It did not specifically address the mirror-image theory. There is an argument that the decision should be read narrowly. One provision struck down by the Court made it an Arizona crime to fail to register with the federal government; the Court concluded that Congress specifically intended the federal immigration registration system to be exclusive. Another provision made it a crime for unauthorized noncitizens to work; the Court concluded that Congress specifically determined not to make that a crime.

On the basis of this decision standing alone, courts could determine that these particular statutes were invalid, while others, where there was no clear evidence of congressional intent for federal exclusivity, might be constitutional. Alternatively, courts could conclude that mirror-image statutes are generally invalid. We argue here that the latter course is correct.

The mirror-image theory is said to be a sibling to the idea of cooperative enforcement, but if so it is an evil twin. Cooperative enforcement is a familiar idea throughout our federal system and a pervasive concept in American criminal justice. Whether the subject is the environment, health and safety, business regulation, or crime, the essential premise of cooperative enforcement is that the federal and state governments either affirmatively work together or work in tandem, and that they do so under either explicit federal authority or independent state authority. In contrast, the recent immigration laws that legislatures justify under the mirror-image theory are an explicit rejection of the federal government's objectives and means, as the Supreme Court majority recognized in *Arizona v. United States*.[3]

Nonetheless, the mirror-image theory is one of the few technical legal concepts to gain currency far beyond the legal academy and legislatures. The idea that states can pass immigration laws based on federal standards[4] has achieved astonishing acceptance in the general political culture, among columnists and commentators,[5] on newspaper editorial boards,[6] among U.S. senators and representatives,[7] and in policy groups.[8] The idea has also succeeded on a rhetorical and popular level, with ordinary citizens asking how the federal government can complain that its own laws are actually being enforced.

What the public and some state politicians may not yet grasp after *Arizona v. United States* is the extent to which the mirror-image idea represents a fundamental legal and policy shift. The idea that states can independently enforce federal *criminal* immigration provisions that deal directly with immigration is inconsistent with immigration jurisprudence, federal law, and federal policy. SB 1070 and its siblings claim an entirely new level of autonomy and discretion for states, an autonomy that has been emphatically rejected by the Court. Through this newfound power, states seek to create and carry out their own immigration-enforcement policies—using their own officers, proceeding in their own courts, and imposing their own punishments, including imprisonment in state prisons.

The explicit purposes of SB 1070 and its copycats are to "make attrition through enforcement the public policy" of the state and to "discourage and deter the unlawful entry and presence of aliens and economic activity by persons unlawfully present in the United States."[9] As proponents of SB 1070 and its imitators often explain, their hope is that illegal immigrants will "self-deport."[10]

A plain reading of a long line of Supreme Court cases suggests that states have no intrinsic sovereign authority to impose criminal sanctions for what they regard as misconduct involving immigration, nor do they have the authority to induce the self-deportation of noncitizens they deem undesirable.

Proponents of SB 1070 and similar laws tried to square the circle by claiming that these laws do not conflict with federal law and policy but instead are efforts at cooperative enforcement. States may regulate immigration, the argument goes, so long as state laws are nearly identical to federal laws.

Part 1 briefly reviews the constitutional text and other legal authority that recognizes exclusive federal control over immigration policy. Saying that federal control is exclusive does not on its own answer the question of whether states can play any role in immigration enforcement—they can and do—or whether states can enact laws incidentally impacting immigration policy—they can. But the recognition that immigration is one of the clearest areas of sole federal authority—along with other matters such as national security and the creation of a single currency—raises the question of whether states can identify either a federal foundation or some other constitutional authority for their new immigration laws and policies.[11]

Part 2 explores the cases and statutes on which the claim of authority for state cooperative enforcement rests. Although both federal case law and the Immigration and Nationality Act (INA)[12] recognize a state role in federal immigration enforcement, these authorities contemplate state cooperation with federal authorities and state authority to arrest for crimes—not independent state criminal prosecution, criminalization, or punishment.

The distinction between arrest, on the one hand, and criminalization and prosecution, on the other, is critical. As the Supreme Court noted in *Arizona v. United States*, criminal arrests leave discretionary decisions in the hands of the federal authorities. Even after an independent state decision to arrest for a federal crime, a suspect is handed over to federal authorities, who decide how to proceed. Under the INA, federal authorities can still decide whether to proceed with a prosecution, use a civil remedy, or grant some form of relief or visa to which the noncitizen is entitled under the law. On the day *Arizona v. United States* was decided, the Obama administration demonstrated both its appreciation of this power and its chutzpah when it reaffirmed the commitment of the federal government to respond only to arrests of undocumented individuals when the acts and record of those individuals fit federal—not state—priorities.

While this point is subtle, it is also absolutely central: the *discretion* inherent in the federal immigration regime, and in federal criminal enforcement more generally—the power to charge or not, to decide what to charge, and to choose whether to pursue civil or administrative measures—is itself a fundamental part of the *law* of immigration.

But there is a deeper theoretical point too that extends beyond the fierce battle over immigration policies. States are free to support federal *civil* policies in various ways, including hearing federal claims in state courts and passing complementary civil laws. In the *criminal* context, the rule is reversed. By Supreme Court decision and under federal statutes dating back to the Judiciary Act of 1789, federal crimes may be tried only in federal courts.

Part 3 explores whether states could pass their own immigration laws if expressly authorized by Congress. Although states can unquestionably do a great deal to aid federal immigration enforcement, Congress has no power to delegate regulatory authority in areas within its exclusive jurisdiction. Further, while Congress can authorize states (or authorize the executive branch to authorize states) to do more in partnership with the federal government, and in some areas under the states' own authority, Congress has no power to delegate the president's duty to carry out the laws to state officers who are wholly outside of presidential control. Accordingly, even if Congress invited the states to legislate in the core immigration sphere, the resulting state laws would still be unconstitutional.

I. The Federal Power to Regulate Immigration

Traditionally, regulation of immigration has been a matter reserved for the federal government. Yet not all state laws that affect immigration or immigrants are automatically unconstitutional. Instead, the Supreme Court has examined whether a given state law is aimed at a legitimate state interest or whether it intends to regulate immigration itself. If a state law is aimed at a legitimate state interest, the Court will examine whether the law interferes or conflicts with federal measures and is, therefore, preempted.

According to proponents of the new state criminal immigration laws, the principle of cooperative enforcement of federal immigration law gives states room to legislate within this constitutional structure.[13] In an article that serves as a playbook for legislators seeking to persuade undocumented citizens to self-deport, Kris Kobach explains,

> The premise is a straightforward one—the way to solve America's illegal immigration problem is to make it more difficult for unauthorized aliens to work illegally in the United States, while incrementally stepping up the enforcement of other laws discouraging illegal immigration. The result is that many illegal aliens self-deport.[14]

Kobach frankly recognizes that "state statutes must be carefully drafted to avoid federal preemption."[15] Even within this cooperative-enforcement scheme, "[t]he federal crimes that are most suited to duplication at the state level are alien smuggling and alien harboring."[16] Federal statutes that establish those crimes impose felony penalties on any person who, "knowing or in reckless disregard of the fact that an alien has come to, entered, or remains in the United States in violation of law," either "transports, or moves or attempts to transport or move such alien within the United States by means of transportation or otherwise, in furtherance of such violation of law; [or] conceals, harbors, or shields from detection, or attempts to conceal, harbor, or shield from detection, such alien in any place, including any building or any means of transportation. . . ."[17]

From a criminal-law perspective, this transportation provision is recognizable as imposing accomplice liability. The law appears to be designed to suppress a particular act—transportation "in furtherance" of the coming, entering, or remaining of noncitizens in violation of the law. Similarly, the provision that prohibits concealment, harboring, or shielding also punishes misprision of the primary wrong of transportation and imposes accomplice liability.

A. Federal Supremacy over Immigration

The Constitution makes the creation of state immigration crimes a tricky proposition. Laws dealing with noncitizens are traditionally divided into two branches. The first is immigration law, which addresses which noncitizens can come to the United States and which must stay out or leave. More specifically, immigration law defines the procedures for admission and exclusion at the border, as well as the procedure for removal—also known as deportation—from the interior of the United States. As recognized in an Arizona State Supreme Court decision from 1975, "federal power over aliens is exclusive and supreme in matters of their deportation and entry into the United States."[18] The states are largely disabled in the field.

The second branch is alienage law, which describes the rights and burdens of noncitizens residing in the United States. Although states have some authority with regard to alienage law,[19] they face a daunting burden when attempting to regulate immigration. That is to say, as a rule of thumb, states have some limited direct power to regulate *immigrants*, but no direct power to regulate *immigration*.

The familiar and fundamental frameworks for assessing conflicts between federal and state power are the Supremacy Clause of the Constitution[20] and the corresponding doctrine of preemption. Preemption of state law comes in three forms: field preemption, whereby federal authority implicitly occupies an entire area; express congressional preemption by statute; and conflict preemption, which occurs when state and federal laws impose conflicting duties, especially when those conflicts are irreconcilable.

The long history of federal authority over naturalization and immigration, along with the history of federal authority over foreign affairs,[21] provides a strong basis for a finding of field and conflict preemption with regard to the regulation of *immigration*. The foundational immigration cases were decided in 1876. *Henderson v. Mayor of New York*[22] and *Chy Lung v. Freeman*[23] invalidated the state immigration regimes of California, Louisiana, and New York that operated before passage of the first general federal immigration laws.[24] The statutes at issue required masters of vessels to post bonds or pay fees when landing passengers. These funds were designed "to protect . . . cities and towns from the expense of supporting persons who are paupers or diseased, or helpless women and children, coming from foreign countries."

In finding the laws invalid, the Court made it clear that the problem with state immigration regulation was not simply that such regulation was preempted by federal law but was instead something more fundamental. The *Henderson* Court recognized that there might be "a kind of neutral ground, especially in that covered by the regulation of commerce, which may be occupied by the State, and its legislation be valid so long as it interferes with no act of Congress, or treaty of the United States." But some matters, the Court stated, are "of such a nature as to require exclusive legislation by Congress."

According to the *Henderson* Court's reasoning, immigration "belongs to that class of laws which concern the exterior relation of this whole nation with other nations and governments," and which therefore "must of necessity be national in its character." As the Court explained, "The laws which govern the right to land passengers in the United States . . . ought to be the same in New York, Boston, New Orleans, and San Francisco." Accordingly, "if there be a class of laws which may be valid when passed by the States until the same ground is occupied by a treaty or an act of Congress, this statute is not of that class."

In addition, the *Henderson* Court rejected the claim that the challenged immigration rules were within the police power of the state. Although the Court recognized that the states had a police power, it nevertheless asserted that no definition of it, and no urgency for its use, can authorize a State to exercise it in regard to a subject-matter which has been confided exclusively to the discretion of Congress by the Constitution.

. . . .

. . . [W]henever the statute of a State invades the domain of legislation which belongs exclusively to the Congress of the United States, it is void, no matter under what class of powers it may fall, or how closely allied to powers conceded to belong to the States.

In *Chy Lung v. Freeman*, the Court emphasized at greater length the foreign-policy and national-security dangers presented by allowing the states to have a discretionary enforcement role in the area of immigration. *Chy Lung* dealt with a California statute aimed at restricting Chinese immigration, a significant domestic and international political issue at the time. The Court recognized that "a silly, an obstinate, or a wicked [state immigration] commissioner may bring disgrace upon the whole country, the enmity of a powerful nation, or the loss of an equally powerful friend";[25] "if citizens of our own government were treated by any foreign nation as subjects of the Emperor of China have been actually treated under this law, no administration could withstand the call for a demand on such government for redress." The Court was concerned that if California "should get into a difficulty which would lead to war, or to suspension of intercourse," not just California but "all the Union" would suffer. The Court concluded that Congress "has the power to regulate commerce with foreign nations: the responsibility for the character of those regulations, and for the manner of their execution, belongs solely to the national government. If it be otherwise, a single State can, at her pleasure, embroil us in disastrous quarrels with other nations."

Chy Lung and *Henderson* established a jurisprudential framework under which, as the Court summarized one hundred years later, "[c]ontrol over immigration and naturalization is entrusted exclusively to the Federal Government, and a State has no power to interfere."[26] This framework has three critical features. First, states' inability to pass immigration legislation comes from a lack of authority, not only preemption by conflicting federal law. Second, the police power of the states does not extend to regulating immigration. Third, both the establishment of substantive immigration laws and the responsibility "for the manner of their execution, belong[] solely to the national government."[27]

It is critical that *Chy Lung* and *Henderson* were decided *before* the first general federal immigration laws. That is, even when the federal government hardly regulated immigration *at all*, the states were still prevented from doing so.

B. State Regulation of Immigrants, Not Immigration

Despite states' inability to regulate immigration, the Supreme Court has consistently left room for some state action in the treatment of undocumented noncitizens. The Court's cases in this area primarily address state responses aimed either at controlling undesirable conduct by noncitizens or at protecting state activities and functions, rather than responses aimed at regulating either noncitizens' presence in the state or the process of immigration itself.

In *De Canas v. Bica*,[28] the Supreme Court held that California could prohibit employers from hiring noncitizens who were not authorized to work under federal law when employment would have "an adverse effect on lawful resident workers." Accordingly, not "every state enactment which in any way deals with aliens is a regulation of immigration and thus *per se* preempted."

The decisive question is whether a particular measure is "a regulation of immigration, which is essentially a determination of who should or should not be admitted into the country, and the conditions under which a legal entrant may remain." Because the California law was designed to "strengthen its economy by adopting federal standards," the Court held that it was valid. Although the Court emphasized that the "[p]ower to regulate immigration is unquestionably exclusively a federal power," the mere fact that a state law "has some purely speculative and indirect impact on immigration" does not make it "a constitutionally proscribed regulation of immigration." In 2011, in *Chamber of Commerce v. Whiting*,[29] the Court, 5-3, upheld Arizona's law punishing employers who hired unauthorized workers. The Court concluded that, notwithstanding an elaborate federal law governing the hiring of undocumented workers, Congress intended to allow the states to impose sanctions on businesses—so long as the state provisions were consistent with federal law. But the case involved neither criminal sanctions nor penalties on individual employees.

Additional important language comes from *Plyler v. Doe*,[30] a 1982 decision. In that case, the Court held that undocumented noncitizens were not a suspect class, but that states nonetheless could not deny public education to undocumented K-12 students to discourage undocumented immigration. *Plyler* did not formally impact state power to regulate immigration because the Court specifically reserved the claim that the state law was preempted and instead decided the case on equal protection grounds. Nevertheless, the decision contained interesting dicta that can be read to support the mirror-image theory.

The *Plyler* Court noted that "undocumented status, coupled with some articulable federal policy, might enhance state authority with respect to the treatment of undocumented aliens." Texas, the state whose statute was being challenged, claimed that it could "protect itself from an influx of illegal immigrants." The Court agreed that a state "might have an interest in mitigating the potentially harsh economic effects of sudden shifts in population." Although it maintained that a state "has no direct interest in controlling entry into this country, that interest being one reserved by the Constitution to the Federal Government," the Court recognized that "unchecked unlawful migration might impair the State's economy generally, or the State's ability to provide some important service." Accordingly, "[d]espite the exclusive federal control of this Nation's borders," the Court refused to "conclude that the States are without any power to deter the influx of persons entering the United States against federal law" when those "numbers might have a discernable impact on traditional state concerns." The Court concluded, "As we recognized in *De Canas v. Bica*, the States do have some authority to act with respect to illegal aliens, at least where such action mirrors federal objectives and furthers a legitimate state goal."

These points did not suffice to enable the *Plyler* defendants to exclude noncitizen children from free public education, as the Court found no evidence that "illegal entrants impose[d] any significant burden on the State's economy" or that "any illegal immigrants c[a]me to this country . . . in order to avail themselves of a free education." Although *Plyler* involved individuals who were not authorized to be in the United States under federal law, the Court explained that "the State has no direct interest in controlling entry into this country, that interest being one reserved by the Constitution to the Federal Government."[31]

In dissent Chief Justice Burger, joined by Justices White, Rehnquist, and O'Connor, concluded that Texas could deny noncitizens access to public schools. Even so, the dissenting opinion agreed that "[a] state has no power to prevent unlawful immigration, and no power to deport illegal aliens; those powers are reserved exclusively to Congress and the Executive."[32] *De Canas* and *Plyler*, then, are properly understood as cases involving alienage, not immigration, and as allowing some state regulation affecting immigrants, but not the direct regulation of immigration itself.

The federal government has exclusive authority not only to establish the standards for the admission and exclusion of immigrants but also to apply and enforce them.[33] Therefore, even scrupulously applying federal standards, New Mexico, for example, could not establish its own border-inspection stations or exclude those it regarded as inadmissible.[34] For the same reason, North Dakota could not establish its own immigration tribunals and order the deportation of undocumented people from the interior of the United States, even if the tribunals carefully applied federal standards.

In addition, deportation by any other name is still deportation. State deterrence that aims to encourage undocumented noncitizens to self-deport to another state or nation confuses a status—potentially deportable alien—with a remedy—deportation. States cannot impose criminal restrictions that are so broadly applicable and onerous that they are tantamount to deportation.

If a state criminal law that prohibits entrance or mandates departure constitutes a regulation of immigration, then some source of federal authority is necessary to sustain it. This much may be consistent with the argument put forward by the supporters of the cooperative-enforcement idea: they contend that state laws such as SB 1070 are indeed authorized by federal case law and legislation. Whether this argument is correct is addressed in the next part.

II. The Doctrinal Foundations of Cooperative Enforcement

States, according to proponents of mirror-image cooperative enforcement, have clear authority under federal law to pass laws mirroring federal immigration crimes. As then-Professor Kobach explains,

> State governments possess the authority to criminalize particular conduct concerning illegal immigration, provided that they do so in a way that mirrors the terms of federal law. In this way, state governments can utilize state and local law enforcement agencies to enforce these state crimes, thereby reinforcing the efforts of federal law enforcement agencies.

The mirror-image theory, then, suggests that state enactments borrow authority from federal law: "As long as such state statutes mirror federal statutory language and defer to the federal government's determination of the legal status of any alien in question, they will be on secure constitutional footing." Kobach does not claim, however, that states have inherent sovereign authority to regulate immigration; rather, in his view, "the states are only permitted to act in ways that are in harmony with federal law and consistent with congressional objectives."

This authority comes from cases from the Ninth Circuit: "Such concurrent enforcement is clearly within a state's authority. As the Ninth Circuit [in *Gonzales v. City of Peoria*][35] opined: 'Where state enforcement activities do not impair federal regulatory interests *concurrent enforcement activity is authorized*.' Where '[f]ederal and local enforcement have identical purposes,' preemption does not occur."[36] Quoting the Second Circuit's 1928 opinion in *Marsh v. United States*,[37] Kobach continues, "In the words of Judge Learned Hand, 'it would be unreasonable to suppose that [the federal government's] purpose was to deny itself any help that the states may allow.'"[38] Kobach thus takes a critical and faulty logical leap. Because *enforcement* of federal law and policy by states is authorized, he argues, so too is state legislation—so long as the state statutes are mirror images of federal provisions.

For two reasons, this argument does not reach as far as Kobach suggests. First, the case law Kobach cites does not support his claim.

Gonzales and *Marsh* allowed state assistance to federal authorities through *arrests*, not through *legislation* or *prosecution*. The power to assist through arrest does not imply the power to legislate or to prosecute, because arrests leave crucial decision-making power in the hands of the federal government, which is free to choose among the criminal, civil, and administrative sanctions and remedies authorized by the INA.

Second, the argument does not account for the structure of the INA, which expressly invites certain forms of state assistance, but only forms—like information sharing and arrests for immigration crimes— that leave the application of the INA to federal authorities. The state assistance contemplated by the INA dovetails with other provisions that grant federal agencies administrative and prosecutorial discretion in particular cases, as well as supplementary lawmaking powers through the promulgation of regulations.

A. *The Power to Arrest versus the Power to Legislate*

On the basis of *Gonzales* and *Marsh*, which allowed states to assist by arresting for federal crimes, Professor Kobach contends that states may also adopt federal crimes as part of state law. But the power to arrest for crime does not necessarily imply the power to legislate. For example, local police are authorized by federal statute to arrest deserters from active-duty service in the U.S. military.[39] This fact does not, however, imply that states and localities are invited to establish rules for the military discipline of active-duty troops or to try them in state courts.[40]

The function of an arrest is to bring a defendant before a court. Delegating arrest authority to the police of another jurisdiction is now routine. The same cannot be said for legislation or prosecution.

As an institutional matter, after arrest by the police, a different official—the prosecutor—determines what charges, if any, are to be filed. Ideally, well-trained police will present well-prepared cases to prosecution agencies that are consistent with their prosecution policies. But prosecutors make charging decisions in most jurisdictions, including in federal courts. Therefore, an arrest does not have the potential to interfere with federal authority in the same way that a prosecution does.

B. Power and Discretion in the INA

1. STATE ASSISTANCE TO FEDERAL AUTHORITIES IN THE INA

Proponents of the mirror-image theory note that, in a variety of ways, the INA seeks help from the states in enforcing civil and criminal immigration law. The most significant example is found in INA § 287(g), which provides for the training of local law-enforcement officers and gives them the power of federal immigration agents, pursuant to a written agreement between the agency and the federal government.[41] While remaining in their regular jobs, under § 287(g), state and local officers participate in the "investigation, apprehension, or detention" of aliens who are removable under the INA.

Section 287(g) does not, however, contemplate that local law-enforcement agencies have the power to establish their own policies or even to enforce federal law at their discretion. The INA provides that "an officer or employee of a State or political subdivision of a State shall be subject to the direction and supervision of the Attorney General." Thus, § 287(g) officers work for the federal immigration authorities, under their direction and control.

Several other provisions of federal law give local law-enforcement agencies authority independent of § 287(g), but there too the authority is exclusively to assist the federal government, not to make policy or independent decisions about enforcement. The provision creating the § 287(g) program provides that an agreement is not required for local law enforcement "(A) to communicate with the Attorney General regarding the immigration status of any individual, including reporting knowledge that a particular alien is not lawfully present in the United States; or (B) otherwise to cooperate with the Attorney General in the identification, apprehension, detention, or removal of aliens not lawfully present in the United States."

Thus, the INA authorizes the free sharing of information in § 287(g)(10)(A), and it allows local police to "cooperate with the Attorney General" in § 287(g)(10)(B). But the INA contains no invitation to draft laws, complementary or otherwise, nor does it even imply that mere arrests can be made other than in cooperation with the attorney general.

2. FEDERAL AUTHORITY IN THE INA

Federal law contemplates that states will be involved in enforcing federal immigration law, but only by providing information and working cooperatively under the supervision of federal enforcement authorities. In contrast to the limited state role, the INA explicitly gives federal authorities broad administrative and prosecutorial discretion, along with the power to supplement the statute itself through regulations. The primary point here is not that the INA takes away from the states any authority they might have had in the absence of federal legislation, but that the INA is not a source of state policy discretion or legislative authority, except in the very limited ways it expressly provides.

Consistent with the background principle of constitutional law that immigration is primarily a federal responsibility, Congress has assigned its enforcement to federal authorities:

> The Secretary of Homeland Security shall be charged with the administration and enforcement of this chapter and all other laws relating to the immigration and naturalization of aliens, except insofar as this chapter or such laws relate to the powers, functions, and duties conferred upon the President, Attorney General, the Secretary of State, the officers of the Department of State, or diplomatic or consular officers. . . .[42]

Specified federal agencies, but no others, can enact regulations.

For many kinds of conduct—including conduct that might trigger federal criminal immigration statutes—federal law authorizes several possible responses. At the broadest level, federal law assigns responsibility for deciding which judicial penalties to seek. Congress has reserved "the conduct of litigation in which the United States, an agency, or officer thereof is a party, or is interested . . . to officers of the Department of Justice, under the direction of the Attorney General."[43] This general power to choose between acting and not acting, and among pursuing criminal charges, civil sanctions, administrative remedies, such as voluntary deportation or removal, or some combination thereof, is also an inherent and explicit part of the structure of the INA.

Take, for example, an undocumented person who has entered the United States by surreptitiously crossing the border into Arizona. That person will have committed the most common immigration crime: entering the United States "at any time or place other than as designated by immigration officers" in violation of 8 U.S.C. § 1325(a)(1). But § 1325 specifically provides for an alternative civil penalty of between $50 and $250, "in addition to, and not in lieu of, any criminal or other civil penalties that may be imposed." That is, although neither is required, the statute itself recognizes that there could be a mix of civil penalties and criminal penalties imposed at the discretion of federal immigration officers.

The problem of discretion is even more profound in an administrative regime like the INA. Under the INA, the Department of Homeland Security and the Department of Justice have a range of options when dealing with a particular undocumented person, including criminal prosecution under 8 U.S.C. § 1325(a)(1). The individual could also be formally removed from the United States[44] or could be allowed to depart voluntarily.[45] Each of these options has substantially different legal consequences.

The INA authorizes benefits as well as sanctions. For example, federal law creates opportunities for an undocumented person to remain in the United States temporarily or permanently. Through the "deferred action" program, a noncitizen, on the basis of compelling circumstances, may be allowed to stay and work in the United States.[46] Noncitizens may have the right to remain in the United States because of a threat in their home country.[47] A noncitizen may also be entitled to some other form of temporary or permanent relief, such as "registry"[48] or a T visa, both of which are available, at the discretion of the secretary of homeland security, to individuals who have been trafficked and to certain relatives of those individuals.[49]

The agencies have elaborate administrative regimes to evaluate and consider claims. These include immigration judges and the Board of Immigration Appeals, both of which are part of the Justice Department. The fact that states are unquestionably disabled from applying most of the provisions of the INA is solid evidence that they have no power to administer any of it, except as it expressly provides.

Further militating against the assumption of implied state criminal authority in immigration cases is the near certainty that such efforts will be motivated by *disagreement* with federal enforcement policy. If state efforts were actually aimed at supporting federal authority, then separate state charges, trials, or punishments would make little sense. Because state officers can arrest suspected violators for federal immigration crimes, they already have the power to deliver offenders to the federal government. And from a fiscal perspective, the state has an excellent financial reason to do so: prosecution and incarceration would be paid for by the federal government. Arizona and other states have previously (and unsuccessfully) sued the United States for reimbursement of the cost of housing undocumented prisoners, demonstrating that states are not eager to incur these expenses.

It seems likely that a state would assume the costs of prosecution and punishment itself not because it sincerely wanted to help the federal government, but rather because the United States was not targeting the noncitizens whom the state expected to prosecute under its new immigration laws. Prosecution by states in cases in which federal immigration authorities would not have prosecuted "presents a serious danger of conflict with the administration of the federal program" and runs the risk of "hampering . . . uniform enforcement of [the federal government's] program by sporadic local prosecutions."[50]

C. The Special Problem of State Criminal Immigration Policy

The decision in Arizona to enforce state immigration law through criminal sanctions is so out of keeping with longstanding authority that its criminal oddness has been overlooked, even in the *Arizona v. United States* decision. But it is nevertheless important to step back and recognize that there is no history or tradition of states enforcing federal criminal claims in state court.

In the *civil* context, the Supreme Court has "consistently held that state courts have inherent authority, and are thus presumptively competent, to adjudicate claims arising under the laws of the United States."[51] Indeed, the Court has held that the Supremacy Clause sometimes requires state courts to hear federal civil causes of action.[52] This policy is ancient: in the Judiciary Act of 1789, the first Congress provided that "the circuit courts shall have original cognizance, concurrent with the courts of the several States, of all suits of a civil nature at common law" involving the United States as a plaintiff, as well as several of the other familiar categories.[53]

The presumption is reversed, however, with respect to federal crimes. Again, the authority is foundational: the Judiciary Act of 1789 established the general rule that federal courts "shall have, exclusively of the courts of the several States, cognizance of all crimes and offences that shall be cognizable under the authority of the United States."[54] The policy was later enshrined in 18 U.S.C. § 3231, which provides, "The district courts of the United States shall have original jurisdiction, exclusive of the courts of the States, of all offenses against the laws of the United States." Accordingly, in the criminal context, Congress generally neither wants nor allows the help of the states in prosecuting federal crimes.

That an identical or similar federal crime is on the books does not necessarily prevent "the State from prosecuting where the same act constitutes both a federal offense and a state offense under the police power."[55] For example, in *Fox v. Ohio*,[56] the Court held that states have the authority to prohibit *passing* counterfeit currency, even though the national government had exclusive jurisdiction over counterfeiting itself. According to the Court, state legislative action in that area is justified because fraudulent transactions can have damaging local effects.[57] Thus, the Court later indicated that the question of whether a state has the power to criminalize turns on whether the subject matter is "within the scope [of the state's] police powers."[58]

A substantial range of exclusive federal criminal jurisdiction may seem startling given the historical state primacy in criminal law more generally[59] and the tradition of concurrent criminal enforcement. Indeed, the increasing overlap of federal and state law—often characterized as the "federalization of criminal law"—has been driven primarily by the creation of new federal crimes and policies.[60] The existence of dual and independent federal and state criminal power over identical acts has been highlighted for more than fifty years by double-jeopardy cases that have recognized the states and the United States as "dual sovereigns."[61]

But the Supreme Court has long recognized that both dual and concurrent sovereignty require states to have some basis for their authority and that neither theory applies in areas of exclusive federal jurisdiction. According to the Court, these theories "will be found to relate only to cases where the act sought to be punished is one over which both sovereignties have jurisdiction. . . . [They have] no application where one of the governments has exclusive jurisdiction of the subject-matter and therefore the exclusive power to punish."[62] Because there are a number of truly national interests, there are a number of areas of exclusive federal jurisdiction created by the Constitution, by statute, and by case law. These include jurisdiction over Indian reservations,[63] military facilities,[64] national banks,[65] and national parks.[66] Exclusive federal criminal jurisdiction, then, is not particularly anomalous.

III. Could Congress Authorize State Enforcement of Federal Criminal Law?

The Supreme Court's decision in *Arizona v. United States* does not represent the first time in American legal history that state attempts to regulate immigration have been judicially rebuffed. On several occasions, however, the political forces demanding state regulation have subsequently moved Congress to respond by passing federal immigration statutes. For example, after courts invalidated state efforts to regulate Chinese immigration in the 1870s, Congress passed the Chinese Exclusion Act of 1882. And after a federal court enjoined California's efforts to regulate undocumented immigration in the 1990s, Congress expressly authorized local police to cooperate with federal enforcement efforts.

Accordingly, it is at least possible that a future Congress will respond to the decision in *Arizona v. United States* and to state concerns about immigration by explicitly authorizing states to adopt complementary immigration statutes. In other words, Congress might actually do what supporters of state immigration enforcement erroneously claim Congress has already done. This part of the chapter suggests that Congress could not constitutionally pass such legislation because Congress cannot delegate its exclusive legislative authority, nor can it authorize states to carry out federal executive powers.

A. State Legislative Power to Enact Criminal Immigration Laws

Could states, with the permission of Congress, enact criminal legislation that would be litigated in their own courts if the field would otherwise fall within exclusive federal jurisdiction? In the celebrated 1816 decision *Martin v. Hunter's Lessee*,[67] the Supreme Court observed that "[n]o part of the criminal jurisdiction of the United States can, consistently with the constitution, be delegated to state tribunals." The literal truth of this dictum is debated.[68] Surely Congress can draw lines, even in favor of the states, delimiting the authority of the state and national governments in areas of shared responsibility. But *Martin* correctly indicated that Congress may not delegate legislative authority over matters that the Constitution identifies as exclusively federal.

A contrary rule would make it possible for Congress to repudiate the Constitution by mere statute without going through the amendment process prescribed in Article V. If, for example, Congress could authorize states to decide, at their discretion, who is to be admitted or excluded, who may be naturalized, and what the relevant procedure is—or, for that matter, if Congress could provide that the states could make treaties or declare war—then the constitutional structure would be dramatically changed. Indeed, in *De Canas*, the Court referred to "a constitutionally proscribed regulation of immigration that Congress itself would be powerless to authorize or approve." The Court seemed to conclude, albeit in dicta, that if a state action were a regulation of immigration, it would be unconstitutional even with the permission of Congress.

A number of holdings suggest that Congress cannot delegate its exclusive powers. In the 1920 decision in *Knickerbocker Ice v. Stewart*,[69] the Court held that Congress could not make state workers' compensation laws applicable within the exclusive admiralty and maritime jurisdiction of Congress. The Court reasoned that "Congress cannot transfer its legislative authority to the States—by nature this is non-delegable."[70]

Although *Knickerbocker Ice* is nearly a century old and the nondelegation doctrine is in some disrepute, when applied to exclusive powers, the decision still stands for a vital principle. For example, in *Clinton v. City of New York*,[71] the line-item-veto case, the six-justice majority explained that Congress could not delegate "lawmaking authority, or its functional equivalent, to the President"; "[t]he fact that Congress intended such a result is of no moment."

B. Presidential Authority over Federal Criminal Prosecutions

A congressional decision to allow state officers to execute federal law would create a serious constitutional question. The problem is

exacerbated in the immigration context, in which—because of the connection among immigration enforcement, national security, and foreign
policy—presidential authority is particularly important.

1. EXECUTIVE AUTHORITY TO EXECUTE THE LAWS

It would very likely be unconstitutional for state prosecutors to prosecute violations of federal criminal law.[72] A federal criminal prosecution is "an exercise of the sovereign power of the United States."[73] This
is particularly so because prosecutorial authority is not mechanical or
rote; it includes the affirmative power to charge, discretion as to what
offenses to charge, *and the negative power to not charge even if probable
cause exists.* In a case rejecting the prosecution of a federal defendant
for the felony of "using a communication facility" when the defendant
had used a cell phone to commit the underlying crime—a misdemeanor
purchase of cocaine—the Supreme Court noted that "Congress legis-
lates against a background assumption of prosecutorial discretion."[74]
The power to prosecute is the power to make policy.[75]

Substantial authority exists for the proposition that the power to
execute federal laws cannot be delegated to individuals entirely outside the presidential chain of command. *Printz v. United States*[76] made
this clear after the Court held that part of the Brady Handgun Violence
Prevention Act[77] was unconstitutional because it delegated discretionary enforcement authority to local law-enforcement agencies: "The
Constitution does not leave to speculation who is to administer the
laws enacted by Congress; the President, it says, 'shall take Care that
the Laws be faithfully executed.'"[78] The Court held that the Brady Act
"effectively transfer[red] this responsibility to thousands of [Chief Law
Enforcement Officers] in the 50 States, who are left to implement the
program without meaningful Presidential control (if indeed meaningful Presidential control is possible without the power to appoint and
remove)."[79]

In the 2010 decision in *Free Enterprise Fund v. Public Co. Accounting
Oversight Board*,[80] a five-justice majority held that the tenure provisions
governing the Public Company Accounting Oversight Board (PCAOB),
a subsidiary agency of the Securities and Exchange Commission (SEC),
were unconstitutional because PCAOB commissioners could only be
removed for good cause by the SEC. The dissenters did not deny that

some presidential control was required; rather, they argued that given the president's influence over the SEC, and further, given the SEC's statutory control over the PCAOB, "as a practical matter, the President's control over the Board should prove sufficient as well."

The president has absolutely no legal or practical ability to direct state prosecutors, who are not appointed, supervised, or removable by the president. State prosecutors, therefore, almost certainly cannot exercise federal executive authority.

The Department of Justice has an existing statutory mechanism for making state prosecutors special assistant U.S. attorneys.[81] A state interested in immigration prosecution is likely to turn down the opportunity to support federal immigration enforcement only if, for some reason, it does not want to follow the directions of the president, the attorney general, and the officers appointed under them. An end run around this mechanism, either by Congress or by a state, would seem to be aimed at undermining federal executive discretion.

2. EXECUTIVE AUTHORITY OVER IMMIGRATION

There is no question that the president is entitled to execute federal immigration law just like all other federal laws. When, in the mid-1990s, Arizona and other states sued the United States, demanding that it more aggressively enforce immigration laws, the Ninth Circuit rejected the claim. It held, borrowing words from the Supreme Court, that "[a]n agency's decision not to prosecute or enforce, whether through civil or criminal process, is a decision generally committed to an agency's absolute discretion."[82]

Indeed, this general principle applies with special force to immigration. For example, in *United States ex rel. Knauff v. Shaughnessy*,[83] the Court explained, "The exclusion of aliens is a fundamental act of sovereignty. The right to do so stems not alone from legislative power but is inherent in the executive power to control the foreign affairs of the nation." Professors Adam Cox and Cristina Rodríguez explain that the *Knauff* view has not been the Court's only approach; sometimes the Court seems to consider the regulation of immigration to be an ordinary congressional power.[84] Nevertheless, even assuming that the president may not contradict or defy a particular congressional direction, the Court understands that administration of the immigration laws implicates foreign policy and national security in ways in which other executive decisions might not.

Thus, in *Reno v. American-Arab Anti-Discrimination Committee*,[85] the Court rejected a claim of selective prosecution in the immigration context. The Court explained the particular difficulties with "invad[ing] a special province of the Executive—its prosecutorial discretion" in the immigration context. As the Court acknowledged, simply inquiring into the executive's reasons for prosecution could cause harm:

> What will be involved in deportation cases is not merely the disclosure of normal domestic law enforcement priorities and techniques, but often the disclosure of foreign-policy objectives and (as in this case) foreign-intelligence products and techniques. The Executive should not have to disclose its "real" reasons . . . and even if it did disclose them a court would be ill equipped to determine their authenticity and utterly unable to assess their adequacy.

Accordingly, if Congress authorized states to regulate immigration by passing and carrying out their own laws, or by carrying out existing federal laws, it would not only be delegating power assigned by the Constitution to the president, but it would also be impermissibly invading the areas of foreign affairs and national security.

Conclusion

Imagine lawfully admitted immigrants traveling by automobile from Albuquerque, New Mexico, to Dallas, Texas; in Dallas, they plan to buy food and rent lodging. The driver is licensed, the car is registered, and traffic laws are obeyed. The car is free of drugs, weapons, and other contraband; the occupants commit no breach of the peace. Texas could not criminalize the presence or travel of those people on the basis of lack of citizenship; not only would such a state crime be inconsistent with federal immigration law but also the occupants have engaged in no acts or omissions within the police power of the state to regulate.

Changing the hypothetical to make the individuals undocumented does not alter the absence of a basis for regulation under the police power, apart from the impermissible desire to regulate immigration itself. To criminalize the otherwise-lawful presence or transportation of otherwise law-abiding people, the state must pinpoint precisely how undocumented status is related to a legitimate state interest other than the desire to regulate immigration. In the absence of any permissible end other than keeping undocumented people out, the police power justifies such regulation only if it permits states to regulate immigration directly. A premise of the mirror-image theory, consistent with existing law, is that the police power does not.

Why has American law generally rejected the proposition that states have the power to prosecute federal crimes in state courts?[86] Early in the nation's history, the answer to this question turned in part on the battles between federalists, who wanted more expansive federal courts with more sweeping jurisdiction, and antifederalists, who wanted to cabin federal power generally and supported the use of state courts to try federal as well as state claims. Although the allocation of powers between the federal government and the states remains a vital topic, the theory and practice of federalism has increasingly come to recognize the "polyphony" of overlapping and intertwined power and action on many topics.[87]

Modern federalism theorists have spent relatively little time focusing on the criminal law. One of the leading articles on the question of whether federal crimes should be enforceable in the states continues to be an article written in 1925 by Professor Charles Warren.[88] Yet the new initiative to increase state enforcement of immigration-related laws and, in particular, the claim that states have the authority to do so in support of federal law, has brought these more general questions to the fore.

As *Arizona v. United States* has forcefully suggested, immigration law and policy remains a uniquely national power. Although many immigration laws have passed under the bridge since 1876, the central holdings of *Henderson* and *Chy Lung* remain fully relevant today. The federal government can, and does, work with the states. Authorizing states to assist with immigration enforcement under the supervision of federal authorities may be good or bad immigration policy. But the decision to make such an authorization is a choice that stems from, and that should be left within, federal control.

States have some authority to regulate noncitizens, but they may not attempt to regulate immigration itself. Inevitably, this distinction will lead to close questions. Even when regulating immigrants and not immigration, states must rely solely on their own regulatory justifications and their own sovereign interests, both of which will be tested for consistency with federal authority.

Under the prevailing legal doctrine, the Supreme Court invalidated the criminal provisions of SB 1070. Similar provisions in other states could stand on the mirror-image theory, even with the permission of Congress. Nor could the state of Arizona prosecute federal offenses directly in state courts. These new state crimes would be valid only if the states could persuade the Supreme Court that states have the inherent authority to regulate immigration with respect to undocumented noncitizens. Arizona tried to do precisely that, and failed. Instead, the Court followed nearly a century and a half of immigration jurisprudence establishing federal power over immigration as supreme.

NOTES

Copyright © 2012 by Gabriel J. Chin & Marc L. Miller. This is a revised and shortened version of our article *The Unconstitutionality of State Regulation of Immigration through Criminal Law*, 61 Duke L.J. 251 (2011).

1. Support Our Law Enforcement and Safe Neighborhoods Act, ch. 113, 2010 Ariz. Sess. Laws 450 (codified in scattered sections of Ariz. Rev. Stat. tits. 11, 13, 23, 28, 41), *as amended by* Act of Apr. 30, 2010, ch. 211, 2010 Ariz. Sess. Laws 1070; *see also id.* § 1 ("The legislature finds that there is a compelling interest in the cooperative enforcement of federal immigration laws throughout all of Arizona.").

2. Arizona v. United States, 132 S. Ct. 2492 (2012).

3. For another important critique of the mirror-image theory, see Margaret Hu, *Reverse-Commandeering*, 46 U.C. Davis L. Rev. 535 (2012), which explains that subfederal immigration laws allow states and localities to impose costs on the federal government at their discretion, and interfere with federal enforcement priorities.

4. *See* Kris W. Kobach, *Attrition through Enforcement: A Rational Approach to Illegal Immigration*, 15 Tulsa J. Comp. & Int'l L. 155, 157–62 (2008) [hereinafter Kobach, *Attrition*] (describing how state laws may encourage self-deportation); Kris W. Kobach, *Reinforcing the Rule of Law: What States Can and Should Do to Reduce Illegal Immigration*, 22 Geo. Immigr. L.J. 459, 463–82 (2008) [hereinafter Kobach, *Reinforcing*; a version of this article is reprinted as chapter 4 of the present volume] (outlining steps that states can take to affect immigration). An unsigned student note from 1954—a time when an author and journal could use

the term "wetback" in the title of an article without irony or embarrassment—
makes a similar argument. *See* Note, *Wetbacks: Can the States Act to Curb Illegal
Entry?* 6 Stan. L. Rev. 287, 303–16 (1954) (arguing that state actions against illegal
immigrants should be permissible).

5. *See, e.g.*, George F. Will, Op-Ed, *A Law Arizona Can Live With*, Wash. Post, April
28, 2010, at A21 ("Arizona's law makes what is already a federal offense—being
in the country illegally—a state offense. Some critics seem not to understand
Arizona's right to assert concurrent jurisdiction."); *Hannity* (Fox News television program April 27, 2010) (transcript available at http://www.foxnews.com/
story/0,2933,591654,00.html) ("Because, again, this law in Arizona that has
recently been signed, it essentially replicates, duplicates the federal law anyway.
So I don't know why Obama has a problem with that. . . ." (quoting Sarah
Palin)); Rush Limbaugh, *Judge Rips Guts out of AZ Law: It's No Longer Illegal
to Be Illegal*, Rush Limbaugh Show (July 28, 2010), http://www.rushlimbaugh.
com/daily/2010/07/28/judge_rips_guts_out_of_az_law_it_s_no_longer_ille-
gal_to_be_illegal ("The Arizona law mirrors the federal law."); David A. Patten,
Experts: "Ridiculous" Lawsuit Won't Nix Arizona Law on Illegals, Newsmax.com
(July 6, 2010, 8:05 PM), http://www.newsmax.com/Headline/arizona-lawsuit-
illegals-obama/2010/07/06/id/363929 ("Arizona's law is designed to help federal
immigration authorities enforce their own laws against illegals—statutes that
the feds have largely ignored. The Arizona law, S.B. 1070, was crafted carefully
to mimic federal laws on the books precisely to avoid a lawsuit based on federal
supremacy.")

6. *See, e.g.*, Editorial, *A Contemptible Suit*, N.Y. Post, July 8, 2010, at 24 ("Arizona's
statute, after all, essentially mirrors existing federal law. . . ."); Editorial, *Judicial
Activism against Arizona*, Wash. Times, July 29, 2010, at B02 ("However, the
case at hand doesn't deal with pre-emptive law but with parallel enforcement.
Arizona's law does not define who has broken immigration laws; it deals with
what to do when police apprehend these criminals.").

7. *See, e.g.*, Brief of *Amici Curiae*, Members of the United States Congress Trent
Franks et al. at 5, United States v. Arizona, 703 F. Supp. 2d 980 (D. Ariz. 2010)
(No. 2:10-CV-01413-SRB), *aff'd*, 641 F.3d 339 (9th Cir. 2011) ("In encouraging
cooperative enforcement of immigration law, Congress did not displace State
and local enforcement activity."); *id.* at 10 ("Congress has continuously encouraged states to assist in enforcing federal immigration law. S.B. 1070 is consistent
with that intent."); *Hannity* (Fox News television program July 23, 2010) (transcript available at http://www.foxnews.com/story/0,2933,597704,00.html) ("[W]
e know that the law was written in order to mirror federal law and not to go
expand beyond the limits of federal law." (quoting Congressman Steve King)).

8. *See, e.g.*, Steven A. Camarota, *Center for Immigration Studies on the New Arizona
Immigration Law, SB1070*, Ctr. for Immigration Studies (Apr. 29, 2010), http://cis.
org/Announcement/AZ-Immigration-SB1070 ("The law is designed to avoid the
legal pitfall of 'pre-emption,' which means a state can't adopt laws that conflict

with federal laws. By making what is a federal violation also a state violation, the Arizona law avoids this problem.").

9. Support Our Law Enforcement and Safe Neighborhoods Act, ch. 113, § 1, 2010 Ariz. Sess. Laws 450, 450.

10. *E.g.*, Kobach, *Attrition, supra* note 4, at 157–62.

11. *Compare* Egelhoff v. Egelhoff, 532 U.S. 141, 151 (2001) (noting "a presumption against pre-emption in areas of traditional state regulation"), *with* Buckman Co. v. Plaintiffs' Legal Comm., 531 U.S. 341, 347 (2001) ("Policing fraud against federal agencies is hardly 'a field which the States have traditionally occupied' such as to warrant a presumption against finding federal pre-emption of a state-law cause of action." (citation omitted) (quoting Rice v. Santa Fe Elevator Corp., 331 U.S. 218, 230 (1947))).

12. Immigration and Nationality Act, 8 U.S.C. §§ 1101–1537 (2006).

13. *See, e.g.*, Kris W. Kobach, Op-Ed, *Why Arizona Drew a Line*, N.Y. Times, April 29, 2010, at A31 ("While it is true that Washington holds primary authority in immigration, the Supreme Court since 1976 has recognized that states may enact laws to discourage illegal immigration without being pre-empted by federal law."); Julia Preston, *A Professor Fights Illegal Immigration One Court at a Time*, N.Y. Times, July 21, 2009, at A10 ("To rigidly separate local government from federal government when we think about immigration enforcement is not only legally incorrect, it's also bad policy. . . ." (quoting Kobach) (internal quotation marks omitted)).

14. Kobach, *Reinforcing, supra* note 4, at 472.

15. *Id.* at 464.

16. *Id.* at 475.

17. 8 U.S.C. § 1324(a)(1)(A)(ii)–(iii) (2006).

18. State v. Camargo, 537 P.2d 920, 922 (Ariz. 1975).

19. State "classifications based on alienage," the Court has said, "are inherently suspect and subject to close judicial scrutiny." Graham v. Richardson, 403 U.S. 365, 372 (1971) (invalidating an Arizona law that restricted legal aliens' access to benefits).

20. Article VI, Clause 2 of the U.S. Constitution provides as follows:
    This Constitution, and the Laws of the United States which shall be made in Pursuance thereof; and all Treaties made, or which shall be made, under the Authority of the United States, shall be the supreme Law of the Land; and the Judges in every State shall be bound thereby, any Thing in the Constitution or Laws of any State to the Contrary notwithstanding.

21. The Constitution grants the federal government the power to "establish an uniform Rule of Naturalization," U.S. Const. art. I, § 8, cl. 4, and to "regulate Commerce with foreign Nations," *id.* art. I, § 8, cl. 3. *See also* Erin F. Delaney, Note, *In the Shadow of Article I: Applying a Dormant Commerce Clause Analysis to State Laws Regulating Aliens*, 82 N.Y.U. L. Rev. 1821 (2007).

22. Henderson v. Mayor of New York, 92 U.S. 259 (1876).

23. Chy Lung v. Freeman, 92 U.S. 275 (1876).

24. *See generally* Gerald L. Neuman, *The Lost Century of American Immigration Law (1776–1875)*, 93 Colum. L. Rev. 1833 (1993) (reviewing immigration law in the United States before the passage of a general federal immigration law).

25. Chy Lung v. Freeman, 92 U.S. 275, 279 (1876).

26. Nyquist v. Mauclet, 432 U.S. 1, 10 (1977); *see also* De Canas v. Bica, 424 U.S. 351, 354 (1976) ("Power to regulate immigration is unquestionably exclusively a federal power.").

27. *Chy Lung*, 92 U.S. at 280.

28. De Canas v. Bica, 424 U.S. 351 (1976).

29. Chamber of Commerce v. Whiting, 131 S. Ct. 1968 (2012).

30. Plyler v. Doe, 457 U.S. 202 (1982).

31. *Plyler*, 457 U.S. at 228 n.23.

32. *Id.* at 242 n.1 (Burger, C.J., dissenting).

33. *See* 8 U.S.C. § 1229a(a)(3) (2006) ("[A] proceeding under this section shall be the sole and exclusive procedure for determining whether an alien may be admitted to the United States or, if the alien has been so admitted, removed from the United States.").

34. *See* Tom Gerety, *Children in the Labyrinth: The Complexities of* Plyler v. Doe, 44 U. Pitt. L. Rev. 379, 384–85 (1983).

35. Gonzales v. City of Peoria, 722 F.2d 468, 474 (9th Cir. 1983), *overruled on other grounds by* Hodgers-Durgin v. de la Vina, 199 F.3d 1037 (9th Cir. 1999).

36. Kobach, *Reinforcing, supra* note 4, at 475 (second alteration in original) (footnote omitted) (quoting *Gonzales*, 722 F.2d at 474).

37. Marsh v. United States, 29 F.2d 172 (2d Cir. 1928).

38. Kobach, *Reinforcing, supra* note 4, at 475 (alteration in original) (quoting *Marsh*, 29 F.2d at 174).

39. 10 U.S.C. § 808 (2006) ("Any civil officer having authority to apprehend offenders under the laws of the United States or of a State . . . may summarily apprehend a deserter from the armed forces and deliver him into the custody of those forces.").

40. *See also* Robertson v. Baldwin, 165 U.S. 275, 279 (1897) (allowing state officers to perform preliminary functions in federal cases, such as arrest).

41. 8 U.S.C. § 1357(g)(1) (2006). Notwithstanding this law's U.S. Code citation, it is often referred to by its INA section number: 287(g).

42. 8 U.S.C. § 1103(a)(1).

43. 28 U.S.C. § 516 (2006).

44. *See id.* § 1182(a)(6)(A)(i).

45. *See id.* § 1229c(a)(1).

46. *See* 8 C.F.R. § 274a.12(c)(14) (2011) (authorizing deferred action, "an act of administrative convenience to the government which gives some cases lower priority, if the alien establishes an economic necessity for employment").

47. *See* 8 U.S.C. § 1158 (outlining the requirements and procedures for gaining asylum); *id.* § 1231(b)(3).

48. *See id.* § 1259.

49. *See id.* § 1101(a)(15)(T).

50. Pennsylvania v. Nelson, 350 U.S. 497, 505 (1956).

51. Tafflin v. Levitt, 493 U.S. 455, 458 (1990).

52. *See, e.g.,* Haywood v. Drown, 129 S. Ct. 2108, 2117–18 (2009) (holding that a state statute divesting state courts of authority to hear claims under 42 U.S.C. § 1983 (2006) was unconstitutional under the Supremacy Clause).

53. Judiciary Act of 1789, ch. 20, § 11, 1 Stat. 73, 78–79.

54. *Id.* § 9.

55. *Nelson,* 350 U.S. at 500.

56. Fox v. Ohio, 46 U.S. (5 How.) 410 (1847).

57. *Id.* at 434.

58. Fla. Lime & Avocado Growers, Inc. v. Paul, 373 U.S. 132, 146 (1963). In this case, the Court concluded that the regulation of food for sale is "traditionally regarded as properly within the scope of state superintendence." *Id.* at 144.

59. *See, e.g.,* Murphy v. Waterfront Comm'n, 378 U.S. 52, 96 (1964) (White, J., concurring) ("[T]he States still bear primary responsibility . . . for the administration of the criminal law; most crimes . . . are matters of local concern; federal preemption of areas of crime control traditionally reserved to the States has been relatively unknown and this area [may] be at the core of the continuing viability of the States in our federal system.").

60. *E.g.,* Task Force on the Federalization of Criminal Law, ABA, The Federalization of Criminal Law 5–16 (1998) (discussing the growth of the federal criminal-justice system and the effects of that growth); Sara Sun Beale, *Federalizing Crime: Assessing the Impact on the Federal Courts,* 543 Annals Am. Acad. Pol. & Soc. Sci. 39, 40 (1996).

61. *E.g.,* Abbate v. United States, 359 U.S. 187, 194 (1959) ("We have here two sovereignties, deriving power from different sources, capable of dealing with the same subject-matter within the same territory. . . . Each government in determining what shall be an offense against its peace and dignity is exercising its own sovereignty, not that of the other." (omission in original) (quoting United States v. Lanza, 260 U.S. 377, 382 (1922)) (internal quotation mark omitted)).

62. S. Ry. v. R.R. Comm'n, 236 U.S. 439, 445–46 (1915).

63. *E.g.,* Solem v. Bartlett, 465 U.S. 463, 466 (1984).

64. *E.g.,* State v. Smith, 400 S.E.2d 405, 407 (N.C. 1991) (citing United States v. Unzeuta, 281 U.S. 138 (1930)).

65. Watters v. Wachovia Bank, N.A., 550 U.S. 1, 14 (2007) (quoting Easton v. Iowa, 188 U.S. 220, 229, 231–32 (1903)).

66. *E.g.,* Bowen v. Johnston, 306 U.S. 19, 30 (1939).

67. Martin v. Hunter's Lessee, 14 U.S. (1 Wheat.) 304 (1816).

68. *See generally* Michael G. Collins, *The Federal Courts, the First Congress, and the Non-Settlement of 1789*, 91 Va. L. Rev. 1515, 1519–20 (2005) (describing the debate regarding the allocation of Article III business to non–Article III tribunals).

69. Knickerbocker Ice Co. v. Stewart, 253 U.S. 149 (1920).

70. *Id.* at 164 (citation omitted). Justice Holmes dissented for himself and three others, but the coalition agreed with the majority on the general point: "I assume that Congress could not delegate to state legislatures the simple power to decide what the law of the United States should be in that district." *Id.* at 169 (Holmes, J., dissenting).

71. Clinton v. City of New York, 524 U.S. 417 (1998).

72. *See* Michael G. Collins & Jonathan Remy Nash, *Prosecuting Federal Crimes in State Courts*, 97 Va. L. Rev. 243, 247–51 (2011) (arguing that it would be unconstitutional to allow state prosecutors to prosecute federal crimes).

73. United States v. Providence Journal Co., 485 U.S. 693, 700 (1988).

74. Abuelhawa v. United States, 129 S. Ct. 2102, 2107 n.3 (2009); *see also* Gonzales v. Oregon, 546 U.S. 243, 296 (2006) (Scalia, J., dissenting) (recognizing "the policy goals and competing enforcement priorities that attend any exercise of prosecutorial discretion").

75. *See* Dan M. Kahan, *Is* Chevron *Relevant to Federal Criminal Law?* 110 Harv. L. Rev. 469, 475 (1996) ("Whenever Congress resorts to general statutory language . . . it necessarily transfers lawmaking responsibility to courts (or prosecutors)."). This is equally true in the context of immigration. *See, e.g.*, Hiroshi Motomura, *Immigration outside the Law*, 108 Colum. L. Rev. 2037, 2060–65 (2008) (discussing the discretionary nature of enforcing immigration laws).

76. Printz v. United States, 521 U.S. 898 (1997).

77. Brady Handgun Violence Prevention Act, Pub. L. No. 103-159, tit. I, 107 Stat. 1536, 1536–44 (1993).

78. *Printz*, 521 U.S. at 922 (quoting U.S. Const. art. II, § 3).

79. *Id.*; *see also* Morrison v. Olson, 487 U.S. 654 (1988).

80. Free Enter. Fund v. Pub. Co. Accounting Oversight Bd., 130 S. Ct. 3138 (2010).

81. *See* 28 U.S.C. § 543 (2006).

82. California v. United States, 104 F.3d 1086, 1094 (9th Cir. 1997) (alteration in original) (quoting Heckler v. Chaney, 470 U.S. 821, 831 (1985)) (internal quotation marks omitted). Arizona's suit was rejected for the same reason. *Id.* at 1089 n.1; Arizona v. United States, 104 F.3d 1095, 1096 (9th Cir. 1997). *See generally* Motomura, *supra* note 75, at 2060–65 (discussing the role of discretion in immigration law); Gerald L. Neuman, *Discretionary Deportation*, 20 Geo. Immigr. L.J. 611 (2006) (same); Shoba Sivaprasad Wadhia, *The Role of Prosecutorial Discretion in Immigration Law*, 9 Conn. Pub. Int. L.J. 243 (2010) (same).

83. United States *ex rel.* Knauff v. Shaughnessy, 338 U.S. 537 (1950).

84. Adam B. Cox & Cristina M. Rodríguez, *The President and Immigration Law*, 119 Yale L.J. 458, 476–78 (2009).

85. Reno v. Am.-Arab Anti-Discrimination Comm., 525 U.S. 471 (1999).

86. *See generally* Adam H. Kurland, *First Principles of American Federalism and the Nature of Federal Criminal Jurisdiction*, 45 Emory L.J. 1, 8–12 (1996) (describing the constitutional limitations that prevent states from prosecuting federal crimes); Charles Warren, *Federal Criminal Laws and the State Courts*, 38 Harv. L. Rev. 545 (1925) (reviewing the nineteenth-century experience with vesting some federal criminal jurisdiction in state courts).

87. *See generally* Robert A. Schapiro, Polyphonic Federalism: Toward the Protection of Fundamental Rights (2009) (arguing that polyphonic federalism is more efficient, democratic, and protective of liberties than other forms).

88. *See supra* note 86 and accompanying text. For a more recent take on the same issue, see Collins & Nash, *supra* note 72.

7

The Role of States in the National Conversation on Immigration

Introduction

What is the role of states in immigration policy and enforcement? Though this question has long been an issue of concern for jurists and policymakers, developments in recent years have made it all the more pressing. One reason is the sheer volume of immigration-related activity on the state level; since 2005, more than four hundred state bills concerning immigration have been enacted to diverse effect. Another reason lies in the increasing severity of the state response, especially with states like Arizona and Alabama competing to pass the "toughest" laws on immigration.

Immigration is, of course, a national issue and a federal responsibility. As a result, most of the commentary to date has focused on the constitutionality and consequences of state involvement. There are ongoing debates over what power, if any, states have to regulate immigration, especially in light of the federal government's extensive occupation of the field. At the same time, there is much disagreement over not only the costs and benefits of state involvement generally but also those associated with policies of particular states. Indeed, as interest and concerns about state efforts to regulate immigration grow, these two debates have become the predominant lens through which the role of states is understood.

But it is worth asking what the near-exclusive focus on the constitutionality and consequences of the state laws fails to capture. Consider, for example, Arizona's controversial immigration enforcement law S.B. 1070. From the perspective of the law itself, it can be said that S.B. 1070 has proved to be relatively inconsequential. Two years after its enactment, most of its provisions have been struck down. And while a key provision of the law still stands—the so-called show-your-papers provision—there also appears to be flagging enthusiasm toward its enforcement at the local level, and signs that the federal government will be more selective going forward in responding to the state referrals they produce. From this perspective, it can be argued that like other sensational state efforts to regulate immigration in the past (e.g., California's Proposition 187 in the 1990s, state employer sanctions in the 1980s), there is a good chance that, in the end, the regulatory impact of S.B. 1070 will ultimately prove to be minimal.

Yet from another perspective, it can be said that even while S.B. 1070 has yet to be effectively enforced, its most significant impacts have already been made. The state law ignited an intense national debate, prompted an immediate federal response, and continues to frame the broader conversation over immigration—all of which were accomplished long before the constitutionality and enforceability of the laws was even settled in court. Indeed, considering how many "failed" state efforts at immigration regulations in the past went on to make their mark on the development of federal immigration policies, it is likely that S.B. 1070's influence will be felt regardless of whether it is ever actually implemented in Arizona.

A central theme of this chapter is that the way a state law affects the national political conversation on immigration is more important than what the law purports to do. It is through this frame that I wish to explore the role and impact of states. The fact is that state efforts to address immigration do not exist in a regulatory vacuum or in political isolation. Notwithstanding concerns about challenges to federal exclusivity or the rise of a patchwork system of immigration regulations, the most sensational state efforts thus far have largely been geared toward reforms at the national level. Rather than seeking to carve out an independent regime, state efforts are often specifically designed to influence the way the federal government administers our nation's immigration laws, or to elicit an eventual legislative response. Accordingly, more often than not they represent the beginning of a broader political negotiation as states seek to effectuate legal change more widely.

Of course, recognizing the discursive impact of states on immigration policy and enforcement is only the first step. Even more important is understanding how states are situated with respect to this conversation and what impact their involvement is having. To this end, this chapter begins by exploring the way states have come to assume this discursive role. Rather than focusing on the differences between states—red states versus blue states, traditional immigration-receiving areas versus those just beginning to attract immigrants—I focus instead on the evolving role of states more generally in our federal system. In part 1, I contextualize the role of states in immigration policy and enforcement by focusing on the role of the state generally within the contemporary structure of federalism. I argue that recent state immigration regulations are best understood as a product of national political disputes and interlocal conflicts, all of which are mediated at the state level. Part 2 builds upon this model by applying it to the recent enactment of S.B. 1070 in Arizona. Taken together, these two parts stress that states should be understood foremost as intermediaries between federal and local—uniquely situated with respect to immigration debates from above and local immigration controversies from below. Treating states as intermediaries not only better comports with the emerging position of states in our federal system; it also explains the particular manner in which states are regulating immigration and the impact that such regulations have.

Framing the role of states as intermediaries also allows us to more fully assess the impact of their involvement on the political conversation over immigration. This will be the focus of the second half of this chapter. Drawing upon the idea of states as intermediaries, and looking beyond standard arguments about "experimentation" and "tailoring," part 3 examines four different ways in which the involvement of states both enhances and distorts the manner in which immigration is understood and discussed as a matter of policy—the values and countervalues of states in the national conversation over immigration. Part 4 suggests some ways to expand the discursive value of states. This is followed by a brief conclusion.

I. Reexamining the Role of States in Our Federal System

There have been many attempts to explain state efforts to regulate immigration. Some have focused on the states' political characteristics, while others have looked at the aggregate or relative impact of immigration on those states and over time. This part suggests another approach by examining the role of states in immigration from the perspective of our federal system. If states are increasingly seen as an important political forum in the immigration debates, the perception is foremost a result of the way this role is changing. Here, I argue that rather than being defined by their separation from the national and their representation of the local, states today are better understood as intermediaries between the two. What this means is that when it comes to immigration, states are increasingly involved as a political forum for national controversies from above and local conflicts from below.

A. Federalism and the Relationship between the Federal Government and the States

Federalism is traditionally understood as a system of sovereign rights and constitutional limits, all of which are predominantly discussed in the language of trumps and vetoes. Yet in past decades, scholars have started to paint a very different picture of our federal system, one that emphasizes cooperation, negotiation, and discourse.[1] Rather than highlighting the separate and distinct nature of states in relation to the federal government, descriptive accounts of federalism have been more likely to focus on how they interact and overlap. Similarly, moving beyond the traditional value of states as "laboratories" for policy experimentation, normative accounts of federalism are increasingly attuned to principles of collaboration, interaction, and the mutual working out of shared values and norms.

How did we get to this point? To be sure, describing the federal system in the United States as a platform for intergovernmental collaboration and cross-jurisdictional discourse seems at odds with traditional views about the basic structure and purpose of our federal system. The conceptual shift in the federalism literature, however, is foremost a recognition of the shortcomings of traditional accounts of the structure and purpose of our federal system. Though federalism has traditionally been based on a jurisdictional divide between the nation and the state, it is increasingly difficult to define a natural and enduring line separating those issues entrusted to the federal government from those left in the care of the states. From education and financial regulation to housing and environmental protection, it is almost impossible to distinguish the "truly national" from the "truly local," as the Supreme Court once admonished.[2] Moreover, whether out of comity, legislative design, or the strategic use of enticements, intergovernmental collaboration and mutual delegation are increasingly becoming the norm for federal programs and many state initiatives.

What is striking about this growing overlap between federal and state is that it has not undermined the relevance of states in our federal system. Instead, the role and influence of states are more expansive than they have ever been, particularly with respect to policy matters that traditionally have not been understood to be matters of state concern. The tremendous reliance on states to implement federal programs has given them significant influence over the crafting of such federal policies as highly influential "interest groups," as well as much discretion in their implementation.[3] In addition, because states retain their role as government regulators, even if their sovereign sphere is increasingly less exclusive, the jurisdictional overlap offers additional opportunities to exert influence through the exercise of their regulatory powers—to in effect "dissent by deciding."[4]

All of this, of course, has dramatically changed the way states are positioned relative to the federal government. For example, the role of states is often characterized less by what they do and more by how their actions influence policies more broadly, especially at the national level. Another consequence is that it is no longer accurate to think of the state as a parochial or isolated political forum. With growing power to influence policies, states have in many cases turned explicitly into a secondary battleground over contentious national issues, such as national health care reform or same-sex marriage. In some instances, the use of states in this regard has raised concerns about exploitation and "carpetbagging," especially with respect to the influence of outside money in state politics. At the same time, states are hardly unwilling victims; they often use their politics strategically as a platform to exert pressure on national policymaking.

Turning to immigration only further strengthens this view of state integration in the national political conversation. To be sure, federalism scholars are only just beginning to extend this new framework into the context of immigration. Yet a collaborative view of federalism actually fits the development of immigration law quite well. For the past few decades, federal immigration enforcement strategies have become increasingly reliant on state and local participation. Moreover, as federal immigration controls have steadily expanded beyond admission quotas and entry requirements at the border, into domestic areas traditionally considered to be in the province of the state, the federal-state entanglement has intensified as a matter of legal doctrine and practice.

The integration of the federal government and the states with respect to immigration regulation and enforcement goes a long way toward explaining the growing interest of states in immigration as a matter of state policymaking. Another reason for their interest, however, is that the structure of our immigration laws allows these state efforts to be particularly influential in the public discourse over immigration. The debate surrounding the role of states in immigration cannot be easily reduced to a question of federal authority versus state rights. If there is a problem with immigration today, it is not that the federal government's authoritative voice is being challenged; none of the state efforts to regulate immigration suggests any desire to supplant the federal government as the primary regulator of immigration. The real issue is that the federal voice has been far from authoritative. It is often argued that exclusive federal control over immigration is necessary to ensure clarity and uniformity. Yet uncertainty hangs over every aspect of our immigration regime, and the development and interpretation of the law has in actuality been quite volatile. This means that, although the authority over immigration is centralized, the interpretation of the law is not.

Uncertainty and volatility not only pervade ongoing debates over immigration reforms but are also embedded in the legal regime that currently exists. The layered, complex, and expansive structure of our immigration laws makes it difficult to draw clear lines around the multitude of immigrant statuses, including those separating "legal" from "illegal." Nor is it easier to agree upon or reconcile the many goals of our immigration regime: to promote economic growth, to ensure national security, to adhere to our founding principles, or to preserve our cultural characteristics. All of this is exacerbated by the large amount of executive discretion accorded by both Congress and the courts, as well as by the large and persistent gap that exists between our immigration law as written and our immigration law as enforced. With major legislative overhauls nearly every decade, and often dramatic shifts in administrative priorities from one presidential term to another, immigration law is notoriously unsettled. At any given point in recent history, we seem to be simultaneously looking back in disappointment, and looking forward in anticipation of some iteration of comprehensive immigration reform.

When uncertainty and volatility pervade an area of law, as they do in the area of immigration, opportunity for divergent voices to enter and shape the conversation is greatly expanded. What makes these voices even more influential is that they can all lay claim to a competing yet well-entrenched conceptualization of our immigration regime. In their effort to regulate immigration, states are assuming this role. Sometimes their appeals choose to highlight certain provisions of our federal immigration regime, while at other times the immigration law is taken together as a whole to stand for an overarching intent or principle. In each instance, however, states are increasingly invoking, referring to, and consulting federal sources of law in their response to immigration. In this manner, it can be argued that the states see themselves as engaged in a larger interpretive project over the meaning and implementation of *existing* immigration laws.

This explains why state regulations of immigration often mirror, rather than deviate from, existing federal law. The first major wave of state regulations targeting undocumented immigrants in such states as Missouri and Oklahoma in the mid-2000s largely focused on replicating existing federal employment restrictions that many believed were underenforced. Moreover, in doing so, many of these laws mandated the use of newly developed federal databases like E-verify, which the federal government was eagerly promoting but had been reluctant to mandate. The wave of "anti-sanctuary" measures in recent years, which seek to prevent localities and local law enforcement agencies from limiting their officers' participation in federal immigration enforcement efforts, are also modeled almost entirely after a federal antisanctuary provision enacted in 1996. The same applies to the most recent wave of state efforts to create criminal penalties against immigration-related activities, such as harboring or transporting undocumented immigrants or the failure to carry immigration documents: Nearly all of them have similar, if not identical, federal counterparts. States defend these replications on the ground that their federal counterparts have not been adequately enforced by the federal government. They rarely characterize these state laws, however, as direct challenges to the letter of existing federal law, or at least their interpretation of the spirit of that law.

At the same time, even when states do strike out on their own with new legislation, they often do so explicitly, with an eye toward creating a new national baseline rather than a unique state niche. It is worth noting here that earlier state efforts in this regard have been quite successful in influencing future federal developments, irrespective of whether these state laws ultimately either withstood legal scrutiny or were effectively enforced. Efforts to limit immigrant access to Medicare benefits in Pennsylvania and Arizona were struck down by the Supreme Court in *Graham v. Richardson*, yet an almost identical federal version of the law was later enacted and upheld in *Matthews v. Diaz*. Anti-Chinese statutes in the nineteenth century and the more recent Proposition 187 in California lost their respective federalism battles in federal court; yet they played a large role in influencing the federal reforms that followed—from Chinese exclusion in the late nineteenth century to the restriction of federal means-tested benefits for legal immigrants in the mid-1990s. And although the California employer restriction upheld in *DeCanas v. Bica* is widely recognized as having been subsequently preempted by federal law, the reason for that preemption was an almost identical measure adopted a few years later in the federal Immigration Reform and Control Act of 1986. Even today, the roots of the DREAM Act now gaining support in Congress, which would offer a path to citizenship for undocumented children who attend college, can be seen in the fierce state-by-state battles over whether to grant in-state tuition to undocumented children, many of whom are now leading the charge for the bill's adoption. If this trend holds, there is no telling what influence recent laws pushing for local enforcement of immigration laws will have on the next round of federal immigration reforms even if they are ultimately struck down as preempted.

B. *Localism and the Relationship between States and Their Localities*

The states' position as intermediaries is reflected not just in their role as forums for national disputes from above. One of the most overlooked aspects of states is their role as forums for negotiating local conflicts from below. To be sure, in the traditional two-tiered model of federalism, the state is usually considered the lowest sovereign and thus representative of "local" interests. Most accounts of our federal structure make no distinctions between state and local governments at all. But from the vantage point of the truly local—the myriad cities, towns, and neighborhoods in which state residents live—the state can often appear as remote and distant a centralized power as the federal government. Moreover, as political and cultural divides intensify within the states themselves, state policymaking increasingly reflects a struggle between competing local interests: upstate versus downstate, urban versus suburban, metropolitan versus rural. As a result, just as the role of states should be understood as an extension of the national political debates, state policies should also at times be seen as the result of increasingly fierce interlocal conflicts within states.

At the heart of this shift is the changing locus of geographic identity in this country. It is often said that the purpose of a federalist arrangement in America is to accommodate the political and cultural distinctiveness of the several states. Yet in today's world, this underlying premise seems at times woefully outdated. We have long rejected many of the political compromises that our federalism purported to justify, from slavery to Jim Crow. More important, even if tangible differences among states continue to exist, those divisions are fast eroding. The political trend in most states is increasingly toward purple—more prone to sway from one side of the political spectrum to another in accordance with national sentiment rather than local distinctiveness. At the same time, even while states and regions retain some unique cultural identifiers, the rise of a national cultural framework is also undeniable, spurred in large part by the nationalization of popular media and consumer culture. All the while, increasing mobility among states diminishes whatever differences remain among states. This is not to say that long conversations cannot still be had on the differences between a New Yorker and a Texan. It is simply that in today's world, the differences that remain no longer seem a sufficient justification for a federalism of independent sovereigns.

Yet, the declining distinctiveness among states does not mean that American society is homogenizing. Nor does it mean that political and cultural differences are no longer geographical in nature. As Bill Bishop recently argued, in the past few decades there has been a dramatic increase in the sorting of "like-minded people" into geographic enclaves.[5] Not only has segregation based on long-standing divisions persisted, but new cleavages also seem to be appearing, often leading to the emergence of distinct and disparate cultural frameworks. The difference is that these cleavages are more likely to be found within states rather than across state lines. In other words, even while interstate distinctiveness is eroding, divisions *within* states are proliferating. Moreover, these two trends are not only reconcilable; they are also in many cases mutually reinforcing. Consider, for example, the state of Colorado: While explosive in-migration of new residents from other parts of the country moved the state as a whole toward the national norm, the concentration of this growth in distinct metropolitan regions has further exacerbated political and cultural divisions within the state.

From this perspective, it is becoming increasingly difficult to say that states represent a cohesive or distinct identity. Rather, states are better understood as an agglomeration of varied interests, often geographically defined and, at times, worlds apart. It is no surprise then that national controversies once marked by federal-state conflicts are today increasingly likely to feature interlocal battles both vertically between the state and localities, and horizontally among different localities in a state. The Supreme Court's first step toward recognizing the civil rights of gay men and lesbians in *Romer v. Evans*, for example, pitted anti-discrimination statutes enacted in Denver, Boulder, and Aspen against a statewide law in Colorado that sought to repeal them. Similarly, in a modern spin on the classic bussing debate, the Court's decision in *Washington v. Seattle Sch. Dist. No. 1* featured a school integration program in Seattle based on race and a Washington state law that forbade any subdivision to institute such programs.

In the context of immigration, the salience of interlocal divisions within states is even more pronounced. In other words, "where immigrants live matters."[6] Though it is the initial act of immigration into this country that dominates the immigration conversation, the geography of immigrant settlement has long played an underlying role in the development of federal immigration policies more broadly. Indeed, the escalation of federal immigration restrictions at the dawn of the twentieth century was motivated in large part by concerns about the deleterious effects and political power of immigrants concentrated in major cities and urban enclaves. Though the residential patterns of the most recent wave of immigrants have changed somewhat from those of their predecessors—most notably in following the broader societal trend toward suburbanization—the cities and neighborhoods in which immigrants live continue to remain largely distinct. In many metropolitan regions, the communities that immigrant labor has helped to create and maintain are often not those in which they can afford to live. A similar pattern is starting to take shape in rural communities as well, where newly recruited immigrant residents often live in poor, underserviced, and unincorporated areas outside the geographic confines of the incorporated towns in which the factories and plants where they work are often located.

In the past, the geographic patterns of immigrant settlement led to many sensational standoffs between native-dominated state houses and immigrant-supported city halls. Indeed, even while the role of cities ascended as a result of the Industrial Revolution in the late nineteenth and early twentieth centuries, many states radically decreased the scope of local power, in part because of growing concerns that their interests were too aligned with immigrant residents as opposed to those of the state as a whole. Signs of similar tension can also be seen in state efforts to address immigration today. Motivated by concerns that certain localities are too accommodating toward undocumented immigrants or soft on immigration enforcement, state regulations have increasingly targeted local policies. When public controversy erupted over so-called sanctuary cities—localities that put limits on their involvement in federal immigration enforcement—several states responded by enacting laws that specifically forbid localities from imposing limits in this manner. When the debate over undocumented immigrants became associated with the presence of day laborers, states like Arizona enacted laws that specifically withheld state funding from any locality that sponsored day-laborer centers, even for the sole purpose of eliminating the congregation and solicitation of workers on the street.[7]

Upon closer examination, even the most well known of state efforts to regulate immigration reveal a localist bent. Take for example the landmark decision *Plyler v. Doe*, in which the Supreme Court famously affirmed the right of undocumented students to receive a free public education. The Texas law that was struck down did not directly seek to exclude undocumented students from public schools in the state. Rather, it tried to do so indirectly by withholding the state's share of educational funding for any pupil that the district could not confirm as a citizen or as lawfully present in the United States. Interestingly, it was almost two years after the state withheld funding that a school district tried to pass on the costs by requiring those students who could not show citizenship or lawful residency to pay "tuition" equivalent to the loss of state grants, thereby prompting a legal challenge of the Texas law. Moreover, given the way the Texas law imposed on local governments both the costs and the responsibility of implementing the statute, it is not surprising that on appeal, localities and local school districts appeared as amici on both sides of the case.

C. States as Intermediaries in the National Conversation on Immigration

The foregoing sections suggest that one of the primary roles of the state today is not only that of an alternative political forum for contentious national issues like immigration but also that of a forum uniquely situated with respect to the federal and local spheres. In other words, rather than being defined by their separation from the national and their representation of the local, states today are better understood as intermediaries between the two.

On the one hand, this model complicates the standard view of state regulations as direct challenges against federal authority over immigration. In most cases, states are not attempting to create an independent regulatory framework on immigration. They are certainly not eager to assume primary responsibility over immigration. Rather, the goal is often to effectuate some kind of response or reform on the federal level. In this respect, states are increasingly becoming an explicit secondary battleground in the immigration debates. Moreover, rather than carving out regulatory niches, states seem to be specifically oriented toward influencing federal policymaking. It is for this reason that, even when there is strong evidence to suggest that a certain regulation will be struck down as unconstitutional, states often continue to pursue it fervently. It also explains why controversial immigration laws are often passed at the state level with substantial fanfare and publicity, and why there is often less enthusiasm for enforcement when such a law actually goes into effect.

On the other hand, rather than reflecting a monolithic local sentiment, underneath the surface of state immigration regulations is often tremendous conflict and discord at the local level. Applying this localist lens reveals how the varying perspectives and contentious disputes commonly associated with immigration policymaking at the federal level are increasingly being replicated in the local interactions within states. To be sure, states have not always been conciliatory actors or neutral forums with respect to these interlocal tensions; depending on the representative mix in the state house, they are often eager to take sides. Yet it does suggest the existence of a rich and often overlooked set of local circumstances that influence state policymaking on issues such as immigration.

Admittedly, none of this offers much insight into what type of state immigration regulations, if any, are constitutionally permissible. Yet, despite the enormous attention that this question has drawn, one purpose of this part has been to suggest that constitutionality may not matter all that much—either for states that are seeking to implement these regulations or for the policymaking process by which federal regulations are made. In the long run, state responses to immigration often reflect the first word in a discursive controversy, not the last. The public outcry that a state response generates is part of the intended impact. The legal challenges that states often expect, if not solicit, can be thought of as a continuation of the conversation—especially given that preemption challenges often expand the debate to include the wisdom of the underlying federal law that is said to preempt the state law in question. Moreover, as history has shown, irrespective of the legal disposition of the state law, the next step is usually an extensive national conversation and an explicit federal response.

II. Analyzing S.B. 1070 in Arizona

In the preceding part, I developed a new model for understanding state efforts to regulate immigration by reexamining the role of states more generally in our federal system. This part demonstrates how this framework operates in the context of one of the most recent, and thus far the most controversial of such state efforts: Arizona's immigration enforcement law, S.B. 1070.

A. Conventional Account of Arizona's New Immigration Law

S.B. 1070 was enacted by Arizona in the summer of 2010, sparking a firestorm of controversy. On the one hand, it was praised as a road map for how the federal capacity for immigration enforcement can be greatly expanded through state involvement. On the other hand, by promoting enforcement by many local officials neither trained nor experienced in enforcing federal immigration law, it was criticized for encouraging racial profiling and the harassment of Latinos and other minority residents in the state. When it was first enacted, there was little agreement on the legality and wisdom of S.B. 1070. Yet all sides seem eager to cast the controversy in the familiar framework of federal power versus state rights.

Though by far the most prominent, S.B. 1070 was not the first comprehensive state effort to regulate immigration in the country. Nor was it even the first such effort in Arizona. In the years prior to S.B. 1070's enactment, both Missouri and Oklahoma passed and touted their own versions of the "strictest" immigration law in the country. Similarly, on the same day that S.B. 1070 was enacted, the Supreme Court announced that it would review the constitutionality of the Legal Arizona Workers Act, an immigration statute that the state had passed a year earlier. Indeed, in many ways, S.B. 1070 was merely the latest development in a long series of state efforts to regulate immigration, particularly the presence of undocumented immigrants.

At the same time, the fact that S.B. 1070 triggered such an immediate and intense public debate was in large part a product of the way the new law both built upon and evolved beyond its predecessors. Whereas earlier state efforts largely had focused on preventing undocumented immigrants from receiving some kind of benefit or accommodation in the state—such as employment, housing, education, or public assistance—S.B. 1070 was focused directly on effectuating removal through enforcement. It did so not simply by creating state laws to penalize conduct often thought to be associated with undocumented immigration. Nor was it content to encourage local enforcement indirectly, as the federal government and other states had done, by attacking so-called sanctuary cities. In addition to all of this, S.B. 1070 also *mandated* that all state and local law enforcement officials participate in immigration enforcement directly by checking for immigration status in two circumstances: (1) when an individual had been arrested and (2) at any lawful stop where there was reasonable suspicion of an individual's unlawful presence in the United States.

The difference between Arizona's S.B. 1070 and other state efforts to address immigration lies not only in its scope but also in the legal challenges that it received. True, almost every major state effort to regulate immigration had faced a lawsuit. However, S.B. 1070 was one of the few state laws ever, and the first one concerning immigration in recent history, to be challenged directly by the federal government itself. A little more than two months after S.B. 1070 was signed into law and weeks before it would go into effect, the Department of Justice took the remarkable step of filing a legal challenge against S.B. 1070. It argued that the Arizona law not only was directly preempted by existing federal law but also impermissibly infringed upon the federal government's exclusive power to set national immigration policy. The federal government's challenge prevailed at both the district and appellate level. Before the Supreme Court, however, the outcome was mixed. On the one hand, the Court struck down nearly all of the provisions the federal government challenged, including those that sought to create state penalties for immigration-related activities. On the other hand, the Supreme Court upheld S.B. 1070's most controversial provision: the mandate that all law enforcement officials in the state verify the immigration status of any individual they arrest or reasonably suspect of being an undocumented immigrant.

Given the federal lawsuit and the manner in which it has been portrayed, the controversy that unfolded over Arizona's S.B. 1070 appears to be a classic federalism battle between the federal government and a state. As the federal government argued in its case against Arizona, even more important than the individual components of S.B. 1070 is the fact that Arizona enacted a comprehensive legislative scheme that represented a unique policy position on how immigration should be regulated and enforced. In this way, Arizona's actions reflected a fundamental challenge to the federal government's plenary power over policymaking with respect to immigration. The federal government also stressed the danger this law posed to federal uniformity, especially if, as they have in fact done, other states began to follow Arizona's lead in enacting their own state policies on immigration. In all of this, of course, Arizona played its part. Not only was S.B. 1070 clear in stating that the purpose of the law was to effectuate a specific policy of "attrition through enforcement," but its sponsors have not been shy in describing the law's passage as a direct challenge to existing federal policy and administration. All the while, the mantra of "state rights" has served as a rallying cry for its supporters. When these challenges are combined with the concerns about racial profiling and police harassment, it is no wonder that many are comparing the fight over S.B. 1070 to the famed federalism struggles of an earlier era: the civil rights movement and the dismantling of Jim Crow.[8]

From another perspective, however, this portrayal of S.B. 1070 as a classic struggle between federal power and state rights seems too simple. At best, it fails to account for much of the complexity surrounding the passage of S.B. 1070. At worst, it risks distorting the underlying intent and motivations of S.B. 1070's enactment. Even if the title of the lawsuit against S.B. 1070—*United States v. Arizona*—suggests a straightforward federalism dispute, one need only look at the declarations and amicus briefs filed in the litigation to see a hint of the competing interests at play. Not only was the federal government's initial complaint filed with supporting declarations from the police chiefs in Phoenix and Tucson and the sheriff of Santa Cruz County; its case on appeal was also supported by amicus briefs from several cities in Arizona and several cities in other states, including Santa Clara and New Haven, along with the National League of Cities. The state of Arizona's brief on appeal was not only joined by an amicus brief filed by attorneys general of eight states and one U.S. territory but was also supported by a brief signed by eighty-one members of Congress. As we saw with state involvement in immigration regulations more generally above, the enactment of and controversy around S.B. 1070 can similarly be seen as reflecting conflicts from both above and below.

B. Federalism Account of Arizona's S.B. 1070

Since its enactment, efforts to explain S.B. 1070 have often centered on trying to explain Arizona. Many have noted the unique political climate of the state, with some pointing to its legislative culture of challenging federal legislation. Others have pointed to the unique position of Arizona with respect to immigration; as a border state with a significant proportion of unauthorized crossings, Arizona has a special relationship to immigration and has borne witness to the casualties of our enforcement regime. All of these factors are important. But in some ways, much of the story behind S.B. 1070 isn't really about Arizona at all. Although S.B. 1070 has been widely portrayed as unprecedented, nearly every aspect of the law has deep roots in existing federal law and ongoing policy debates over how those laws are to be enforced. In this respect, its passage can also be understood as part the see-saw of national politics surrounding the federal immigration regime's meaning, scope, and priorities. In other words, the controversy over S.B. 1070 is simply a reflection of existing controversy over federal immigration laws and regulation more generally.

The roots of S.B. 1070 are firmly embedded in federal law. Nearly all of the new state penalties that it creates target conduct that is already illegal under federal law. The enforcement mandates that it imposes on local law enforcement officials are all structured around their cooperation with federal authorities in identifying and removing undocumented immigrants. In addition, the legal standards that S.B. 1070 employs draw heavily from existing federal standards and practices: Cities are forbidden from adopting or implementing any policies that limit local immigration enforcement to anything "less than the extent permitted by federal law"; no officer may consider "race, color or national origin" in implementing the law "except to the extent permitted by the United States . . . Constitution." I do not wish to suggest, as some have argued, that just because a state regulation of immigration "mirrors" federal law, it is necessarily constitutional. Yet, at its core, S.B. 1070 does not seek to directly challenge federal law or present a competing policy; rather, it seems to be an effort to draw attention to federal law itself.

Indeed, the fact that Arizona felt empowered to involve state and local law enforcement officials in immigration enforcement may reflect developments at the federal level. For the past couple of decades the federal government has been actively encouraging the kind of "cooperation" that underlies S.B. 1070. Congressional priority in the 1990s was to prohibit states and localities from *refusing* to participate in immigration enforcement. The Bush administration in the 2000s actively solicited their participation, going so far as to draft and rely on a legal opinion suggesting that states and localities have "inherent authority" to enforce federal immigration laws even in the absence of federal authorization. In furtherance of promoting state and local involvement, both Congress and the administration created an elaborate infrastructure around such assistance: Federal law now requires the Department of Homeland Security to respond to any and all inquiries regarding immigration status that it receives from state and local law enforcement, and several databases and a hotline have been established to accomplish that goal. To be sure, the Obama administration has reversed course on many of these policies. Yet state involvement continues to be featured prominently in federal immigration initiatives like Operation Secure Communities and the increasing outsourcing of immigration detention to state prisons. Indeed, this was one reason why the federal government's lawsuit against S.B. 1070 did not actually argue that the underlying conduct that S.B. 1070 sought to mandate—e.g., inquiring about immigration when there is a lawful stop, detention, or arrest—was itself preempted. Rather, it focused specifically on Arizona's effort to mandate such actions.

From this perspective, the controversy over S.B. 1070 seems less an example of a federalism challenge involving a defiant state, and more like an internal debate about the development of federal immigration policy. Indeed, as the timing of S.B. 1070 suggests, much of this has to do with the recent change in presidential administrations. The legal architect of S.B. 1070, Kris Kobach, had been a central figure in developing federal immigration policy in the Bush administration. Thus, the policy positions that undergird S.B. 1070—"attrition through enforcement" and "inherent authority"—are now touted by Arizona as in accordance with federal law in large part because those are the same positions that Kobach and others had adopted as federal policy through most of the 2000s. In this respect, the battle between the federal government and Arizona today is in many ways a reflection of the debates over immigration policy within the federal government.

Its assertion about state rights notwithstanding, Arizona seems to recognize this; its primary interest seems to be in shifting federal policy rather than establishing an independent legal regime. Supporters of S.B. 1070 have spent more time using the law as a platform for attacking existing federal immigration practices than trying to explain why the law is good for Arizona. Despite the talk about what makes Arizona special, there is still a clear sense that the main issue is federal immigration law and the prospects of comprehensive reform.

C. Localist Account of Arizona's S.B. 1070

Just as state immigration regulations can be understood as a part of a broader national conversation at the federal level, they can also be seen as responses to local disputes from below. Indeed, the passage of S.B. 1070 was preceded by a steady escalation of tensions among several of Arizona's local communities with respect to immigration and immigration enforcement. Although this aspect was largely overlooked in the early days following S.B. 1070's passage, much of the law was directed downward at local governments within the state. In this regard, S.B. 1070 can be understood as a state effort to resolve (or suppress) growing interlocal tensions within the state.

S.B. 1070 is part of a larger debate about the role of state and local law enforcement with respect to immigration. One of the most overlooked aspects of the law is the extent to which it seeks to increase immigration enforcement in the state by attacking local discretion and control. Even before the passage of S.B. 1070, local law enforcement officials in Arizona had long been involved in immigration enforcement at varying levels, both with and without the federal government's explicit approval. What the state law sought to do was not to empower local enforcement but rather to force *all* communities to prioritize immigration enforcement regardless of local policies or priorities. Moreover, S.B. 1070 took the novel step of creating a private cause of action against cities that try to limit enforcement in any respect. As a result, it did not affect only cities with near-complete bans on immigration enforcement, if any such cities existed in Arizona. The law's scope was such that the vast majority of Arizona communities were implicated, even those that participated in immigration enforcement but simply not to the degree that S.B. 1070 required. In this regard, although the enactment of S.B. 1070 may have been intended to target federal policy as a political matter, its legislative focus was on the conscription of local resources to accomplish state ends. Not surprisingly, some of S.B. 1070's most vocal critics were its own communities, particularly officials in Arizona's largest cities.

But this state-local conflict over immigration is all the more significant because it is so easily overlooked. Take, for example, the original preliminary injunction issued by the district court against S.B. 1070. Much attention was focused on the provisions that the district court enjoined. Yet, equally significant were the provisions that the preliminary injunction and the federal challenge that led to it did not (and arguably could not) address, namely, the parts of the S.B. 1070 involving state-local relations. The provision prohibiting cities from limiting their law enforcement officials' involvement in immigration matters was never enjoined, nor was the private cause of action designed to compel cities to participate in immigration enforcement to the furthest extent possible. As a result, while the federal challenge against S.B. 1070 set the stage for the federal-state showdown on immigration that would eventually be resolved two years later, the preliminary injunction that emerged first immediately placed cities in legal limbo: not required to enforce federal immigration laws, on the one hand, but also prohibited from taking any steps not to enforce it.

The limited relief that cities received from the original preliminary injunction against S.B. 1070 is illustrated by what little effect it had in blocking disruptive immigration-enforcement efforts in cities that did not want such enforcement to take place. For example, after the preliminary injunction against S.B. 1070 was issued, Sheriff Joe Arpaio of Maricopa County immediately announced an aggressive immigration sweep in the city of Phoenix. The chaotic results were predictable. Yet considering the extent of the disruption, it is worth noting that the sweep was not authorized by Phoenix, and that city officials had been critical of similar sweeps in the past. This, of course, was not the first time Sheriff Arpaio had carried out immigration sweeps, or targeted cities like Phoenix in his county. Indeed, the sweep was only the most recent installment of an ongoing local conflict over immigration.

Arpaio's penchant for aggressiveness and publicity are well known and documented, and he has been an icon for both supporters and critics of local immigration enforcement, albeit for different reasons. What is less well known outside of Arizona is that Arpaio faces local opposition not only in the neighborhoods that he raids but also from the political officials in the cities and towns that he frequently targets. Rather than spreading his enforcement efforts throughout Maricopa County, Arpaio targets neighborhoods in specific cities. He does so not only because these are the areas with large concentrations of Latino residents but also because he feels the cities in which they are located are "soft" on immigration enforcement. Moreover, he has been able to carry out these sensational raids without approval from local leaders in those cities. Arizona law grants county sheriffs and municipal police departments concurrent jurisdiction to operate in Arizona cities. As a result, the cities themselves have no power to influence the way these county raids are carried out, much less prevent them altogether.

This has led to some sensational standoffs. In the city of Mesa, Arizona's third-largest municipality, Arpaio drew sharp criticism from both the mayor and the police chief after conducting an unannounced predawn raid on City Hall and the public library. In the city of Phoenix, the consequences of Arpaio's raids so disturbed the city's mayor that he wrote a letter directly to the Department of Justice asking the federal government to initiate an investigation of Arpaio for civil rights violations. By several accounts, the letter triggered a federal investigation that eventually led to the partial removal of Maricopa County from the federal government's 287(g) program. Yet it is ironic that the mayor of Phoenix had to seek federal assistance in an effort to control law enforcement activity in his own city, and to address potential civil rights violations against his own residents.

The enactment and battle over S.B. 1070 can be understood as an escalation of this fight. Communities in Arizona have different interests with respect to immigration enforcement. Those like Maricopa County succeeded through the enactment of S.B. 1070, which immediately preempted all conflicting policies within the state. Other communities have played a significant role in supporting the federal government's efforts to strike down Arizona's law. On the surface, the controversy over S.B. 1070 may look like one between the federal government and the state of Arizona as a whole. But on the ground, the interlocal conflicts that both led to the enactment of S.B. 1070 and contributed to the federal challenge are not lost on the individuals and institutions most affected by the outcome.

III. Assessing the Discursive Role of States in the Immigration Conversation

The symbolic tendencies of state responses to immigration and states' ultimate desire to influence national policymaking should not lead us to overlook the unique impact of states involved in the immigration conversation as states. Thus, having set forth a discursive framework of how states shape the perception of immigration as an issue and its development as a body of law, we turn now to an evaluation of that discursive impact. In other words, how does the involvement of states contribute to framing immigration as an issue in the national conversation? Here, I suggest that states offer both unique promises and particular dangers in this regard.

A. Grounding and Bridging the Immigration Debates

First, the use of states as a political forum may ground and contextualize issues that might tend toward abstraction in the national arena. For contentious national issues like immigration, in which controversies can often seem remote, intractable, and unimaginative, states may offer a more intimate and tangible forum in which the costs, benefits, and consequences of policies are more concrete. This is not to say that political discourse at the state level is entirely free from the partisan bickering or emotional impulses that plague the major political issues dominating national politics. Rather, the structural position of states is unique and accordingly suggests a greater ability to put faces, places, and names to what might otherwise be a vague and unmoored conversation. This may be particularly important given that the issue of immigration has steadily been narrowing to focus almost entirely on enforcement and undocumented immigration, while the human face and divergent interests involved are fading from view.

Related to their ability to ground and contextualize national conversations, states are also uniquely situated to bridge and negotiate what may seem like intractable conflicts within states and on the local level.

The impact of immigration is at times sharply delineated among different local communities, not only because of the concentration of immigrant settlement but also because the economic and political organization of our regions often means that the benefits of immigration are not necessarily locally concentrated in the areas where the costs are most directly incurred. I have argued before that local immigration controversies need to be understood against the backdrop of localist structures that foster fierce interlocal competition for the right kind of residents, the right kind of growth, and the right kind of tax base.[9] Any immigration compromise will not only need to include a wide range of stakeholders at the local level and reconcile a number of competing interests but will also need to address the legal incentive structure that exacerbates local tensions over immigration. This is a task and a conversation for which states may be well suited.

B. Mirrors on Federal Law and Policy

The involvement of states not only creates an alternative forum; it can also greatly expand existing conversation over federal immigration policy at the national level. It does so by indirectly calling attention to federal laws that would ordinarily be insulated by the perceived finality of federal policymaking or the doctrinal deference mandated by the plenary power doctrine. The reason for this is that, as noted earlier, state immigration regulations are so often exact or near-exact copies of provisions already in federal law. Thus, even if it is the state attempt to replicate federal law that draws public scrutiny, that scrutiny also indirectly calls into question aspects of federal law that may have remained unexamined.

Compare, for example, the judicial approach taken in *Graham v. Richardson* with that in *Matthews v. Diaz*, both of which presented the Supreme Court with a near-identical restriction of health benefits to certain legal immigrants. When the restriction was presented in the form of a federal law in *Matthews*, the Supreme Court penned an extremely deferential opinion that avoided nearly any substantive consideration of the law itself. Yet, when the same restriction had been presented earlier in the form of a state law in *Graham*, the court engaged in a robust equal protection analysis that called the motivation and wisdom of the law into serious question. To be sure, this critical analysis in *Graham* had no impact on the Court's decision in *Matthews*—in fact, that Court specifically refused to consider those arguments on the ground that they were now dealing with an exercise of the federal government's plenary power. But absent the state's initial attempt, that scrutiny would not have even existed; and notwithstanding the Court's dismissal of those concerns in *Matthews*, they applied with equal force against the motivations behind the federal law as they did against the state law in *Graham*.

Indeed, because so many state regulatory efforts adopt or mirror existing federal law, they have triggered widespread conversations and debates over federal policies that do not necessarily occur otherwise. When the federal government enacted its law against "sanctuary cities" in 1996, there was little to no public discussion about its merits. This was the case even after New York City famously filed a facial constitutional challenge against the provision in federal court on the ground that it constituted a commandeering of local officials and the local policymaking process. Yet, as states have proposed copycat antisanctuary legislation, the wisdom of such prohibitions has been subject to extensive debates at both the local and the national level. State legislative efforts to require the use of E-verify, a federal database designed to allow employers to check the legal status of potential employees, have also prompted a broader conversation over the federal program's accuracy and reliability. To be sure, E-verify had already been subject to criticism when it was first announced by the federal government. State efforts to push the use of E-verify even further prompted more extensive public scrutiny about the database, along with the federal government's continuing efforts to encourage its use among employers.

One can also argue that a similar development is taking place around the controversy over S.B. 1070. Recall that one of the main concerns is that by requiring all state and local law enforcement officials to inquire about immigration status when there is a reasonable suspicion of unlawful status, the law promotes racial profiling. The drafters of S.B. 1070 sought to counter these allegations by amending the law to prohibit the consideration of race "except to the extent permitted by the United States . . . Constitution." As many of S.B. 1070's critics pointed out, however, the Supreme Court has long held that the consideration of race is permissible in the enforcement of immigration laws in certain circumstances, and recent years have expanded those circumstances substantially. In other words, while S.B. 1070 sought to deflect fears about racial profiling by specifically incorporating federal standards on the use of race in immigration enforcement, the law also drew increased attention to how paltry those federal standards actually are. Though these aspects of federal law had thus far largely escaped public scrutiny, it appears that the controversy over Arizona's immigration law may draw them back into the spotlight.

C. Cost Distortion

As the above suggests, states may simultaneously ground national conversation and bridge local divisions and, in so doing, provide a more contextualized picture of what is at stake with respect to immigration. Yet, there is also the risk that framing policy choices through the lens of states may actually do the opposite; it may distort the costs and benefits of a regulatory proposal. That is the case because, as an intermediate tier of government, states have the ability to frame issues and regulatory schemes in a way that shifts the costs up to the federal government or down to localities.

Indeed, Arizona's S.B. 1070 was crafted largely in this manner. On the one hand, the fiscal and social costs of implementing the law on the front end fell almost entirely on local governments. One feature of our uniquely decentralized system of criminal law enforcement is that cities, towns, and counties fund the vast majority of criminal enforcement costs through local taxes. By mandating local enforcement of federal immigration laws, the state essentially imposed an additional burden on already-cash-strapped departments across the state. It also took the additional unique steps of making local governments and law enforcement agencies (1) monetarily liable for failing to enforce federal immigration laws and (2) financially responsible for indemnifying any officer who is sued for enforcing federal immigration laws pursuant to S.B. 1070. None of this was offset with any funding from the state or even any additional revenue-raising authority for local governments. It is no wonder that even while critics criticized S.B. 1070 for authorizing local immigration enforcement, many local leaders and law enforcement officials denounced the law for imposing an unfunded mandate. In the debates over the law at the state and federal level, however, many of these costs were ignored, much less balanced against S.B. 1070's anticipated benefits.

But financial costs are only part of the overall equation. The state-wide dragnet envisioned by S.B. 1070 also posed the danger of substantial social costs in increased police inquiries, detention, and community harassment. The residential geography of Arizona, however, ensured that such costs were not going to be shared evenly statewide—Latino and other immigrant communities would be targeted, with citizens and legal residents of those communities facing the added scrutiny and surveillance, while other communities would probably be insulated from the law entirely. The uneven burden of local immigration enforcement had long been a point of contention among communities in Arizona. Indeed, the sensational clashes between Sheriff Arpaio in Maricopa County and local leaders in Phoenix and Mesa were due in large part to the fact that neighborhoods in the two cities bore the brunt of the costs associated with Arpaio's enforcement sweeps while he was reaping the publicity.

On the other hand, while all the financial and social costs of detection were imposed on local governments, the processing, detention, and removal costs of carrying through Arizona's immigration law at the back end were foisted entirely on the federal government. Arizona has neither the ability nor the desire to be primarily responsible for immigration enforcement. Its intention was to require more federal enforcement by taking more initiative on the front end. By mandating that local law enforcement officials cooperate in federal immigration enforcement activities, however, the law also effectively required the federal government to cooperate. This involved not only responding to the flood of status inquiries that enforcement of S.B. 1070 would produce[10] but also bearing the detention and removal costs of those identified as undocumented in this manner, even if these individuals are not considered high-priority targets by the federal government. These costs were not lost on the federal government. Indeed, the extent to which Arizona's law will impose financial burdens on the federal government and "impermissibly shift the allocation of federal resources away from federal priorities" was one of the federal government's primary argument against S.B. 1070.

As the above demonstrates, S.B. 1070 imposed substantial costs that needed to be balanced against its purported gains. At the state level, however, few if any of these costs were readily apparent, and thus many of the actual costs that the law would have imposed on both the federal government and local communities in Arizona went unexamined. This is not to say that similar distortions do not also appear in debates at other levels; indeed, as was the case in Postville, Iowa, and New Bedford, Massachusetts, the federal government often underestimates the costs of its enforcement activities on local communities. Yet being able to hide costs by shifting them up or down the governmental hierarchy, state policymaking poses a particular concern in this regard.

D. Outsourcing and Shirking

Related to cost distortion is that state involvement in the immigration debates may also lead to narrowing of the states' perception of their own role. Of concern are not external constraints imposed by the federal government or other states, but rather the danger of "self-imposed" limitations. I refer to this as the dual problem of "outsourcing" and "shirking"—outsourcing in that states may come to expect and rely on the blunt and ill-suited tools of federal legislation to solve local problems, while shirking the state's own role and responsibility in this regard.

One of the problems with immigration regulation is that it is too often treated as a panacea for a host of problems that require more tailored and specific solutions. In the past, we have looked to immigration regulations as a means of solving problems associated with urbanization, industrialization, political corruption, economic recession, and America's perceived moral decline. In addition, immigrants today, particularly undocumented immigrants, are blamed for crime, drugs, educational overcrowding, unbalanced budgets, housing congestion, traffic, and terrorism. This is not to say that immigration is wholly unassociated with these issues or that an effective immigration regime will not help. Rather, the expectations of what immigration regulations can achieve, whether it be comprehensive immigration reform or perfect enforcement, are simply too high.

There are reasons to believe that such expectations are of particular concern for states. For state leaders, immigration has long been an effective means of deflecting attention away from past mistakes and hard decisions at times of crisis, not only because immigrants are easy to scapegoat but also because it makes local issues seem like federal problems and federal responsibilities. Indeed, the tactic of raising alarms about immigration at the state level has been employed during almost every recession as a means of compelling federal "reimbursement" to balance strained budgets; it was a major factor behind California's pursuit of Proposition 187.

More worrisome than state efforts to outsource their problems to the federal government as an immigration issue, however, is the prospect that states will then be inclined to "shirk" the important and critical role that they can play with respect to immigration and the fundamental problems that they wish to pass off as immigration issues. As Christina Rodriguez and Hiroshi Motomura have argued, states and localities are well situated to contribute to the process of assimilation and community building—roles vital to any well-functioning immigration regime.[11] Moreover, solutions to many of the problems now commonly attributed to immigration and immigrants are still best found at the state and local level. In a world of jurisdictional divide, this intergovernmental allocation problem may not arise. With increasing federal-state overlap not only on the issue of immigration but also more generally, the dangers of outsourcing and shirking are pronounced. By relying on this view of immigration, states risk overlooking the powers that they already have.

IV. Toward a More Integrated Conversation

The descriptive reframing thus far has largely relied on a neutral portrayal of state immigration regulations as a whole. But in so doing, it has not directly addressed what is for many the primary concern: States are making bad decisions. Arizona's immigration enforcement law will be a destructive and costly policy if it is ever allowed to be enforced as written. The nascent yet burgeoning state-led efforts to repeal the Fourteenth Amendment guarantee of birthright citizenship for American-born children of undocumented immigrants would pose even more disastrous long-term consequences if they were to succeed. To be sure, these represent but a few of the diverse and quite pragmatic state responses to immigration that have been considered and enacted. Yet that fact seems to offer little comfort when these severe measures are receiving the most attention and the most support. And as this chapter has argued, it might not actually matter whether state laws on immigration survive legal scrutiny, or even whether states truly intend to dedicate the resources to enforce them even if they could. Their very enactment is often sufficient to reshape the national conversation on immigration, and it is often in the federal laws to come that the most lasting legacy of these laws are made.

Given this scenario, it makes sense that the instinct for many has been to remove the states from involvement in this conversation. Their aim appears to be a return to a discourse located entirely at the national level and in a federal forum. This goal, of course, is not new, and history has shown it to be very difficult to implement through legal means. Yet, even if it were possible to achieve this goal, it is not necessarily clear that we would want to, especially in light of the structure of our federal system and the particularities of immigration as an issue. It may now be cliché, but the solution to "bad talk" in this regard may be to promote more talk, as well as to focus on the institutional structure of that relationship. States are fractured and often sufficiently diverse to produce robust conversations that are balanced, grounded, and rich. That they do not always produce such conversations is often a result of the restricted manner in which they are formally allowed into the larger conversation. Consequently, rather than trying to exclude the states from the conversation or marginalize their concerns in the name of federal exclusivity, it might be more productive to take affirmative steps to incorporate them directly into the discourse and promote them as a forum for conversations about immigration.

Such practices can arise even where they are least expected. Consider, for example, the federal 287(g) program, which authorizes federal immigration officials to enter into memorandums of understanding with state and local law enforcement officials to assist with the local enforcement of federal immigration laws under federal supervision. The intent of the program may have been simply to increase the national capacity for immigration enforcement by recruiting local law enforcement officials, especially as undocumented migrants are settling in areas where there is not yet a robust infrastructure for federal interior enforcement. The program has been abused in many jurisdictions, and has been subjected to a scathing internal investigation. But at the same time, as a mechanism of collaboration and negotiation, the formalization of this federal-local relationship has shown some promise. Rather than developing into a uniform enforcement dragnet involving local officials, the program seems to be evolving into a flexible and tailored approach to immigration enforcement; 287(g) participants have not only been sanctioned or removed for abuses but have also felt free to drop out when they perceived federal demands as endangering rather than enhancing local safety.[12] In the long run, it may be that such formal federal-state arrangement may curb excesses across the enforcement spectrum. The risk of immigration laws being used by local law enforcement to harass residents has been tempered by federal involvement. At the same time, federal inclination toward sensational and sometimes unwarranted employer raids and neighborhood sweeps may be moderated by the concerns of state and local law enforcement officials, given their long-term and ongoing relationship with the communities and given that immigration enforcement might be just one among many of their public safety priorities.

More effort, however, can be made to fully integrate the voice of states into the immigration conversation. Canada has moved in this direction by specifically allowing provincial governments to negotiate an accord with the national government with respect to immigration. This arrangement has not only given provinces some measure of control over national immigration policy as it pertains to them, but it has also given the national government more leeway in allocating the terms and responsibilities of provinces.[13] It may be too early to assess how well these arrangements will work in the long run. Yet, at this point it appears to be a more transparent and productive way of engaging states than the system we have now.

Let us be clear that even if one is not convinced about the benefits of state involvement, the choice as it now stands in our federal system does not appear to be a choice between state involvement or no state involvement. Given that prompting preemption challenges and instigating constitutional confrontations are part of the strategy of state engagement in the national discourse, I see no easy way of removing states entirely from the conversation. What I suggest here is that it may be better to engage the concerns of states openly and to utilize the states as a forum directly than to adhere dogmatically to a doctrinal presumption against state involvement that does not seem to serve its purpose and threatens to distort the conversation.

NOTES

1. *See, e.g.,* Robert A. Schapiro, Polyphonic Federalism 98–101, 104–8 (2009); Paul W. Kahn, Comment, *Interpretation and Authority in State Constitutionalism*, 106 Harv. L. Rev. 1147, 1161–63 (1993); Erin Ryan, *Negotiating Federalism*, 52 B.C. L. Rev. 1, 4–5 (2011); Jessica Bulman-Pozen & Heather K. Gerken, *Uncooperative Federalism*, 118 Yale L.J. 1256 1284–92 (2009).

2. United States v. Morrison, 529 U.S. 598, 599 (2000).

3. *See generally* Anne Marie Cammisa, Governments As Interest Groups: Intergovernmental Lobbying and the Federal System (1995).

4. *See* Heather K. Gerken, *Dissenting by Deciding*, 57 Stan. L. Rev. 1745, 1784 (2005).

5. *See generally* Bill Bishop, The Big Sort: Why the Clustering of Like-Minded America is Tearing us Apart (2008).

6. Richard Wright & Mark Ellis, *Race, Region, and the Territorial Politics of Immigration in the US*, 6 Int. J. Popul. Geogr. 197, 197 (2000).

7. Ariz. Rev. Stat. §§ 9-500.24, 11-269.08.

8. *See* Kevin R. Johnson, *Sweet Home Alabama? Immigration and Civil Rights in the "New" South*, 64 Stan. L. Rev. Online 22 (2011).

9. *See generally* Rick Su, *A Localist Reading of Local Immigration Regulations*, 86 N.C. L. Rev. 1619 (2008).

10. The Department of Homeland Security is required by federal law to respond to any and all inquiries in this regard. *See* 8 U.S.C. § 1373(c).

11. *See* Cristina M. Rodriguez, *The Significance of the Local in Immigration Regulation*, 106 Mich. L. Rev. 567, 581 (2008); Hiroshi Motomura, *Immigration outside the Law*, 108 Colum. L. Rev. 2037, 2077–78 (2008).

12. *See* Maria Sacchetti, *Agencies Halt Their Immigrant Scrutiny: Barnstable Sheriff, Framingham Police Say No*, Boston Globe, October 2, 2009, at 1.

13. *See* Organisation for Economic Co-operation and Development, OECD Territorial Reviews: Toronto, Canada 2009, at 119–20 (2009); Local Economic and Employment Development, From Immigration to Integration: Local Solutions to a Global Challenge 83, 127–28 (2006).

8

Post-Racial Proxy Battles over Immigration

MARY FAN

Introduction

Amid economic and political turmoil, anti-immigrant legislation has flared again among a handful of fiercely determined states.[1] To justify the intrusion into national immigration enforcement, the dissident states invoke imagery of invading hordes of "illegals"[2]—though the unauthorized population actually fell by nearly two-thirds, decreasing by about a million people, between 2007 and 2009 as the recession reduced the lure of jobs.[3]

Arizona's Senate Bill 1070—recently invalidated in part by the U.S. Supreme Court in *Arizona v. United States*[4]—led the charge.[5] By pre-election-year summer 2011, several states enacted laws patterned after Arizona's controversial Senate Bill 1070, including Alabama's even more aggressive HB 56.[6] A host of lawsuits are pending against the new laws,[7] which are at least partially invalid after *Arizona v. United States*. Other controversial proposals circulate, such as eliminating birthright citizenship or branding the birth certificates of alleged "anchor babies" implanted in the United States by foreigners.[8]

This chapter examines how the spurt of state legislation is a proxy way to vent resurgent racialized anxieties and engage in friend-enemy politics founded on conflict with the "Other"—the foreign enemy within—in a time of economic and political turmoil. Despite the ostensibly a-racial construct of the illegal alien used to legitimize the lashing out, it is suffused with racialized perception.[9] Current tactics parallel the overtly racialized hostility of past episodes of states enacting out anti-immigrant legislation. The oft-raised concern in such a fiercely polarized time is racial discrimination. Antidiscrimination law, however, does not offer the remedy for this concern.

The chapter explores alternate frames for rendering antidiscrimination commitments legally legible. Rather than striking dissident state immigration legislation because of the interests of "them"—the marginalized people most impacted by the laws—invalidation is grounded in shared interests and constitutional commitments. Convergent interests include the constitutionally designed balance of federal power on issues requiring coordinated rather than conflicting approaches. Such an approach mitigates polarization by making convergent interests, rather than racial divergence, salient. Hearteningly, recent landmark decisions, including *Arizona v. United States*, do not ignore antidiscrimination values. Rather, the decisions illuminate the shared interests impacted by discrimination concerns, such as impairment of foreign relations and commerce. This chapter analyzes the way antidiscrimination values inform preemption analyses used to invalidate encroaching state immigration laws fueled by fear and loathing.

Part 1 analyzes two hot-button forms of resurgent state and local anti-"alien" laws of our times—laws patterned on the Arizona template and the anti–birthright citizenship movement. It explores the dominance of racialized anxieties behind the seemingly race-neutral construct of the vilified alien. Part 2 contrasts the friend-enemy politics and legislation of our contemporary scene with the state and local legislation and furor against the Chinese during the turbulent politics of the last quarter of the nineteenth century. Part 3 examines the polarization-ameliorating bases for decisions to cut back on overreaching state and local laws in order to make shared interests, rather than racial difference, salient while protecting underlying antidiscrimination values. The approach helps build bridges between dissonant worldviews to navigate the profoundly polarized politics and legislation of our times.

I. The Resurgence of Aggressive State Anti-"Alien" Laws

Two of the most aggressive and controversial forms of state and local anti-immigrant legislation include (1) the "attrition-through-enforcement"-type laws patterned after Arizona Senate Bill 1070 that aim to drive out perceived aliens by creating a hostile environment through a multifront attack and (2) and the anti–birthright citizenship movement aimed against U.S.-born children of aliens.

A. The "Attrition-through-Enforcement" Attack Strategy

The strategy behind the "attrition through enforcement" approach is to create an atmosphere of fear that drives undocumented people to "self-deport." As the bill's cosponsor, Arizona State Representative John Kavanagh, explained, "it's about creating so much fear they will leave on their own."[10] The details of the laws vary somewhat, but they share a similar strategy of creating a totalizing atmosphere of hostility through a multipronged attack.

For example, Arizona's template law directs police to check immigration status during mundane traffic and other temporary stops if there is a "reasonable suspicion" of unlawful status.[11] Though it generally is not a crime for a removable alien to remain in the United States, the legislation also authorizes police to arrest people without warrant based on probable cause of removability due to commission of a public offense.[12] Reaching into private interactions, some of the new laws also criminalize such mundane but vital activities as job seeking by aliens, giving a ride or renting to a suspected undocumented person, or leaving home without carrying alien registration documents.[13]

To take Alabama's particularly aggressive example, the state's controversial House Bill 56 criminalized, among other things, transporting someone or entering into a rental agreement in "reckless disregard[]" of a person's undocumented status.[14] The controversial rental provision was later legislatively deleted in May 2012.[15] Plainly, the criminalization of such mundane things as giving rides or renting—without even requiring knowledge of undocumented status—chills interaction with people who might be undocumented. Alabama's legislation even reaches into the schoolhouse, requiring school officials to determine the immigration status of children.[16]

The laws press public officials and private actors—willing or not— into creating an atmosphere of surveillance and suspicion.[17] In the process, the laws upend previous policies aimed at building community trust.[18] To prevent the problem of crime victims fearing to turn to police or to bear witness, many police agencies have assured immigrant communities that they are not immigration-law enforcers.[19] Upending the wisdom built on experience, the new breed of laws bars police from nonparticipation in federal immigration enforcement.[20] Arizona's template law also authorizes warrantless arrests of persons the officer believes has committed "any public offense that makes the person removable from the United States."[21] The Arizona law also requires that law enforcement officers in any lawful stop, detention, or arrest attempt to determine immigration status if "reasonable suspicion exists that the person is an alien who is unlawfully present" unless "the determination may hinder or obstruct an investigation."[22]

As originally enacted, the law provided that officers "may not *solely* consider race, color or national origin,"[23] apparently taking advantage of the Supreme Court's 1975 decision in *United States v. Brignoni-Ponce* providing that race can be a relevant—albeit not sole—factor in establishing reasonable suspicion of alienage.[24] *Brignoni-Ponce* held that "[t]he likelihood that any given person of Mexican ancestry is an alien is high enough to make Mexican appearance a relevant factor, but standing alone it does not justify stopping all Mexican-Americans to ask if they are aliens."[25]

In response to the firestorm of controversy, the Arizona legislature amended Senate Bill 1070 to delete the adjective "solely."[26] As amended, the law provides that officials may not consider race, color, or national origin "except to the extent permitted by the United States or Arizona Constitution"[27]—which under *Brignoni-Ponce* means what the law said before: that race can be a relevant but not a sole factor.[28] The amendment gave Arizona some cover, however, in the ensuing political and legal battles. Indeed, the district court of Arizona apparently missed the wiggle clause and analyzed the law as if it barred consideration of race, color, or national origin.[29] The states claim that their legislation avoids impermissibly intruding on the federal power over foreign affairs,[30] foreign commerce,[31] and nationality rules[32] because they merely mirror and enforce federal standards.[33] A host of other provisions in the Arizona law were constructed as mirror images—in some instances imperfectly so—of federal immigration crimes in an attempt to further thrust Arizona into immigration law and policy.[34] The state law criminalizes failing to carry alien registration documents, transporting aliens, inducing aliens to enter Arizona, and employing illegal aliens, among other actions.[35] The act also goes further than federal law in criminalizing the actions of applying for work, soliciting work, or performing work by an undocumented person.[36]

Arizona's template for the new breed of state laws was fueled by incendiary politics painting Arizona as a state under siege. Bill sponsor Senator Pearce explained that his impetus was to stem the flood of Mexicans, proclaiming, "We have been overrun. . . . [M]illions more will come behind them, and we will be overrun to the point that there will no longer be a United States of America. . . . How long will it be before we will be just like Mexico?"[37] Arizona governor Jan Brewer proclaimed, "We cannot afford all this illegal immigration and everything that comes with it, everything from the crime and [sic] to the drugs and the kidnappings and the extortion and the beheadings and the fact that people can't feel safe in their community."[38] The president of the Arizona Sheriff's Association, Paul Babeu, also helped sound the crime and immigration alarm, telling FOX News that criminal "illegals" were to blame for Arizona having "the highest crime rates in America."[39]

In reality, Arizona is experiencing as much of a decline in crime as the national average, if not more.[40] Figures 8.1 and 8.2 plot crime rate data from the FBI's Uniform Crime Reports for Arizona compared to the nation as a whole. As depicted, Arizona's crime rate, like that of the nation overall, has been falling dramatically in recent years. Indeed, in 2009, Arizona enjoyed a lower violent crime rate than the nation overall. And while the curve for Arizona's property crime rate has been higher than the national average, by 2009, the gap was narrowing because Arizona has experienced a steeper decline in property crimes than the national average.

Indeed, sociologists have argued that rather than aggravating crime, immigrants have a "protective" effect against crime. The protective effect stems from such factors as immigrants diluting violent street culture

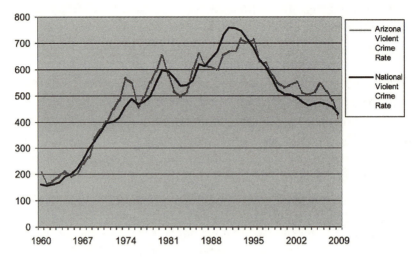

Figure 8.1. Arizona vrs. national violent crime rate per 100,000 of the poplulation.

with new norms: downplaying violence as the appropriate response to perceived slights, emphasizing strong family and ethnic ties, and revitalizing abandoned or malaised neighborhoods.[41] A new study using pooled time-series cross-sectional data found that cities with the greatest declines in homicides and robberies had the largest influx of immigrants.[42] But perception—and social cascades of misperception spurred by opinion leaders—are what count in politics. And the immigration-crime paradigm helped spur passage of Arizona Senate Bill 1070.

The Arizona attrition attack strategy is not the first of recent state legislation attempting to intervene in regulating immigrant life. During another intense anti-immigrant political broil, for example, Arizona enacted the Legal Arizona Workers Act of 2007.[43] The law makes it a state-law offense to "knowingly" or "intentionally" employ "an unauthorized alien," defined so as to incorporate the federal-law definition of illegal status.[44] The law also mandates that employers verify the employment eligibility of new hires using the E-Verify system,[45] though under federal law, E-Verify is only a voluntary-use pilot program, in part because of concerns about the risk of error and resultant discrimination. The mandates are backed by penalties centered on licensing revocation, relying on a savings clause for "licensing and similar laws" in the

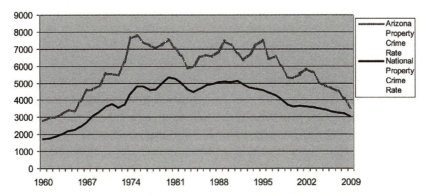

Figure 8.2. Arizona vrs. national property crime rate per 100,000 of the poplulation.

express preemption provision of the federal Immigration Reform and Control Act (IRCA). The Supreme Court ruled that the law was valid under the licensing savings clause, noting that the law was confined to licensing of in-state businesses, not an area of traditional federal dominance.[46]

The distinguishing aspect of the new breed of laws, however, is the multifront attack with the aim of "attrition" —interfering in the admission and expulsion of suspected aliens—by rendering suspected foreigners into an untouchable caste.[47] Because of the prevalence of race, language, and culture-based heuristics for outsider alienage—cognitive rules of thumb that may generate persistent biases—the laws sweep overbroadly to impact people perceived as foreign, even if lawfully present. Concern over the impact on people perceived as foreign has roused protest not only within the United States but also abroad, interfering with diplomatic relations.[48]

Decades ago, the Supreme Court explained that in enacting a uniform national immigration system, Congress manifested the purpose of leaving the law-abiding "free from the possibility of inquisitorial practices and police surveillance. . . ."[49] The new breed of laws aggressively transgresses this approach in aiming for an atmosphere of fear and hostility that impacts not only those who are unlawfully present but also those who are suspected to be so because of race, culture, and language.

B. *The Attack on U.S.-Born Children of Noncitizen Parents*

Another movement afoot is the attack on U.S.-born children of alien parents. Proponents would overrule longstanding Supreme Court precedent and rewrite the Constitution to deny citizenship to native-born people whose parents are noncitizens.[50] The movement capitalizes on anti–illegal alien hostility to claim a righteous struggle against the sinister, sneaking "anchor baby" and the alleged incentive to enter the United States illegally in order to gain birthright citizenship for the baby.[51] But behind the anti–"illegal alien invasion" banner, the movement has an even more aggressive aim.

Proponents argue that even native U.S.-born children of many lawfully present noncitizens should not be birthright citizens.[52] Legislative proposals aim to exclude children of parents lawfully present on temporary visas.[53] Most broadly, theorists trying to justify the attack suggest that children of foreign nationals in general, lawfully present or not, are ineligible for birthright citizenship.[54] Proponents would exclude from the purview of the Fourteenth Amendment's Citizenship Clause, for example, first-generation Americans, such as this writer, born of people who lawfully immigrated to America to attend school or lawfully reside in America on work visas. The scope of the attack shows the enduring wisdom behind Martin Niemöller's poem that begins, "First they came for the [vilified group] and I did not speak out / Because I was not a [member of the vilified group]." The poem ends, "Then they came for me—and there was no one left to speak for me."

To achieve their aim, proponents strain constitutional text and seek to overrule Framer intent, longstanding precedent, and the progress of American history and antidiscrimination values. Forged in the post–Civil War era of progress in humanity and equality values, Section 1 of the Fourteenth Amendment provides, "All persons born or naturalized in the United States, and subject to the jurisdiction thereof, are citizens of the United States and of the state wherein they reside."[55] Automatic citizenship for U.S.-born people bound the nation to the mast against the demons of racial loathing and caste carving that resulted in decisions such as *Dred Scott v. Sandford*, ruling that descendants of African slaves, even if emancipated, cannot be citizens.[56]

The criterion that U.S.-born people must be "subject to the jurisdiction" of the United States is a narrow exception to birthright citizenship for the children of foreign ambassadors, hostile enemies in occupation, and Native Americans of sovereign tribes not taxed. The scope of the restrictive clause was settled by the Supreme Court's decision in *United States v. Wong Kim Ark* in 1868.[57] The Court ruled that a Chinese American born in the United States to legal permanent resident parents was a U.S. citizen within the meaning of the Fourteenth Amendment.[58]

Wong Kim Ark linked the interests of first-generation Chinese with those of first-generation Europeans in explaining its interpretation of the Citizenship Clause. The Court reasoned, "To hold that the fourteenth amendment of the constitution excludes from citizenship the children born in the United States of citizens or subjects of other countries, would be to deny citizenship to thousands of persons of English, Scotch, Irish, German, or other European parentage, who have always been considered and treated as citizens of the United States."[59] The Court concluded that whatever the animosities that led the political branches to exclude Chinese, the judiciary branch must "give full effect to the peremptory and explicit language" of the Fourteenth Amendment.[60]

Latter-day revisionists argue that the notion of citizenship flowing from birth within the dominion (*jus soli*) is a feudal notion that clashes with American values. They argue for citizenship based on consent of the subject and of the nation. While they claim that this is a progressive vision, it is in actuality a cruelly regressive attempt to unbind ourselves from the mast of interests joined across racial lines that has weathered the shifting racial animosities of the day. Community consent to belonging is influenced strongly by race. Without the automaticity of place of birth as a unifying force of belonging, there is a danger that racial fear and loathing would split the nation.

Campaigners against U.S.-born children of noncitizens are also wrong in oversimplifying the choice as between a supposed outmoded feudal concept and the purported progressive notion of consent. The heritage and purpose of American birthright citizenship is not the feudal tradition of the past but rather the realization that leaving citizenship to the vagaries of racial animosities would lose the progress hard won in the Civil War that ravaged the nation.

II. Friend-Enemy Politics

In another society under strain, riven by economic woes and fierce doubt, Carl Schmitt argued that the fundamental distinction on which political life rests is that of friend and enemy.[61] The enemy is "the other, the stranger; and it is sufficient for his nature that he is, in a specially intense way, existentially something different and alien, so that in the extreme case, conflicts with him are possible."[62] As for the friend side of the equation, the "us" in a democratic polity, Schmitt argued that homogeneity was crucial and necessitated—"if the need arises—elimination or eradication of heterogeneity."[63] He cited as examples the expulsion of the Greeks from Turkey and the prevalence of national laws, such as those of Australia at the time, restricting immigrants to the "right type of settler."[64]

Schmitt wrote during the economic travails of the Weimar Republic preceding the Third Reich, for which he would be later the "crown jurist."[65] He openly voiced a logic that flares with particular ferocity when nations struggle with economic travails and doubts. In the past and our present, the political[66] and the polity reinvigorate in times of doubt and turmoil through conflict with the "Other" and attempts to purge this foreign enemy within. Dissident political groups try to rouse support against current power holders using a rallying cry of threat with an explicitly or implicitly racialized face. This process of pronounced differentiation is a means through which faith and fervor in an "us" as an identity is regenerated despite the travails of the times.

Those vilified and used to define the boundary between our national "us" and the threatening "Other" have historically taken different—generally raced—forms. Nativists of the past have vilified the Italians, Jews, Eastern Europeans, Irish, Blacks, Japanese, and Chinese, among others.[67] Demonstrating the acutely racialized nature of animosity, out-group Caucasians were often not perceived as white but instead as degraded "swarthy types" in the Social Darwinian scale.[68] In this multitextured history of animosity, the story of the intensification of hostility and state and local laws against the Chinese in California around the time of the severe recession of the 1870s has resonances with, and insights for, our contemporary political and legal scene.

A. Déjà Vu Politics

In 1878, Representative Horace Davis of California said of the "Chinaman,"

> Twenty-eight years ago the pioneer Chinaman was welcomed with an eager curiosity, but with no foresight of the eventful consequences of his coming. To-day, he is found in every village, in every mining camp, utterly an alien in the body-politic, and like some foreign substance in the human body, breeding fever and unrest till that system is relieved of its unwelcome presence.[69]

Times were getting tougher after the boom years of the 1850s drew the Chinese to the gold fields, swamps, and mountains of California to clear the land and lay the tracks for the then-expanding economy. By the time of the severe recession that seized the United States in the 1870s, "many thousands of unemployed men" were saying "with great bitterness that but for [the Chinese] presence work and bread would be plenty."[70] The Chinese were accused of degrading labor and displacing white workers, of being by nature "voluntary slaves," capable of subsisting and living cheaply like vermin.[71] Opponents warned that masses of Chinese would render America an "Asiatic state."[72] The fear over the racial transformation of the nation and states presents a parallel with contemporary fears, voiced, for example, by Senator Russell Pearce, sponsor of Arizona Senate Bill 1070, of America being "overrun" by "illegal aliens" and transformed into Mexico.[73]

In another tactic with parallels to our present, the vilified alien "Chinaman" was associated with crime; advocates of anti-Chinese legislation warned that China was sending masses of its unwanted criminals.[74] The Chinese were accused of, among other things, selling and buying their women, gambling, prostitution, thievery, and violence against whites.[75]

In a third striking parallel with our present, fractious political groups campaigned against the presidential administration tenuously in power by whipping up anti-immigrant sentiment. In the last quarter of the nineteenth century, national politics were closely divided, with control of Congress and the presidency frequently shifting between the two parties.[76] Two "minority presidents" failed to win a majority of the vote and two presidents were elected on close splits, with a bare majority of less than twenty-five thousand votes.[77] In an example of the tactics of the anti-administration reform politics of the era, a "Committee of Fifty" assembled in San Francisco decried the president and national government for "wantonly den[ying] to the people of the Pacific . . . relief from a scourge that menaces their very existence"—the "invasion of the subjects of the Mongolian empire."[78] They castigated the Republican presidents for opposing their calls to purge the Chinese, ignoring their "pleading for deliverance."[79]

B. Déjà Vu Laws

In this foment of overtly racialized hostility, state and local laws were deployed in an attempt to expel the Chinese through direct and indirect methods. These state immigration interventions sometimes tried to skirt and sometimes unabashedly usurped the federal power over foreign commerce and admission of aliens.

In 1849, the Supreme Court held in *The Passenger Cases* that states may not interfere with the federal power to regulate foreign commerce by imposing passenger head taxes on ships entering a port.[80] In one of eight opinions in the case, Justice McLean suggested that while "the municipal power of a State cannot prohibit the introduction of foreigners brought to this country under the authority of Congress," the state could "guard its citizens against diseases and paupers" by denying foreigners residence unless "security" was posted "to indemnify the public should they become paupers."[81] Apparently acting on this suggestion, in 1852 the California legislature enacted a law requiring a bond of five hundred dollars per noncitizen passenger.[82]

By 1855, the legislature had gotten bolder and enacted a direct tax titled "An Act to Discourage the Immigration to This State of Persons Who Cannot Become Citizens Thereof"[83]—in other words, to discourage the immigration of nonwhites because, since 1790, Congress had limited naturalization to "a free white person."[84] The 1855 California law required ship masters or owners to pay a fifty-dollar head tax for any person "incompetent" to become a citizen.[85] This unsubtle law was struck down two years later by the California Supreme Court in *People v. Downer*, which arose from an action to exact $12,750 from a ship bearing Chinese passengers.[86]

Undaunted, the California legislature in 1858 enacted another unsubtle law in an attempt to steer immigration policy—"An Act to Prevent the Further Immigration of Chinese or Mongolians to This State"—which forbade Chinese or Mongolians from entering the state or its ports.[87] The act made it a misdemeanor, punishable by fine or imprisonment for three months to a year, for Chinese to land or to bring Chinese in.[88] When California attempted to enforce the law, the California Supreme Court declared it void and unconstitutional in an opinion never reported.[89]

In 1876, the U.S. Supreme Court invalidated a modified version of the California statute requiring the posting of a $500 bond for every incoming passenger that a state-appointed "Commissioner of Immigration" deemed "lunatic, idiotic, deaf, dumb, blind, crippled, or infirm," a convict or "lewd or debauched woman," or otherwise "a public charge, or likely soon to become so."[90] Justice Field, riding circuit, had earlier ordered the release of Chinese women held under the statute as an impermissible state interference with the exclusive federal power over "the intercourse of foreigners with our people, their immigration to this country and residence therein."[91]

Enfolded in Justice Field's analysis were burgeoning equality concerns. He stated that anti-Chinese feelings could not "justify any legislation for their exclusion, which might not be adopted against the inhabitants of the most favored nations of the Caucasian race, and of Christian faith."[92] He deplored the discriminatory application of laws by state officials who were "shocked when a frail child of China is landed on our shores, and yet allow[] the bedizened and painted harlot of other countries to parade our streets and open her hells in broad day, without molestation and without censure."[93] He suggested that an alternative basis for invalidating the legislation was the newly enacted legislation of 1870, implementing the equal protection guarantee of the recently adopted Fourteenth Amendment.[94] In *Chy Lung v. Freeman*, a unanimous Supreme Court ruled that the law impermissibly interfered with the power of Congress to regulate commerce with foreign nations, reasoning in essence that one state could not inflict nationwide externalities marring foreign relations and trade.[95]

While the Court did not address the discrimination argument Justice Field had made, it obliquely deplored the "extraordinary statute" that gave the commissioner arbitrary discretion to require bonds for any passenger who appeared to him to be an "idiot" or a potential "pauper" or "lewd woman."[96] Such unbounded discretion opened the door to "systematic extortion of the grossest kind," the Court wrote.[97] The specter of discrimination was thus obliquely acknowledged in the guise of concern over the law's conferral of open-ended discretion through the use of vague terms. *Chy Lung's* arbitrariness analysis was thus an intriguing precursor to vagueness doctrine cases a century later, such as *Papachristou v. Jacksonville*, which addressed antidiscrimination concerns in the guise of arbitrariness and vagueness analysis.[98]

The legislature and localities also tried alternative ways to drive out the Chinese, such as through licensing, taxes, and employment and housing laws.

California was particularly hard hit by the 1870s recession, the worst the fledgling nation had experienced, and widespread unemployment, mortgage foreclosures, and homelessness stirred radical reactions and calls for state constitutional reform.[99] The anti-Chinese campaign was intensifying, stirred by rabble rousers such as Dennis Kearney of the self-styled "Workingmen's Party."[100] The resulting revised California Constitution of 1879 included an article, simply titled "Chinese," that forbade corporations from employing any Chinese or Mongolian and forbade the employment of Chinese in any state, county, municipal, or other public work "except in punishment for crime."[101] Lest there be any doubt about the intent behind the legislation, the final section declared, "The presence of foreigners ineligible to become citizens of the United States is declared to be dangerous to the well-being of the State, and the Legislature shall discourage their immigration by all the means within its power."[102]

In response, the legislature enacted laws criminalizing the employment of Chinese on pain of fines, imprisonment of at least two hundred days and up to two years, and, upon a second conviction, forfeiture of the corporate charter, franchise, and privileges.[103] Businessman Tiburcio Parrott was imprisoned for an alleged violation of the law.[104] He appealed his conviction, arguing first that the anti-Chinese law was void because it violated the Fourteenth Amendment and legislation implementing the equal protection guarantee.[105] Two judges wrote for the federal Circuit Court for the District of California, which invalidated the conviction and voided the anti-Chinese employment laws. Judge Hoffman noted, in an early interest-tying type of argument, that the law "might equally well have forbidden the employment of Irish, or Germans, or Americans, or persons of color, or it might have required the employment of any of these classes of persons to the exclusion of the rest."[106]

Judge Hoffman ultimately framed his decision, however, not in the violation of the rights of the Chinese but in the violation of the rights of corporations, many of which, he noted, had ceased operations or faced closure if the anti-Chinese laws were enforced.[107] He held that the right of corporations "to utilize their property, by employing such laborers as they choose" could not be overridden by the prohibited purpose of driving the Chinese out.[108] Judge Sawyer, in contrast, was less shy about directly ruling that the California law was in violation of treaty protections, as well as the Fourteenth Amendment and laws implementing the Fourteenth Amendment that gave "all persons" the "same right" to make and enforce contracts and enjoy "full and equal benefit of all laws."[109]

These skirmishes with aggressive state anti-immigrant legislation thus enfolded antidiscrimination concerns within alternate frames of invalidation that made shared interests in foreign commerce and vibrant business salient. The deployment of alternate frames for vindicating antidiscrimination values helped transition a fractured and polarized polity in a time of social strain. These alternate modes of analysis underscored the shared interests at stake in ameliorating the harsh state legislation. Ultimately, these transitional frames paved the way for the development of antidiscrimination doctrine—including *Yick Wo v. Hopkins*, which invalidated the selective prosecution of Chinese laundry operators on equal protection grounds.[110] The Supreme Court famously held,

> Though the law itself be fair on its face, and impartial in appearance, yet, if it is applied and administered by public authority with an evil eye and an unequal hand, so as practically to make unjust and illegal discriminations between persons in similar circumstances, material to

their rights, the denial of equal justice is still within the prohibition of the constitution.[111]

The many skirmishes with aggressive state legislation directly or indirectly interfering with the admission and expulsion of the Chinese had sensitized the judicial eye to the underlying impact and intent behind formal legal guises.

Part of the point of examining the history of unruly state and local passions is to show how even as law evolves, new forms can be vehicles for old impulses to drive out racially distinctive others. The lesson is important for our avowedly "postracial" times when racialized anxieties cannot be voiced openly aloud and must be dressed in legitimizing constructs that still pursue old goals.

III. Alternate Frames for Antidiscrimination Values

While the legislation creating proxy vehicles for venting racialized animosities rightly rouse fears of racialized harms, antidiscrimination law supplies scant succor. The Equal Protection Clause has a very high hurdle for plaintiffs to surmount, requiring proof of discriminatory intent behind the law[112] or discrimination in the claimant's case, if discriminatory application is alleged.[113] Savvy officials socialized in contemporary forms and conventions of behavior generally no longer provide such blatant evidence.

Moreover, the Equal Protection Clause's conscious-purpose standard altogether neglects the problems of implicit bias or racialized anxieties and angers that are unconscious or not fully acknowledged to ourselves but that nonetheless generate racialized harm.[114] Constitutional criminal-procedure protections also offer no succor for racial harms because criminal-procedure doctrine simply directs claimants to the strictures and blind spots of equal protection doctrine.[115] Antidiscrimination concerns can, however, inform alternate frames for assessing the validity of the laws. The dangers of discrimination posed by the most aggressive forms of new state laws can conflict with the balance struck by federal law between enforcement and antidiscrimination and be impliedly preempted. The risk of harm against suspected foreign nationals poses foreign policy complications that impermissibly intrude on the federal power over foreign affairs. And the unleashing of discriminatory exclusion posed by the campaign against native-born children of noncitizens should inform interpretation of constitutional text framed to protect against the dangers of carving out a lower caste.

A. Informing Conflict Analyses

The recent opinion in *Arizona v. United States* offers excellent examples of how preemption analysis can reframe—and be enriched by—the shared interest in antidiscrimination values. Writing for the Court in affirming the invalidation of three controversial provisions of Arizona Senate Bill 1070, Justice Kennedy captured the harms to the national interest posed by the new state immigration laws. In crafting the opinion, Justice Kennedy took care to explain how federal coordination and control in setting immigration policy serve shared national interests. He explained that the "broad, undoubted power" of the national government over immigration policy benefits "trade, investment, tourism and diplomatic relations for the entire Nation, as well as the perceptions and expectations of aliens in this country who seek the full protection of its laws."[116] National enforcement discretion served shared interests in "this Nation's international relations" and "immediate human concerns."[117] This approach deftly linked individual and collective interests and harms.

Portions of Justice Kennedy's preemption analysis explained how the risk of harassment of disfavored groups also impaired national interests. He began the opinion by explaining the longstanding wisdom that "[o]ne of the most important and delicate of all international relationships . . . has to do with protection of the just rights of a country's own nationals when those nationals are in another country."[118] Invalidating § 6 of the Arizona law, he noted that allowing state officers the power to arrest aliens on the basis of their assessment of removability—in disregard of federal procedures and safeguards—risked "unnecessary harassment of some aliens (for instance, a veteran, college student, or someone assisting with a criminal investigation) whom federal officials determine should not be removed."[119] The conflicting state provision presented an obstacle to the full design and purposes of federal law and the important national interests served by entrusting removal to the procedures and discretion of national enforcers.

At this early juncture, Justice Kennedy did not invalidate § 2(B) of the Arizona law, which requires state officials to make reasonable attempts to check the immigration status of any person stopped and detained or arrested on reasonable suspicion of unlawful alien status.[120] Noting the "basic uncertainty about what the law means and how it will be enforced" at this early stage, he stated that the opinion did not "foreclose other preemption and constitutional challenges to the law as interpreted and applied after it goes into effect."[121] Nevertheless, he gave Arizona incentive to construe the law in a manner that mitigates the risk of harassment and prolonged detention.

He warned that "[d]etaining individuals solely to verify their immigration status would raise constitutional concerns" and referred to the line of cases invalidating prolonged detention after formally valid (and potentially pretextual) stops.[122] He also noted that the opinion did not address "whether reasonable suspicion of illegal entry or another immigration crime would be a legitimate basis for prolonging a detention, or whether this too would be preempted by federal law."[123] Thus, though the opinion did not directly address the great fear sparking waves of protests across the nation that people would be harassed on the basis of racial, linguistic, and cultural heuristics for "looking illegal," it gave Arizona incentive to mitigate this concern. This warning was a judicial nudge rather than a dictate, leaving states space to develop policies while relying on the utility of uncertainty to provide incentive not to transgress constitutional values.[124]

B. The Virtues of Alternate Frames for Equality Values

Alternate frames can make shared interests rather than racial difference and divergence of interests salient, helping ameliorate inflamed perceptions. We become particularly parochial and polarized during times of economic and political turmoil, and resort to the politics of ferocity toward the threatening Other to rally a fearful, fractured, and doubting polity. Racial differentiation and divergence of interests become particularly salient and can operate as blinders. Negative stereotypes can be particularly pronounced.

Studies have found that an "ego threat" to self-regard activates negative ethnic stereotypes and heightens prejudice against out-groups.[125]

Social psychologists have theorized that part of the function of negative stereotypes is to help bolster self-regard.[126] It is particularly important in such times for law to help deactivate the tendency to resort to heightened out-group vilification and remind us of common ground and interest convergence.

Invalidating the Arizona-style attrition-through-fear laws based on foreign affairs conflict, as proposed by concurring Judge Noonan in *United States v. Arizona*,[127] makes shared interests salient. Legislation is invalidated not to "accommodate" the minorities against the majority will, but to preserve shared interests in unimpaired commerce and international cooperation on important issues such as counternarcotics and counterterrorism. Ultimately, Justice Kennedy's opinion for the Court in *Arizona v. United States* eloquently rendered antidiscrimination norms majoritarian. Vindicating antidiscrimination norms did not entail a countermajoritarian pitting of an out-group's interests against the desires of an already-riled polity. Rather, vindicating antidiscrimination interests was about vindicating the shared interest in federal structure and not allowing a patchwork of rogue jurisdictions to undermine a carefully crafted national balance.

Another virtue of alternate frames is the ability to bridge across disparate worldviews.[128] Someone with a hierarchical worldview, for example, might value federalism structure and foreign affairs power even if the protection of underprivileged minorities does not have strong appeal. Someone with an individualistic orientation may find resonant due process concerns against arbitrary and unchecked government power, whereas the notion that individual interests should give way to antidiscrimination and equality interests could be riling. Alternate frames for antidiscrimination norms can thus help communicate the import of these interests to the fractious skeptical whose support is most needed.

Why should the palatability of bases for decisions matter to courts, which, after all, are customarily conceived as set above the political fray?[129] To be effective and realized in reality, decisions need to be socially contextualized. For the values implanted by courts to be realized in practice, they must take root and be accepted by the polity. Part of the art of crafting a judgment is to implant ideas that cultivate affinity among those who disagree.[130] Judges adjudicating some of the most heated questions in our society must craft their standards carefully, cognizant of the risk of backlash and resistance that entrench the very attitudes and legislation that their decisions are trying to ameliorate.[131] The risk of resistance and divergence between pronouncement and practice is particularly acute on polarizing issues in polarized times.

Commentators have argued in different registers about the value of grounding equality interventions in shared interests.[132] In the context of the African American struggle for equality, Derrick Bell argued that progress toward racial equality "will be accommodated only when it converges with the interests of whites."[133] He recalled how couching the import of enforcing school desegregation orders in terms of federalism principles and respect for the courts' role of interpreting law had more widespread appeal.[134] In contrast, racial divergence in interests would undermine realization of equality protections, despite normative commitments and claims.[135] Early campaigners for civil rights also apparently recognized the import of making interest-convergence arguments. For example, countering the spate of anti-Chinese laws, Dr. J. G. Kerr wrote, "In this warfare against the Chinese, the rights and liberty of the white man are just as much at stake as those of the Chinaman. Both must stand or fall together."[136] While Bell's theory was positivistic, describing the world as it *is* rather than as it *ought* to be, there are prescriptive ramifications to the insight about behavior. As a pragmatic matter, choosing frames that make interest convergence salient is a way to better secure necessary majoritarian support for decisions vindicating equality values.

Besides appealing externally to the polity, alternate frames that make social cohesion and interest convergence salient may also appeal internally to judicial centrists. Reva Siegel recently has illuminated how "racial moderates" on the Supreme Court adhere to an "antibalkinization perspective" that "privileges laws that expressively affirm universalism and commonality rather than difference and division."[137] This preference for approaches that ameliorate estrangement and division may also influence the approach taken to claims of harm posed by laws facially framed in terms of immigration status, but that have a tense relationship with race. Judicial decision making is often a group project wherein internal consensus as well as external consensus must be cultivated. A more palatable pathway that underscores interest convergence rather than difference may thus have the double benefit of securing broader judicial as well as popular support.

The danger of alternate frames is that they may be used to avoid addressing altogether what is often the biggest concern regarding anti-immigrant laws—the risk of racialized harms. Indeed, particularly in polarized and fierce times and contexts, there may be a desire to eschew or elide the vexing and ire-rousing concerns. Who wants to open Pandora's Box, or even slightly raise the lid, when times are tough enough? This approach, however, allows wounds to fester wholly unaired and emboldens the angry and anxious to enact intensifying and multifarious vehicles for venting ire at the expense of out-groups. Alternate frames are constructive rather than destructive when they take into account antidiscrimination concerns and address them in ways that are more palatable across worldviews and less polarizing—not when they ignore some of the biggest concerns altogether.

Conclusion

History's repetitions, in different registers and legal forms, teach us the dangers of overreaching state and local laws used to vent frustrations on out-groups whose members are either overtly or implicitly racialized. In times of fierce politics, the form and mode of judicial intervention to curb divisive and destructive excesses matters. We must be attentive to how to manage the inflammation of feeling that gives rise to the surge of problematic laws. Unity-reinforcing frames of analysis such as preemption doctrine can be deployed in a manner that renders salient in more palatable fashion previous national commitments to antidiscrimination values and help foster the polarization-amelioration and cooperation necessary to curb the excesses and inflamed perceptions of the times.

Closing his opinion for the Court, Justice Kennedy eloquently counseled the wisdom of temperance and deliberation in the fierce and fractious domain:

> With power comes responsibility, and the sound exercise of national power over immigration depends on the Nation's meeting its responsibility to base its laws on a political will informed by searching, thoughtful,

rational civic discourse. Arizona may have understandable frustrations with the problems caused by illegal immigration while that process continues, but the State may not pursue policies that undermine federal law.[138]

As the nation continues to fiercely debate immigration policies, this wisdom provides an important guide for the future in this fractious domain.

NOTES

This chapter is updated and adapted from Mary D. Fan, *Post-Racial Proxies: Resurgent State and Local Anti-Alien Laws and Unity-Rebuilding Frames for Antidiscrimination Values*, 32 Cardozo L. Rev. 905 (2011).

1. *See* Jeffrey S. Passel & D'Vera Cohn, *U.S. Unauthorized Immigration Flows Are Down Sharply since Mid-Decade*, Pew Hispanic Ctr., i, iii, 1–2 (Sept. 1, 2010), http://pewhispanic.org/files/reports/126.pdf (reporting substantial decrease). Unauthorized migration tends to ebb and flow with the ups and downs of the economies of the United States and Mexico. *See* Douglas S. Massey et al., Beyond Smoke and Mirrors: Mexican Immigration in an Era of Economic Integration 111 (2002); Jeffrey S. Passel & Roberto Suro, *Rise, Peak, and Decline: Trends in U.S. Immigration 1992–2004*, Pew Hispanic Ctr., 2–3, 10–11 (Sept. 27, 2005), http://pewhispanic.org/files/reports/53.pdf.

2. Now a noun signifying banned people. *See* Oxford English Dictionary Online (2010), http://oed.com (defining the noun "illegal" to mean "illegal immigrant").

3. Compare Pew Hispanic Ctr. 2010 Report, supra note 1, at i–ii, 1 (decrease data), with, e.g., Russell Pearce, *Enough Is Enough*, http://www.russellpearce.com (follow "SB 1070" hyperlink) (last visited Oct. 8, 2010) (arguing the United States is "overrun" by Mexicans).

4. Arizona v. United States, 132 S. Ct. 2492 (2012).

5. United States v. Arizona, 703 F. Supp. 2d 980, 985, 987, 1008 (D. Ariz. 2010).

6. *E.g.,* Beason-Hammon Alabama Taxpayer & Citizen Protection Act of 2011, HB 56, (Ala.), §§ 4–5, 13–18 (2011); Illegal Immigration Reform and Enforcement Act of 2011, HB 87 (Ga.), § 3, 7–8, 20 (2011); SB 590 (Ind.), ch. 19, § 5, § § 16–26, 21, 24 (2011); Utah Illegal Immigration Enforcement Act of 2011, HB 497 (Utah), §§ 3, 4, 8, 10, 11(5) (2011). A number of these laws have been the subject of litigation, and some have been enjoined.

7. *E.g.,* Hispanic Interest Coalition v. Bentley, Case No. 5:11-CV-2484-SLB (N.D. Ala. Aug. 29, 2011); Georgia Latino Alliance for Human Rights v. Deal, No. 1:11-cv-1804-TWT (N.D. Ga. 2011); Buquer v. City of Indianapolis, No. 1:11-cv-708-SEB-MJD (S.D. Ind. 2011); Parsley v. Bentley, No. 5:11-cv-24 02736 (N.D.

Ala. 2011); United States v. State of Alabama, No.2:11-cv-02746-WMA (N.D. Ala.); Utah Coalition of La Raza v. Herbert, No. 2:11-cv-401 CW (D. Utah).

8. *See, e.g.,* Julia Preston, *Citizenship as Birthright Is Challenged on the Right,* N.Y. Times, Aug. 7, 2010, at A8 (reporting on proposal to eliminate birthright citizenship for children of illegal immigrants and frustration over "anchor babies"); Alia Beard Rau, *Migrant Hard-Liners' Next Target: High Court,* Ariz. Republic, Sept. 12, 2010, at A1 (reporting on Arizona proposal to add notation to birth certificates).

9. Kevin R. Johnson, *The New Nativism: Something Old, Something New, Something Borrowed, Something Blue,* in Immigrants Out! The New Nativism and the Anti-Immigrant Impulse in the United States 165, 171 (Juan F. Perea ed., 1997); *see also, e.g.,* Mae M. Ngai, Impossible Subjects: Illegal Aliens and the Making of Modern America (2004) (tracing the history of how Mexicans emerged as "the iconic illegal alien").

10. *Many Migrants, Legal and Illegal, Say They Are Planning to Leave State,* Ariz. Rep., April 28, 2010, at A1.

11. Ariz. Rev. Stat. § 11-1051(B) (codifying Ariz. S.B. 1070, § 2(B)) (directing officers to make a reasonable attempt to check immigration status of people stopped, detained, or arrested and authorizing arrest if an officer has probable cause to believe a person committed any public offense rendering him or her removable from the United States).

12. Ariz. Rev. Stat. §§ 11-1051(B), 13-3883(A) (codifying Ariz. S.B. 1070, §§ 2(B), 6). *See also* Arizona v. United States, 132 S. Ct. 2492, 2505 (2012) (noting that it generally is not a crime for removable aliens to remain in the United States and explaining the typical removal procedures).

13. *See, e.g.,* Ariz. Rev. Stat. §§ 11-1509(A), 13-2928(C) (codifying Ariz. S.B. 1070, §§ 3, 5(C)) (creating the state misdemeanor crimes of job seeking by unauthorized aliens and willful failure to carry alien registration documents); Beason-Hammon Alabama Taxpayer and Citizen Protection Act, H.B. 56, 2011 Leg., Reg. Sess. §§ 10, 11, 13(3), (4) (2011) (criminalizing job seeking by unauthorized aliens; failure to carry alien registration documents; and renting or transporting people in reckless disregard of potential unlawful status); S.C. S20, 2011–2012 119th Leg. Sess., §§ 4(B), (D), 5 (criminalizing transporting or giving shelter to unlawful aliens in reckless disregard of unlawful status with intent to further the unlawful entry or avoid apprehension or detection of the unlawful immigration status and criminalizing as a misdemeanor the failure to carry a certificate of alien registration). For an overview see Mary D. Fan, *Rebellious State Crimmigration Enforcement and the Foreign Affairs Power,* 89 Wash. U. L. Rev. 1269 (2012).

14. Beason-Hammon Alabama Taxpayer and Citizen Protection Act, H.B. 56, 2011 Leg., Reg. Sess. § 13(3), (4) (2011) [hereinafter Ala. HB 56].

15. Ala. HB 658, 2012 Leg., Reg. Sess. §31-13-13 (2012).

16. Ala. HB 56, § 28.

17. *E.g.,* Ala. HB 56, §§ 5, 12, 18; Ariz. S.B. 1070, § 2(A), (B); Ind. SB 590, §§ 2–3, ch. 18(3), ch. 19(5); Utah HB 497, § 3, 6.

18. See Brief for The Center on the Administration of Criminal Law as Amicus Curiae in Support of Plaintiff's Motion for a Preliminary Injunction at 11, United States v. Arizona, No. 10-1413 (D. Ariz. July 8, 2010), available at http:// www.law.nyu.edu/ ecm_dlv2/groups/public/@nyu_law_website__centers__center_on_administra-tion_of_criminal_law/documents/documents/ecm_pro_066096.pdf (listing examples).

19. *See* David A. Harris, *The War on Terror, Local Police, and Immigration Enforce-ment: A Curious Tale of Police Power in Post-9/11 America,* 38 Rutgers L.J. 1, 36–43 (2006); Orde F. Kittrie, *Federalism, Deportation, and Crime Victims Afraid to Call the Police,* 91 Iowa L. Rev. 1449, 1476–90 (2006); Huyen Pham, *The Constitu-tional Right Not to Cooperate? Local Sovereignty and the Federal Immigration Power,* 74 U. Cin. L. Rev. 1373, 1381–91 (2006).

20. *See, e.g.,* Ariz. Rev. Stat. § 11-1051(A) (codifying Ariz. S.B. 1070, § 2(A)).

21. Id.

22. Ariz. Rev. Stat. § 11-1051(B) (codifying Ariz. S.B. 1070, §2(B)).

23. *Id.* (emphasis added).

24. United States v. Brignoni-Ponce, 422 U.S. 873, 886–87 (1975).

25. *Id.; see also* Gabriel J. Chin & Kevin R. Johnson, *Profiling's Enabler: High Court Ruling Underpins Arizona Immigration Law,* Wash. Post, July 13, 2010, at A15 (critiquing *Brignoni-Ponce* and its consequences).

26. H.B. 2162, 49th Leg., 2d Sess. § 3(B) (Ariz. 2010), available at http://www.azleg. gov/FormatDocument.asp?inDoc=/legtext/49leg/2r/bills/hb2162c.htm.

27. Id.

28. *Brignoni-Ponce,* 422 U.S. at 886–87.

29. United States v. Arizona, 703 F. Supp. 2d 980, 989 (D. Ariz. 2010).

30. *See, e.g.,* Dep't of Navy v. Egan, 484 U.S. 518, 530 (1988) (describing deference to the executive on matters related to foreign affairs and national security); Haig v. Agee, 453 U.S. 280, 293–94 (1981) (noting "the generally accepted view that foreign policy was the province and responsibility of the Executive").

31. *See, e.g.,* U.S. Const. art. I, § 8, cl. 1, 3 ("The Congress shall have Power . . . To regulate Commerce with foreign Nations. . . ."); Chy Lung v. Freeman, 92 U.S. 275, 278–80 (1875) (striking down state statute aimed at deterring immigrant entry as impermissible intrusion on the federal power to regulate foreign commerce).

32. *See* U.S. Const. art. I, § 8, cl. 1, 4 ("The Congress shall have Power . . . To estab-lish an uniform Rule of Naturalization. . . .").

33. For analyses of the flaws in this "mirror theory" see, e.g., Gabriel J. Chin & Marc L. Miller, *The Unconstitutionality of State Regulation of Immigration through Criminal Law,* 61 Duke L.J. 251 (2011), reprinted as chapter 6 of the present vol-ume; Fan, *Rebellious State Crimmigration Enforcement, supra* note 13.

34. For an illuminating critique, see Chin & Miller, *supra* note 33.

35. Ariz. S.B. 1070, §§ 3, 5, 7–13.

36. *Id.* § 5.

37. Pearce, *supra* note 3.

38. Greta Van Susteren, *Arizona Continues Immigration Battle*, FOX News, June 16, 2010, available at 2010 WLNR 12337754 (statement of Gov. Jan Brewer during *On the Record* news show).

39. *See AZ Gov Signs Immigration Bill into Law*, FOX News, Apr. 23, 2010, available at http://www.youtube.com/watch?v=YENGkp6lREo (interview with Paul Babeu, president, Arizona Sheriff's Association).

40. Nicholas Riccardi, *Both Sides in Arizona's Immigration Debate Use Crime Argument*, L.A. Times, May 3, 2010, available at http://articles.latimes.com/2010/may/03/nation/la-na-arizona-crime-20100503.

41. Robert J. Sampson, *Rethinking Crime and Immigration*, 7 Contexts 28, 29–33 (2008), available at http://contexts.org/articles/files/2008/01/contexts_winter08_sampson.pdf; Tim Wadsworth, Is *Immigration Responsible for the Crime Drop? An Assessment of the Influence of Immigration on Changes in Violent Crime between 1990 and 2000*, 91 Soc. Sci. Q. 531, 532–33, 548–49 (2010).

42. Wadsworth, *supra* note 41, at 544–46, 549.

43. Ariz. Rev. Stat. §§ 23-211-23-214 (2010).

44. Ariz. Rev. Stat. §§ 23-212, 212-212-23-214 (2010).

45. *Id.* at § 23-214(A).

46. Chamber of Commerce v. Whiting, 131 S.Ct. 1968, 1981, 1984 (2011).

47. *See* Fan, *Rebellious State Crimmigration Enforcement*, *supra* note 13.

48. *See, e.g., Mexico Roundup: Reactions to Approval of Arizona's SB 1070*, on 27 Apr. 10, World News Connection (Newswire), Apr. 27, 2010, at 22:01:09 (collecting numerous articles expressing protest); Declaration of William J. Burns, Deputy Secretary of State, United States v. Alabama, Case Nos. 5:11-cv-02484, 02736, 02746 (SLB) (N.D. Ala. July 29, 2011) (explaining interference in foreign relations).

49. Hines v. Davidowitz, 312 U.S. 52, 74 (1941).

50. *See, e.g.,* Julia Preston, *State Lawmakers Outline Plans to End Birthright Citizenship, Drawing Outcry*, N.Y. Times, Jan. 6, 2011, at A16.

51. *Id.*

52. *E.g., John C. Eastman, From Feudalism to Consent: Rethinking Birthright Citizenship*, Legal Memorandum (The Heritage Foundation), Mar. 30, 2006, at 2, 5 (arguing children of even lawfully present foreign nationals should not be citizens).

53. *See, e.g.,* Preston, *supra* note 50, at A16 (summarizing state legislative proposals).

54. See id.; Margaret Mikyung Lee, *Birthright Citizenship under the 14th Amendment of Persons Born in the United States to Alien Parents*, Congressional Research Service, August 12, 2010, at 9–14 (summarizing national proposals); Eastman, *supra* note 52, at 5 (suggesting that children of even lawfully present foreign nationals are not fully "subject to the jurisdiction" of the United States).

55. U.S. Const. amend. XIV, § 1.

56. 60 U.S. 393, 403, 407 (1856).

57. 169 U.S. 649, 682 (1898).

58. *Id.* at 693–94.

59. *Id.* at 694.

60. *Id.*

61. Carl Schmitt, The Concept of the Political 26 (George Schwab trans., 1996 [1927]).

62. *Id.* at 27.

63. Carl Schmitt, The Crisis of Parliamentary Democracy 9–12 (Ellen Kennedy trans., 1985); see also Chantal Mouffe, *Carl Schmitt and the Paradox of Liberal Democracy*, in The Challenge of Carl Schmitt 38, 47 (Chantal Mouffe ed., 1999) (explaining that Schmitt conceived of homogeneity as the necessary bond for a democracy and the construction of an "us").

64. Schmitt, The Crisis of Parliamentary Democracy, supra note 63, at 9 (quoting Hugo Grotius, De Jure Belli ac Pacis, bk. I, ch. 3, § 6 (2d ed., Amsterdam 1631)).

65. See Jan-Werner Müller, A Dangerous Mind: Carl Schmitt in Post-War European Thought 3, 39–51, 238–41 (2003).

66. After Schmitt's *das politische*, to convey the realm of political life.

67. *See, e.g.,* Karen Brodkin, How Jews Became White Folks & What that Says about Race in America 25–52 (2002); Ian Haney López, White by Law: The Legal Construction of Race 27–28, 35–37 (2006); Salvatore J. LaGumina, Wop! A Documentary History of Anti-Italian Discrimination 11–15 (2d ed., 1999).

68. LaGumina, *supra* note 67, at 14–16. Italians, for example, were variously referred to as "the Chinese of Europe," "dagoes" and "guineas"—a probable reference to slaves from West Africa. Michael Barone, The New Americans: How the Melting Pot Can Work Again 143 (2001).

69. Congressman Horace Davis, Speech on Chinese Immigration in the House of Representatives, 3 (June 8, 1878) [hereinafter Davis Speech], available at http://content.cdlib.org/ark:/13030/hb7h4nb21q/?order=3&brand=calisphere.

70. *Id.*

71. *See, e.g.,* Comm. of Senate of Cal., Chinese Immigration: The Social, Moral, and Political Effect of Chinese Immigration 7, 41 (1877) [hereinafter 1877 Senate of Cal. Report], available at http://content.cdlib.org/ark:/13030/hb538nb0d6/?order=2&brand=oac (referring to the Chinese as "voluntary slaves" subsisting "like vermin"); Joseph M. Kinley, Remarks on Chinese Immigration 1, 3–5, 11 (1877), available at http://www.oac.cdlib.org/ark:/13030/hb3d5n996b/?order=2&brand=oac4 (quasi-slave labor); Senator Aaron A. Sargent, Speech on Immigration of Chinese in the United States Senate, 1, 6 (May 2, 1876) [hereinafter Sargent Speech], available at http://www.oac.cdlib.org/ark:/13030/hb0j49n3vp/?order=2&brand=oac4 (explaining that the "very industries" of "this strange and dangerously unassimilative people" were a vice displacing white workers); Gen. A. M. Winn, President, Mechanics' State

Council of California, Valedictory Address, 4–5 (Jan. 11, 1871) [hereinafter Winn Valedictory Address], available at http://www.oac.cdlib.org/ark:/13030/ hb2779n54f/?order=2&brand=oac4 (decrying the futility of competing against nomads with no families to support, packed into squalid living conditions and toiling endlessly without spending).

72. Davis Speech, *supra* note 69, at 8.

73. Pearce, *supra* note 3 (asking rhetorically, "How long will it be before we will be just like Mexico?").

74. *E.g.*, 1877 Senate of Cal. Report, supra note 71, at 31–32; Philip A. Roach, Senator of the District of Monterey and Santa Cruz, Minority Report on the Bill to Enforce Contracts for Labor within the State of California (Mar. 20, 1852), reprinted in Winn Valedictory Address, supra note 71, at 7, 8–9.

75. 1877 Senate of Cal. Report, supra note 71, at 5, 20–31 (women in servitude); Winn Valedictory Address, supra note 71, at 5 (describing gambling dens and "other dark dens where crimes that cannot be named are habitually committed").

76. Elmer Clarence Sandmeyer, The Anti-Chinese Movement in California 111 (Illini Books 1991) (1939).

77. *Id.*

78. Address by the Committee of Fifty to the People 1 (n.d.), available at http:// www.oac.cdlib.org/ark:/13030/hb7t1nb2fw/?order=2&brand=oac4.

79. *Id.* at 2–3.

80. Smith v. Turner (The Passenger Cases), 48 U.S. (7 How.) 283 (1849).

81. *Id.* at 406 (McLean, J.).

82. Act of May 3, 1852, ch. 36, §§ 1–2, 1852 Cal. Stat. 78, 78–79, repealed by Act of Apr. 27, 1945, ch. 111, § 5, 1945 Cal. Stat. 424, 465. The 1852 act was struck down by the California Supreme Court two decades later in State v. Steamship Constitution, 42 Cal. 578, 589–90 (1872), as an impermissible interference in foreign commerce.

83. Act of Apr. 28, 1855, ch. 153, §§ 1–2, 1855 Cal. Stat. 194, repealed by Act of Mar. 30, 1955, ch. 46, § 1, 1955 Cal. Stat. 487, 487–88.

84. Act of Mar. 26, 1790, ch. 3, § 1, 1 Stat. 103, repealed by Act of Jan. 29, 1795, ch. 20, 1 Stat. 414.

85. § 1, 1855 Cal. Stat. at 194.

86. 7 Cal. 169 (1857).

87. Act of Apr. 26, 1858, ch. 313, § 1, 1858 Cal. Stat. 295, 295–96, repealed by Act of Mar. 30, 1955, ch. 46, § 1, 1955 Cal. Stat. 487, 487–88.

88. *Id.* §§ 1–2.

89. *See* Lin Sing v. Washburn, 20 Cal. 534, 538 (1862) (recounting that the Supreme Court informed counsel of this history from the bench).

90. Chy Lung v. Freeman, 92 U.S. 274, 280 (1876).

91. In re Ah Fong, 1 F. Cas. 213, 216 (C.C.D. Cal. 1874).

92. *Id.* at 217.

93. *Id.*

94. *Id.* at 218.

95. Chy Lung, 92 U.S. at 278–80.

96. *Id.* at 277–78.

97. *Id.* at 278.

98. Papachristou v. City of Jacksonville, 405 U.S. 156 (1972) (invalidating on vagueness grounds an antivagrancy ordinance that permitted arrests on grounds such as "loafing," being a "vagrant," and "wandering or strolling" without apparent "lawful purpose or object").

99. *See* Harry N. Scheiber, *Race, Radicalism, and Reform: Historical Perspective on the 1879 California Constitution*, 17 Hastings Const. L.Q. 35, 36–37 (1989).

100. *Id.* at 39–40.

101. Cal. Const., art. XIX, § 1–3 (repealed Nov. 4, 1952).

102. *Id.* § 4.

103. *See* In re Tiburcio Parrott, 1 F. 481, 483–84 (C.C.D. Cal. 1880) (summarizing laws at issue).

104. *Id.* at 483.

105. *Id.* at 484.

106. *Id.* at 491 (Hoffman, J.).

107. *Id.* at 492–93.

108. *Id.* at 493–99.

109. *Id.* at 501–10 (Sawyer, J.)

110. 118 U.S. 356 (1886).

111. *Id.* at 373–74.

112. *See, e.g.,* Pers. Adm'r of Mass. v Feeney, 442 U.S. 256, 279 (1979) (requiring, to establish discriminatory intent, proof that the decision maker chose "a particular course of action at least in part 'because of,' not merely 'in spite of,' its adverse effects upon an identifiable group"); Washington v. Davis, 426 U.S. 229, 240–45 (1976) (requiring proof of "a racially discriminatory purpose" and holding that showing substantial disproportionate impact alone is insufficient).

113. *See, e.g.,* McCleskey v. Kemp, 481 U.S. 279, 290–98 (1987) (holding that sophisticated statistical study is insufficient; there must be evidence specific to the claimant's case).

114. *See, e.g.,* Samuel R. Bagenstos, *The Structural Turn and the Limits of Antidiscrimination Law*, 94 Calif. L. Rev. 1, 5–7 & nn.10–20 (2006); Christine Jolls & Cass R. Sunstein, *The Law of Implicit Bias*, 94 Calif. L. Rev. 969 (2006); Linda Hamilton Krieger, *The Content of Our Categories: A Cognitive Bias Approach to Discrimination and Equal Employment Opportunity*, 47 Stan. L. Rev. 1161 (1995); Charles R. Lawrence III, *The Id, the Ego, and Equal Protection: Reckoning with Unconscious Racism*, 39 Stan. L. Rev. 317 (1987). For an overview of the findings in social psychology on implicit bias, see, for example, Jerry Kang, *Trojan Horses of Race*, 118 Harv. L. Rev. 1489, 1497–1530 (2005).

115. An oft-critiqued exemplar of this approach is *Whren v. United States*, 517 U.S. 806 (1996), in which the Court declined to review allegations of racial profiling.
116. Arizona v. United States, 132 S. Ct. 2492, 2498 (2012).
117. *Id.* at 2499.
118. *Id.* at 2498–99 (quoting Hines v. Davidowitz, 312 U.S. 52, 64 (1941)).
119. *Id.* at 2506 (invalidating Ariz. S.B. 1070 § 6).
120. *Id.* at 2507–9.
121. *Id.* at 2510.
122. *Id.* at 2509 (citing Arizona v. Johnson, 555 U.S. 323 (2009); Illinois v. Caballes, 543 U.S. 405 (2005)).
123. *Id.* at 2509.
124. *See* Mary D. Fan, *Beyond Budget-Cut Criminal Justice: The Future of Penal Law*, 90 N.C. L. Rev. 581, 608–10 (2012) (discussing the utility of uncertainty and judicial nudges).
125. *See, e.g.,* Steven Fein & Steven J. Spencer, *Prejudice as Self-Image Maintenance: Affirming the Self through Derogating Others*, 73 J. Personality & Soc. Psychol. 31 (1997).
126. *See, e.g., id.*; Lennart J. Renkema et al., *Terror Management and Stereotyping: Why Do People Stereotype When Mortality Is Salient?* 34 Personality & Soc. Psychol. Bull. 553 (2008).
127. *See* United States v. Arizona, 641 F.3d 339, 366–69 (9th Cir. 2011) (Noonan, J., concurring) (writing that Arizona Senate Bill 1070 is unconstitutional because of incompatibility with U.S. foreign policy).
128. *Cf.* Dan M. Kahan, *The Cognitively Illiberal State*, 60 Stan. L. Rev. 115, 145–48 (2007) (arguing law and policy should be infused with a surfeit of meanings so that divergent worldviews can be simultaneously affirmed and people in a pluralistic society can deliberate with rather than past each other).
129. This customary portrait has long been challenged by scholars who contend that public demand, political majorities, and elite national opinion powerfully influence Supreme Court decision making. *E.g.*, Larry D. Kramer, The People Themselves: Popular Constitutionalism and Judicial Review 240–41, 250–51 (2004); Robert G. McCloskey, The American Supreme Court 260–61 (Sanford Levinson ed., 5th ed. 2010); Robert A. Dahl, *Decision-Making in a Democracy: The Supreme Court as a National Policy-Maker*, 6 J. Pub. L. 279, 280–81, 283–89 (1957), reprinted in 50 Emory L.J. 563, 565–66, 568–75 (2001); Jack M. Balkin, *What* Brown *Teaches Us about Constitutional Theory*, 90 Va. L. Rev. 1537, 1538–46 (2004); Barry Friedman, *Mediated Popular Constitutionalism*, 101 Mich. L. Rev. 2596, 2606–8 (2003).
130. Robert L. Tsai, Eloquence & Reason: Creating a First Amendment Culture 44–48 (2008).
131. Robert Post & Reva Siegel, Roe *Rage: Democratic Constitutionalism and Back-lash*, 42 Harv. C.R.-C.L. L. Rev. 373, 374 (2007); Reva B. Siegel, *Equality Talk:*

Antisubordination and Anticlassification Values in Constitutional Struggles over Brown, 117 Harv. L. Rev. 1470, 1545–46 (2004).

132. *E.g.*, Elizabeth F. Emens, *Integrating Accommodation*, 156 U. Pa. L. Rev. 839, 895–96 (2008) (arguing for framing disability accommodations in terms of third-party benefits); Richard T. Ford, *Hopeless Constitutionalism, Hopeful Pragmatism*, in The Constitution in 2020, at 143, 151–52 (Jack M. Balkin & Reva B. Siegel eds., 2009) (noting the coalition-building power of narrative about "what joins us as a political community"); Vicki Schultz, *Life's Work*, 100 Colum. L. Rev. 1881, 1937–38 (2000) (explaining import of shifting discourse on work-related rights from one emphasizing rights of certain demographic groups to one emphasizing rights for all).

133. Derrick A. Bell Jr., Comment, Brown v. Board of Education *and the Interest-Convergence Dilemma*, 93 Harv. L. Rev. 518, 523 (1980). The proposition, though controversial in its time, has proved to have powerful explanatory force in an array of contexts. *See* Cynthia Lee, *Cultural Convergence: Interest Convergence Theory Meets the Cultural Defense*, 49 Ariz. L. Rev. 911, 922–38 (2007) (analyzing examples).

134. Bell, *supra* note 133, at 530.

135. *Id.* at 523, 528.

136. J.G. Kerr, The Chinese Question Analyzed 5 (1877), available at http://www.oac.cdlib.org/ark:/13030/hb009n96wp/?order=2&brand=oac4.

137. Reva Siegel, *From Colorblindness to Antibalkanization: An Emerging Ground of Decision in Race Equality Cases*, 120 Yale L.J. 1278 (2011).

138. Arizona v. United States, 132 S. Ct. 2492, 2510 (2012).

About the Contributors

Gabriel J. Chin is Professor of Law at the University of California, Davis School of Law. He is the author of several articles on the intersection of immigration, race, and criminal justice, and his scholarship has been cited by the U.S. Supreme Court.

John C. Eastman is the Henry Salvatori Professor of Law & Community Service at Chapman University School of Law. He is the Founding Director of the Center for Constitutional Jurisprudence, a public interest law firm affiliated with the Claremont Institute.

Mary Fan is Associate Professor at the University of Washington School of Law. She specializes in U.S., international, and cross-border criminal law and procedure. She has written extensively about the intersection of criminal law and procedure with immigration, or "crimmigration" for short.

Carissa Byrne Hessick is Professor of Law at the University of Utah's S.J. Quinney College of Law. Her 2010 report (with Jack Chin, Marc Miller, and Toni Massaro) on the legal issues raised by Arizona's SB 1070 has been widely referenced in scholarly articles and news reports, including the *Wall Street Journal* and *The Economist*, for fairly framing the core issues.

Kris W. Kobach is the Kansas Secretary of State and formerly served as a Professor of Law at University of Missouri–Kansas City School of Law (1996–2011). Secretary Kobach is former Counsel to U.S. Attorney General John Ashcroft (2002–2003), Chairman of the Kansas Republican Party (2007–2009), and a frequent litigator of cases involving illegal immigration.

Douglas S. Massey is the Henry G. Bryant Professor of Sociology and Public Affairs at Princeton University. He is a member of the National Academy of Sciences, the American Academy of Arts and Sciences, and the American Philosophical Society. He is the current president of the American Academy of Political and Social Science. He is a member of the Council of the National Academy of Sciences and is coeditor of the *Annual Review of Sociology*. He is the author, most recently, of *Brokered Boundaries: Creating Immigrant Identity in Anti-Immigrant Times*, published in 2010 and coauthored with Magaly Sanchez.

Marc L. Miller is the Dean and the Ralph W. Bilby Professor of Law at the University of Arizona's James E. Rogers College of Law. His 2010 report (with Jack Chin, Carissa Hessick, and Toni Massaro) on the legal issues raised by Arizona's SB 1070 has been widely referenced in scholarly articles and news reports, including the *Wall Street Journal* and *The Economist*, for fairly framing the core issues.

Huyen Pham is Professor of Law at the Texas A&M University School of Law. Professor Pham's most recent scholarship tracks the evolution of subfederal governments on immigration issues and studies the interaction between this evolution and economic growth, demographic movement, and other outcomes. Her work has been cited by various media outlets, including the *Washington Post* and msnbc. com.

Tom I. Romero II is Associate Professor at the University of Denver Sturm College of Law and an affiliated faculty member in the Department of History. His research focuses on race and law in the American West. Professor Romero's work on such topics have appeared in the *Colorado Law Review*, the *Utah Law Review*, the *New Mexico Law Review*, the *Albany Law Review*, the *Journal of Gender, Race, and Justice*, the *Temple Political and Civil Rights Law Review*, the *Seattle Journal for Social Justice*, the *Oregon Review of International Law*, the *Chicano-Latino Law Review*, and *Aztlán: A Journal of Chicano Studies*, among others.

Rick Su is Associate Professor at SUNY Buffalo Law School. Su writes and teaches in the areas of immigration, federalism, and local government law. His work has appeared in the *North Carolina Law Review*, the *William & Mary Law Review*, and the *Houston Law Review*, among others.

Pham Hoang Van is Associate Professor of Economics at Baylor University. His research interests include developing country labor markets, immigration, corruption, retail and international trade, services trade, technology change, and big data.

Index